Fodor's 2000

The U.S. & British Virgin Islands

D1621454

The comple.. guide, thoroughly up-to-date

Packed with details that will make your trip

The must-see sights, off and on the beaten path

What to see, what to skip

City strolls, countryside adventures

Smart lodging and dining options

Essential local do's and taboos

Transportation tips

Key contacts, savvy travel tips

When to go, what to pack

Clear, accurate, easy-to-use maps

Books to read, background essays

Excerpted from *Fodor's Caribbean 2000*

Fodor's Travel Publications, Inc. • New York, Toronto, London, Sydney, Auckland
www.fodors.com/usvi   www.fodors.com/bvi

Fodor's The U.S. and British Virgin Islands

EDITOR: Laura M. Kidder

Editorial Contributors: Pamela Acheson, Carol M. Bareuther, Gary Goodlander, Lynda Lohr, Jordan Simon
Editorial Production: Brian Vitunic
Maps: David Lindroth, *cartographer*; Steven K. Amsterdam and Robert Blake, *map editors*
Design: Fabrizio La Rocca, *creative director*; Guido Caroti, *art director*; Jolie Novak, *photo editor*
Cover Design: Pentagram
Production/Manufacturing: Rebecca Zeiler
Cover Photograph: Bob Krist

Copyright

Copyright © 1999 by Fodor's Travel Publications, Inc.

Fodor's is a registered trademark of Random House, Inc.

All rights reserved under International and Pan-American Copyright Conventions. Published in the United States by Fodor's Travel Publications, Inc., a division of Random House, Inc., New York, and simultaneously in Canada by Random House of Canada, Limited, Toronto. Distributed by Random House, Inc., New York.

No maps, illustrations, or other portions of this book may be reproduced in any form without written permission from the publisher.

ISBN 0–679–00336–3

ISSN 1070–6380

"Beach Picnic" by Calvin Trillin. Excerpted from his book *Travels With Alice,* published by Ticknor & Fields. Copyright © 1989 by Calvin Trillin. Originally appeared in different form in *Travel & Leisure.* "Me? The Dad? On a Spring-Break Cruise?" by Bob Payne (*Sail* Magazine, 1992) is reproduced by permission of the author.

Important Tip

Although all prices, opening times, and other details in this book are based on information supplied to us at press time, changes occur all the time in the travel world, and Fodor's cannot accept responsibility for facts that become outdated or for inadvertent errors or omissions. So **always confirm information when it matters,** especially if you're making a detour to visit a specific place.

Special Sales

Fodor's Travel Publications are available at special discounts for bulk purchases for sales promotions or premiums. Special editions, including personalized covers, excerpts of existing guides, and corporate imprints, can be created in large quantities for special needs. For more information, contact your local bookseller or write to Special Markets, Fodor's Travel Publications, 201 E. 50th Street, New York, NY 10022. Inquiries from Canada should be directed to your local Canadian bookseller or sent to Random House of Canada, Ltd., Marketing Department, 2775 Mattheson Blvd. E, Mississauga, Ontario, L4W 4P7. Inquiries from the United Kingdom should be sent to Fodor's Travel Publications, 20 Vauxhall Bridge Road, London, England SW1V 2SA.

PRINTED IN THE UNITED STATES OF AMERICA

10 9 8 7 6 5 4 3 2 1

CONTENTS

Maps

ON THE ROAD WITH FODOR'S

EVERY Y2K TRIP is a significant trip. So if there was ever a time you needed excellent travel information, it's now. Acutely aware of that fact, we've pulled out all stops in preparing *Fodor's The U.S. and British Virgin Islands 2000.* To guide you in putting together your USBVI experience, we've created multiday itineraries and neighborhood walks. And to direct you to the places that are truly worth your time and money in this important year, we've rallied the team of endearingly picky know-it-alls we're pleased to call our writers. Having seen all corners of the USBVI, they're real experts. If you knew them, you'd poll them for tips yourself.

Pamela Acheson spent 18 years in New York City as a publishing executive before heading south to divide her time between Florida and the Caribbean. She writes extensively about both areas and is a regular contributor to *Travel & Leisure, Caribbean Travel & Life, Fodor's Florida, Fodor's Walt Disney World,* and *Fodor's Caribbean.* She's the author of *The Best of the British Virgin Islands, The Best of St. Thomas and St. John, The Best of the Bahamas, The Best Romantic Escapes in Florida* (with her husband, Richard Myers), and *More of the Best Romantic Escapes in Florida.*

St. Thomas–based writer and dietitian **Carol M. Bareuther** publishes two weekly columns on food, cooking, and nutrition in the *Virgin Islands Daily News* and serves as the USVI stringer for the Reuters News Service International. She also writes about sports and travel for *Islands' Nautical Scene, All at Sea, Southern Boating, Caribbean Travel & Life,* and other publications. She's the author of two books, *Sports Fishing in the Virgin Islands* and *Virgin Islands Cooking.*

Lynda Lohr is a veteran mainland and USVI photojournalist who has spent the last 15 years living in St. John and who contributes regularly to national, regional, and local magazines, newspapers, and Web sites. Although she, her boyfriend, and their two cats live in a tiny cottage overlooking Cruz Bay, they're now building a new home at Ajax Peak. With half a dozen hurricanes to her credit, Lynda hopes that this house will hold up against the elements.

We would like to thank the British Virgin Islands Tourist Board and the U.S.V.I. Government Tourist Offices for helping keep us up to date.

Don't Forget to Write

Keeping a travel guide fresh and up-to-date is a big job. So we love your feedback—positive and negative—and follow up on all suggestions. Contact the USBVI editor at editors@fodors.com or c/o Fodor's, 201 East 50th Street, New York, New York 10022. And have a wonderful trip!

Karen Cure

Karen Cure
Editorial Director

The Virgin Islands

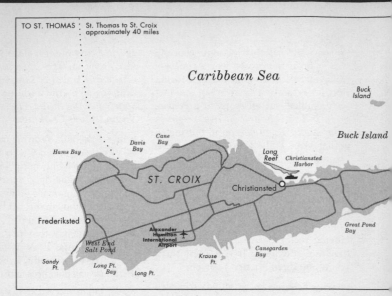

TO ST. THOMAS

St. Thomas to St. Croix
approximately 40 miles

Caribbean Sea

Buck
Island

Buck Island

Hams Bay

Davis
Bay

Cane
Bay

Long
Reef

*Christiansted
Harbor*

ST. CROIX

Christiansted

Frederiksted

West End
Salt Pond

Alexander
Hamilton
International
Airport

Great Pond
Bay

Sandy
Pt.

Long Pt.
Bay

Long Pt.

Krause
Pt.

Canegarden
Bay

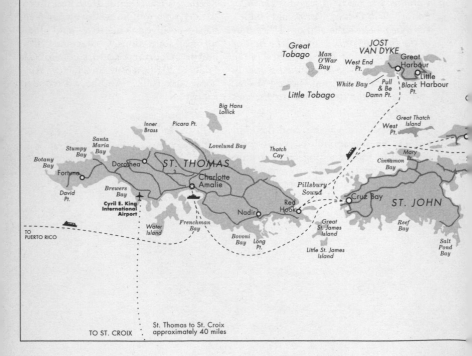

A T L A N T I C

O C E A N

Great
Tobago

Man
O'War
Bay

JOST
VAN DYKE

Great
Harbour

West End
Pt.

White Bay

Pull
& Be
Damn Pt.

Little
Black Harbour
Pt.

Little Tobago

Big Hans
Lollick

Great Thatch
Island

Inner
Brass

Picara Pt.

West
Pt.

Santa
Maria
Bay

Lovelund Bay

Thatch
Cay

Cinnamon
Bay

Mary
Pt.

Stumpy
Bay

Dorothea

ST. THOMAS

Botany
Bay

Fortuna

Charlotte
Amalie

Pillsbury
Sound

Cruz Bay

ST. JOHN

David
Pt.

Brewers
Bay

Cyril E. King
International
Airport

Nadir

Red
Hook

Reef
Bay

TO
PUERTO RICO

Water
Island

Frenchman
Bay

Bovoni
Bay

Long
Pt.

Great
St. James
Island

Little St. James
Island

Salt
Pond
Bay

TO ST. CROIX

St. Thomas to St. Croix
approximately 40 miles

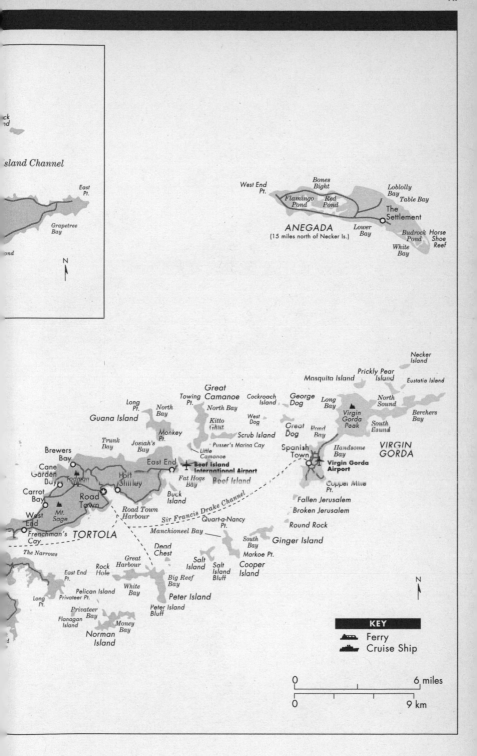

sland Channel

East Pt.

Grapetree Bay

N

West End Pt.

Bones Bight

Loblolly Bay
Table Bay

Flamingo Pond   Red Pond

The Settlement

ANEGADA
(15 miles north of Necker Is.)

Lower Bay

Budrock Pond

White Bay

Horse Shoe Reef

Necker Island

Prickly Pear Island

Eustatia Island

Masquita Island

George Dog

Long Bay

North Sound

Berchers Bay

Great Camanoe

Towing Pt.

North Bay

Cockroach Island

Virgin Gorda Peak

Long Pt.

North Bay

Kitto Ghut

West Dog

South Sound

Guana Island

Great Dog

Pond Bay

VIRGIN GORDA

Trunk Bay

Josiah's Bay

Monkey Pt.

Scrub Island

Pusser's Marina Cay

Spanish Town

Handsome Bay

Brewers Bay

Little Camanoe

East End

Beef Island International Airport

Virgin Gorda Airport

Cane Garden Bay

Fort Shirley

Fat Hogs Bay

Beef Island

Copper Mine Pt.

Todman Pk.

Carrot Bay

Road Town

Buck Island

Fallen Jerusalem

Mt. Sage

Road Town Harbour

Sir Francis Drake Channel

Broken Jerusalem

West End

Quart-a-Nancy

Round Rock

Frenchman's Cay

TORTOLA

Manchioneel Bay

The Narrows

Dead Chest

South Bay

Ginger Island

Markoe Pt.

Great Harbour

Salt Island

Salt Island Bluff

Cooper Island

Rock Hole

East End Pt.

White Bay

Big Reef Bay

N

Long Pt.

Pelican Island

Privateer Pt.

Peter Island

Privateer Bay

Peter Island Bluff

Flanagan Island

Money Bay

Norman Island

KEY

⛴ Ferry

🚢 Cruise Ship

0 _____ 6 miles

0 _____ 9 km

The Caribbean

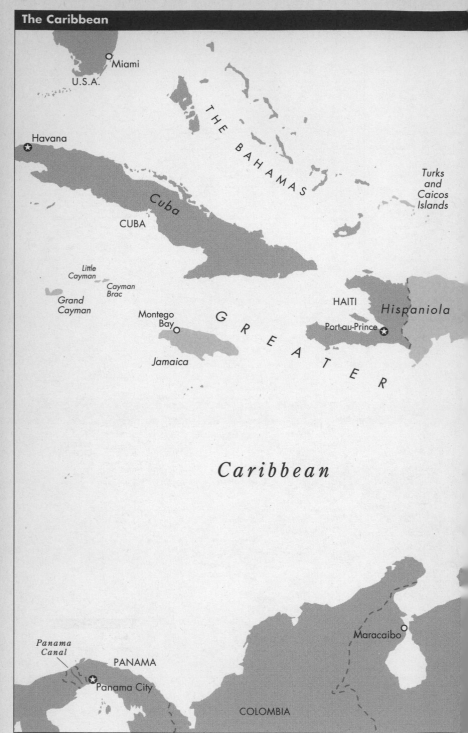

Miami
U.S.A.

THE BAHAMAS

Havana

Cuba

CUBA

Turks
and
Caicos
Islands

Little
Cayman

Cayman
Brac

Grand
Cayman

Montego
Bay

G R E A T E R

HAITI

Hispaniola

Port-au-Prince

Jamaica

T E R

Caribbean

Panama
Canal

PANAMA

Maracaibo

Panama City

COLOMBIA

0   200 miles

0   300 km

N

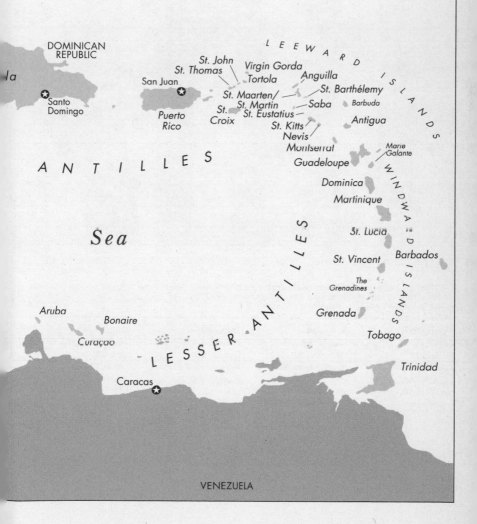

ATLANTIC OCEAN

L E E W A R D   I S L A N D S

DOMINICAN
REPUBLIC

la

★ Santo
Domingo

San Juan ★

Puerto
Rico

St. John

St. Thomas

Virgin Gorda

Tortola

Anguilla

St. Maarten/
St. Martin

St. Barthélemy

Saba

Barbuda

St.
Croix

St. Eustatius

Antigua

St. Kitts

Nevis

Montserrat

Guadeloupe

Marie
Galante

A N T I L L E S

Dominica

Martinique

W I N D W A R D   I S L A N D S

Sea

St. Lucia

St. Vincent

Barbados

The
Grenadines

Aruba

Bonaire

Grenada

Curaçao

L E S S E R   A N T I L L E S

Tobago

Trinidad

Caracas ★

VENEZUELA

x

World Time Zones

+12 +13

MONDAY
SUNDAY

International Date Line

-9

-10

-11

-10

-11

+11

+12

1

2

3

4

5

6

7

8

9

10

11

12

13

14 15

16

17

18

19

20

21

22

23

24

25 0

-4

-3

-4

-5

-4

-3:30

-7

-8

-6

-5

-4

-5

-4

-3

-3

-4

+11 | +12 - | -11 | -10 | -9 | -8 | -7 | -6 | -5 | -4 | -3 | -2

Numbers below vertical bands relate each zone to Greenwich Mean Time (0 hrs.).
Local times frequently differ from these general indications,
as indicated by light-face numbers on map.

Algiers, **29**

Anchorage, **3**

Athens, **41**

Auckland, **1**

Baghdad, **46**

Bangkok, **50**

Beijing, **54**

Berlin, **34**

Bogotá, **19**

Budapest, **37**

Buenos Aires, **24**

Caracas, **22**

Chicago, **9**

Copenhagen, **33**

Dallas, **10**

Delhi, **48**

Denver, **8**

Dublin, **26**

Edmonton, **7**

Hong Kong, **56**

Honolulu, **2**

Istanbul, **40**

Jakarta, **53**

Jerusalem, **42**

Johannesburg, **44**

Lima, **20**

Lisbon, **28**

London
(Greenwich), **27**

Los Angeles, **6**

Madrid, **38**

Manila, **57**

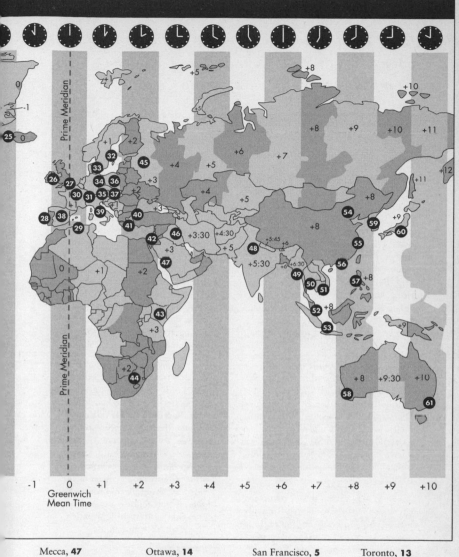

SMART TRAVEL TIPS A TO Z

Basic Information on Traveling in the Virgin Islands,
Savvy Tips to Make Your Trip a Breeze, and
Companies and Organizations to Contact

AIR TRAVEL

BOOKING YOUR FLIGHT

Price is just one factor to consider when booking a flight: frequency of service and a carrier's safety record are often just as important. Major airlines offer the greatest number of departures. Smaller airlines—including regional and no-frills carriers—usually have a limited number of flights. On the other hand, so-called low-cost airlines usually are cheaper, and their fares impose fewer restrictions, such as advance-purchase requirements. Safety-wise, low-cost carriers as a group have a good history—about equal to that of major carriers.

Major carriers include American Airlines, which flies direct from New York and Miami, with connecting flights through those cities and Puerto Rico to St. Thomas and St. Croix; Delta, with direct flights from Atlanta to St. Thomas and St. Croix; and US Airways, which flies from Philadelphia to St. Thomas and continues on to St. Croix.

You can also take a major or no-frills carrier to San Juan, Puerto Rico, where you can connect on a regional airline for one of the United States Virgin Islands and British Virgin Islands (USBVI) or on to another another Caribbean destination. Air Sunshine flies from San Juan to St. Croix and Beef Island/Tortola; Air St. Thomas has flights from San Juan to St. Thomas and Virgin Gorda; American Eagle has service from San Juan to St. Croix, St. Thomas, and Beef Island/Tortola as well as flights between St. Thomas and St. Croix and St. Thomas and Beef Island/Tortola. Gorda Aero Service flies between Beef Island/Tortola and Anegada. Leeward Island Air Transport (LIAT) travels between St. Thomas and most Caribbean islands.

British Airways and Virgin Atlantic fly directly from London to Antigua, an island south of the Virgins, where you can connect to both the BVI and USVI. Air Canada arrives in Antigua from Toronto. Alternatively, you can fly from London to Miami and connect with American Airlines, to Atlanta and connect with Delta, or to San Juan and connect with American Eagle or another island-hopping carrier to St. Thomas, St. Croix, Beef Island/Tortola, or Virgin Gorda. From Australia, British Airways will get you to London, where you can connect with nonstop Caribbean flights. Qantas will get you to Honolulu and Los Angeles, with connections on American Airlines, or to London, with connections on British Airways.

Note that many smaller Caribbean airlines only answer the phone when they're checking in flights, so keep trying. **Research flights through the Internet**—there have been some amazing deals of late, particularly through San Juan. When you book **look for nonstop flights** and **remember that "direct" flights stop at least once.** While you should **avoid connecting flights,** which require a change of plane, that's often difficult when flying to the Virgin Islands.

CARRIERS

➤ MAJOR AIRLINES: **American Airlines** (✆ 800/474–4884), **Delta** (✆ 800/221–1212), and **US Airways** (✆ 800/622–1015).

➤ SMALLER AIRLINES: **Air Sunshine** (✆ 800/327–8900, 800/435–8900 in Florida, or 888/879–8900 in the USVI and Puerto Rico), **Air St. Thomas** (✆ 340/776–2722 in the USVI or 284/495–5935 in the BVI), **American Eagle** (✆ 800/474–4884), **Gorda Aero Service** (✆ 284/495–2271 in the BVI), and **Leeward Island Air Transport (LIAT)** (✆ 340/778–9930 in the USVI).

➤ FROM THE U.K.: **British Airways**
(☎ 0345/222–111), **Virgin Atlantic**
(☎ 0129/374–7747).

➤ FROM ELSEWHERE IN THE WORLD:
Air Canada (☎ 800/776–3000 in the
U.S. or 888/247–2262 in Canada),
British Airways (☎ 02/9258–3399 in
Sydney, 03/9603–1199 in Melbourne,
or 07/3223–3133 in Brisbane), **Qantas** (☎ 13–13–13 in Australia or
0800/808–767 in New Zealand).

CHECK-IN & BOARDING

Checking in, paying departure taxes
(if they aren't included in your ticket),
clearing security, and boarding can
take much longer than you expect at
some island airports. Especially when
heading home, **get to the airport at
least 1½ hours ahead of time**
(2 hours if you plan to squeeze in
some duty-free shopping). From some
islands, there may only be one flight
per day going in the direction you're
headed.

Assuming that not everyone with a
ticket will show up, airlines routinely
overbook planes. When that happens,
airlines ask for volunteers to give up
their seats. In return these volunteers
usually get a certificate for a free
flight and are rebooked on the next
flight out. If there aren't enough
volunteers, the airline must choose
who will be denied boarding. The
first to get bumped are passengers
who checked in late and those flying
on discounted tickets, so **get to the
gate and check in as early as possible,** especially during peak periods.
Always **bring a government-issued
photo ID to the airport** (a passport is
best). You may be asked to show it
before you're allowed to check in.

CUTTING COSTS

The least-expensive airfares to the
USBVI must usually be purchased in
advance and are non-refundable. It's
smart to **call a number of airlines, and
when you are quoted a good price,
book it on the spot**—the same fare
may not be available the next day.
Always **check different routings** and
look into using different airports.
Travel agents, especially low-fare
specialists (☞ Discounts & Deals,
below), are helpful.

Consolidators are another good
source. They buy tickets for scheduled
international flights at reduced rates
from the airlines, then sell them at
prices that beat the best fare available
directly from the airlines, usually
without restrictions. Sometimes you
can even get your money back if you
need to return the ticket. Carefully
read the fine print detailing penalties
for changes and cancellations, and
**confirm your consolidator reservation
with the airline.**

➤ CONSOLIDATORS: **Cheap Tickets**
(☎ 800/377–1000), **Discount Airline
Ticket Service** (☎ 800/576–1600),
Up & Away Travel (☎ 212/889–
2345), **Unitravel** (☎ 800/325–2222),
World Travel Network (☎ 800/409–
6753).

ENJOYING THE FLIGHT

For more legroom **request an emergency-aisle seat.** Don't sit in the row
in front of the emergency aisle or in
front of a bulkhead, where seats may
not recline. If you have dietary concerns, **ask for special meals when
booking.** These can be vegetarian,
low-cholesterol, or kosher, for example. On long flights, try to maintain a
normal routine, to help fight jetlag.
At night **get some sleep.** By day **eat
light meals, drink water** (not alcohol),
and **move around the cabin** to stretch
your legs.

FLYING TIMES

Flights from New York or Atlanta
take about four hours; from Miami,
it's nearly three hours. If you connect
in San Juan, you'll spend another
half-hour in the air. From Antigua to
the USBVI takes about an hour.
Nonstop flights from London to
Antigua are about seven hours. Once
you've arrived in the USBVI, hops
between the islands take about 10 to
20 minutes.

HOW TO COMPLAIN

If your baggage goes astray or your
flight goes awry, complain right away.
Most carriers require that you **file a
claim immediately.**

➤ AIRLINE COMPLAINTS: U.S. Department of Transportation **Aviation
Consumer Protection Division** (✉
C-75, Room 4107, Washington, DC

THE GOLD GUIDE / SMART TRAVEL TIPS

20590, ☎ 202/366–2220). Federal Aviation Administration Consumer Hotline (☎ 800/322–7873).

RECONFIRMING

Be sure to **reconfirm your flights on interisland carriers.** You're often subject to a carrier's whim: If no other passengers are booked on your flight, you may be requested (actually, ordered) to take a more convenient departure for the airline, or your plane may make unscheduled stops to pick up more clients or cargo. It's all part of the excitement—and unpredictability—of Caribbean travel. In addition note that there are usually weight restrictions; **travel light,** or you could be subject to outrageous surcharges or delays in getting very large or heavy luggage, which may have to follow on another flight (☞ *also* Packing, *below*).

AIRPORTS

➤ MAJOR AIRPORTS: The major airports are Beef Island International Airport on Tortola, Cyril E. King International Airport on St. Thomas, and Henry Rohlsen International Airport on St. Croix. There are smaller airports (so small that they don't have phone numbers; call the individual airlines if you need info) on Anegada and Virgin Gorda.

➤ AIRPORT INFORMATION: **Beef Island International Airport** (☎ 284/495–2525), **Cyril E. King International Airport** (☎ 340/774–5100), **Henry Rohlsen International Airport** (☎ 340/778–0589).

DUTY-FREE SHOPPING

Both St. Croix and St. Thomas airports have gift shops where you can pick up last-minute gifts or liquor, but since all items purchased in the USVI are duty-free, you won't find any bargains at the airports. Prices may be lower and the selection greater at off-airport stores. In the BVI, do your shopping in town because airport merchandise consists primarily of T-shirts.

BIKE TRAVEL

The USBVI offer a variety of biking terrains. You can wheel through some truly gorgeous scenery on St. Croix. On St. Thomas, St. John, and the BVI, steep hills and roads that lack shoulders make the going more difficult, but you can always cool off with a swim. Note, however, that traffic moves at a good clip on most islands, and drivers aren't always at their most polite when they encounter cyclists. For more information, *see* Outdoor Activities and Sports *in* individual island chapters.

BIKES IN FLIGHT

Most airlines accommodate bikes as luggage, provided they're dismantled and boxed. For bike boxes, often free at bike shops, you'll pay about $5 (at least $100 for bike bags) from airlines. International travelers can sometimes substitute a bike for a piece of checked luggage at no charge; otherwise, the cost is about $100. Domestic and Canadian airlines charge $25–$50.

BOAT & FERRY TRAVEL

For information, *see* Arriving and Departing by Boat *in* the A to Z section at the end of each chapter.

BUS TRAVEL

St. Thomas's mainland-size Vitran buses are comfortable (and no-smoking) but slow; service is limited to east–west runs to and from Charlotte Amalie. St. John's buses meet departing ferries. St. Croix has Vitran buses with limited service to key destinations. The fares range from 75¢ to $1 (one way), depending on your destination. On St. Croix and Tortola, taxi vans with reasonable fares and regular schedules and routes are also an option. For more information, *see* Getting Around by Bus *in* the A to Z section at the end of each chapter.

CAMERAS & PHOTOGRAPHY

Frothy waves in a turquoise sea and palm-lined crescents of beach are relatively easy to capture on film if you **don't let the brightness of the sun on sand and water fool your light meter.** You'll need to compensate or else work early or late in the day when the light isn't as brilliant and contrast isn't such a problem. Try to **capture expansive views** of waterfront, beach, or village scenes; consider shooting down onto the shore from a clearing on a hillside or from a rock on the beach.

Or **zoom in on something colorful,** such as a delicate tropical flower or a craftsman at work. Always **ask permission to take pictures of locals or their property** and **offer a gratuity.**

EQUIPMENT PRECAUTIONS

Always **keep your film and tape out of the sun.** Carry an extra supply of batteries, and **be prepared to turn on your camera or camcorder** to prove to security personnel that the device is real. Always **ask for hand inspection of film,** which becomes clouded after successive exposures to airport X-ray machines, and **keep videotapes away from metal detectors.**

FILM AND DEVELOPING

You'll find up-to-date Kodak and Fuji film at photo shops, discount stores, and gift shops, but it's priced a dollar or two higher than you probably pay at home. A roll of 36-exposure Kodak Max runs about $7 and costs about $20 to develop. Overnight developing is available throughout the USBVI, but the quality varies, particularly on the smaller islands. It may be best to have your irreplaceable vacation photos processed back home.

➤ PHOTO HELP: **Kodak Information Center** (☎ 800/242-2424). *Kodak Guide to Shooting Great Travel Pictures,* available in bookstores or from Fodor's Travel Publications (☎ 800/533-6478; $16.50 plus $4 shipping).

VIDEOS

Video camera film selection is slim. What exists is available at camera and discount stores for about $8.

CAR RENTAL

Rates range from $50 a day/$300 a week for an economy car with air-conditioning, automatic transmission, and unlimited mileage to $80 a day/$400 a week for a four-wheel-drive vehicle. Both the USVI and the BVI have major companies (with airport locations) as well as numerous local companies (near the airports, in hotels, and in the main towns). Most provide pick-up service; some ask that you take a taxi to their headquarters.

➤ MAJOR AGENCIES: **Avis** (☎ 800/331-1084; 800/879-2847 in Canada; 02/9353-9000 in Australia; 09/525-1982 in New Zealand), **Budget** (☎ 800/527-0700 or 0144/227-6266 in the U.K.), **Hertz** (☎ 800/654-3001, 800/263-0600 in Canada, 020/8897-2072 in the U.K., 02/9669-2444 in Australia, or 03/358-6777 in New Zealand).

CUTTING COSTS

To get the best deal **book through a travel agent who will shop around.** Also **price local car-rental companies,** although the service and maintenance may not be as good as those of a major player. Be sure to **check with several agencies to compare costs.** Remember to ask about surcharges (☞ *below*). If you're traveling during a holiday period, also make sure that a confirmed reservation guarantees you a car.

➤ LOCAL AGENCIES: For information on local companies, *see* Getting Around by Car *in* the A to Z section at the end of each chapter.

INSURANCE

When driving a rented car you're generally responsible for any damage to or loss of the vehicle as well as for any property damage or personal injury that you may cause. Before you rent see what coverage your personal auto-insurance policy and credit cards already provide.

For about $15 to $20 per day, rental companies sell protection, known as a collision- or loss-damage waiver (CDW or LDW), that eliminates your liability for damage to the car. However, **make sure you have enough coverage to pay for the car.** If you don't have auto insurance or an umbrella policy that covers damage to third parties, purchasing liability insurance and a CDW or LDW is highly recommended.

REQUIREMENTS & RESTRICTIONS

In the USVI your own driver's license is acceptable for 90 days. The minimum age is 18, although many agencies won't rent to anyone under 25. You'll pay extra for child seats (about $3 per day), which are compulsory for children under five, and for additional drivers (about $2 per day).

In the BVI a valid BVI driver's license is required and can be obtained for $10 at rental agencies. You must be 25 and have a valid driver's license from another country.

SURCHARGES

Before you pick up a car in one city and leave it in another **ask about drop-off charges or one-way service fees,** which can be substantial. Note, too, that some rental agencies charge extra if you return the car before the time specified in your contract. To avoid a hefty refueling fee **fill the tank just before you turn in the car,** but be aware that gas stations near the rental outlet may overcharge.

CAR TRAVEL

A car gives you mobility. You'll be able to spend an hour browsing at that cozy out-of-the-way shop instead of the 10 minutes allotted by your taxi driver. You can beach-hop without searching for a ride, and you can sample that restaurant you've heard so much about that's a half-hour (and an expensive taxi ride) away. On parts of some of the islands, you may need to rent a four-wheel-drive vehicle to really get out and about.

AUTO CLUBS

➤ IN AUSTRALIA: **Australian Automobile Association** (AAA; ☎ 02/6247–7311).

➤ IN CANADA: **Canadian Automobile Association** (CAA; ☎ 613/247–0117).

➤ IN NEW ZEALAND: **New Zealand Automobile Association** (NZAA; ☎ 09/377–4660).

➤ IN THE U.K.: **Automobile Association** (AA; ☎ 0990/500–600), **Royal Automobile Club** (RAC; ☎ 0990/722–722 for membership; 0345/121–345 for insurance).

➤ IN THE U.S.: **American Automobile Association** (AAA; ☎ 800/564–6222).

EMERGENCIES

For emergencies, dial 911 in the USVI and 999 in the BVI.

GASOLINE

Gas is expensive, ranging from a low of around $1 a gallon on St. Croix up to nearly $2 a gallon on other islands. The USVI stations sell gas by the gallon; in the BVI, you'll buy it by the liter. Most stations take major credit cards. Gas stations abound on St. Croix, St. Thomas, and Tortola; on other islands, be sure to fill up before you leave the main towns. Most stations are open from early morning until early evening. On smaller islands, they may be closed on Sunday.

ROAD CONDITIONS

Main roads and those that go to major attractions are paved, but those to your rental villa may not be. Your best defense is a map, which you can get at rental agencies or tourist offices. Before setting out to a remote location, write down complete directions.

RULES OF THE ROAD

Driving in the USBVI can be tricky. Traffic moves on the left in *both* the USVI and the BVI. (The BVI obviously followed British tradition; no one knows why the USVI followed suit.) Except for the odd right-hand drive car in the BVI, cars on both the BVI and USVI have left-hand drive, the same as cars on the mainland. This means the driver sits on the side of the car next to the road's edge, a situation that makes some people nervous. Note that you may turn left from the left-hand lane when the light is red.

Buckle up before you turn the key. Police in the USVI are notorious for giving $25 tickets to unbelted drivers and front-seat passengers. The police are a bit lax about drunk driver enforcement, but why risk it? Take a taxi or appoint a designated driver when you're out on the town.

Drivers throughout the islands often stop in the middle of the road to chat with people or pick up passengers. Watch out for such situations. Traffic moves at about 10 mph in town; on major highways in St. Croix, for example, you can fly along at 50 mph. On other roads, the speed limit may be less. Traffic jams in major towns such as Christiansted on St. Croix and Charlotte Amalie on St. Thomas aren't unheard of. Try to avoid the 7:30 AM–9 AM and 4 PM–6 PM rush hours.

Main roads in the USVI carry route numbers, but locals may not know them. (Be prepared for such directions as "turn left at the big tree.") Few USVI secondary roads have signs; throughout the BVI, roads aren't very well-marked either. Parking laws are enforced in all major towns. Your best bet is to park in public lots found on all the islands. There are no meters, but there are still fees on some islands, with some lots charging a mere 50¢ an hour.

CHILDREN IN THE USBVI

The USBVI are family-friendly destinations. With endless beaches and outdoor activities, children can run off lots of their excess energy. The beach is also a great place for kids to meet other kids, but make sure you pick one with a lifeguard to safeguard against accidents. Slather on the sunscreen to make sure your child doesn't get a bad burn.

Except at hotels that offer children's programs, there's little in the way of scheduled events for kids. However, there are numerous attractions that children love: Coral World on St. Thomas, the guided hikes offered by the Virgin Islands National Park on St. John, and Ft. Christianvaern on St. Croix. If you're renting a car, don't forget to **arrange for a car seat** when you reserve.

FLYING

If your children are two or older **ask about children's airfares.** As a rule, infants under two not occupying a seat fly at greatly reduced fares or even for free. When booking **confirm carry-on allowances** if you're traveling with infants. In general, for babies charged 10% of the adult fare, you're allowed one carry-on bag and a collapsible stroller; if the flight is full the stroller may have to be checked or you may be limited to less.

Experts agree that it's a good idea to use safety seats aloft for children weighing less than 40 pounds. Airlines set their own policies: U.S. carriers usually require that the child be ticketed, even if he or she is young enough to ride free, since the seats must be strapped into regular seats. Do **check your airline's policy about using safety seats during takeoff and landing.** And since safety seats aren't allowed everywhere on the plane, get seat assignments early.

When reserving, **request children's meals or a freestanding bassinet** if you need them. But note that bulk-head seats, where you must sit to use the bassinet, may lack an overhead bin or storage space on the floor.

FOOD

Your children are welcome at most restaurants, but use common sense. The toniest island eateries probably won't enjoy a visit from your tired children and your children may not appreciate the food anyway. When kids want a taste of home, you'll find McDonald's and Pizza Hut on St. Thomas and St. Croix. On the other islands, hamburgers are standard lunchtime fare.

LODGING

Most USBVI hotels allow children under a certain age to stay in their parents' room for free, but some charge for them as extra adults; be sure to **find out the cutoff age for children's discounts.** Cribs are usually available, but ask before you book. Many of the larger hotels offer children's programs that include supervised care and such activities as beach time, games, and movies. Some include meals. Your hotel may also offer evening babysitting service or have a list of approved local sitters for you to call.

➤ BEST CHOICES IN THE BVI: **Bitter End Yacht Club** (☎ 800/872–2392 or 284/872–2392) on Virgin Gorda, **Brewers Bay Campground** (☎ 284/494–3463) on Tortola, **Little Dix Bay** (☎ 800/238–3000 or 284/495–5555) on Virgin Gorda, **Prospect Reef Resort** (☎ 800/356–8937 or 284/494–3311) on Tortola, and **White Bay Campground** (☎ 284/495–9312) on Jost Van Dyke.

➤ BEST CHOICES IN THE USVI: **Chenay Bay Beach Resort** (☎ 340/773–4408 or 800/548–4457) on St. Croix, **Cinnamon Bay Campground** (☎ 340/776–6330 or 800/539–9998) on St. John, **Maho Bay Campground** (☎ 340/776–6226 or 800/392–9004) on St. John, **Renaissance Grand Beach**

Resort (☎ 340/775–1510 or 800/468–3571) on St. Thomas, **Sapphire Beach Resort & Marina** (☎ 340/775–6100 or 800/524–2090) on St. Thomas, and **Westin Resort, St. John** (☎ 800/937–8461).

SIGHTS & ATTRACTIONS

Throughout this guide, places that are especially good for children are indicated by a rubber duckie icon in the margin.

SUPPLIES & EQUIPMENT

Formula, baby food, and disposable diapers are available throughout the USBVI, but you may not find your favorite brand. The farther you get from St. Thomas and St. Croix, the smaller the selection and the higher the prices. Grocery stores are your best bet for baby food and formula. Discount stores such as Kmart in the USVI may have the best prices on diapers.

COMPUTERS ON THE ROAD

Most large hotels now have modem hookups on their phones, but at the smaller properties you'll need to hunt around for the wall phone jack. On the BVI, some phones have jacks of an unusual size. Bring adapters; a surge protector is also a good idea. All islands have computer stores that can assist with disks and other supplies, but the prices may be higher than at home.

CONSUMER PROTECTION

Whenever shopping or buying travel services in the USBVI, **pay with a major credit card** so you can cancel payment or get reimbursed if there's a problem. If you're doing business with a particular company for the first time, **contact your local Better Business Bureau and the attorney general's offices** in your state and the company's home state, as well. Have any complaints been filed? Finally, if you're buying a package or tour, always **consider travel insurance** that includes default coverage (☞ Insurance, *below*).

➤ LOCAL BBBs: **Council of Better Business Bureaus** (✉ 4200 Wilson Blvd., Suite 800, Arlington, VA 22203, ☎ 703/276–0100, FAX 703/525–8277).

➤ ISLAND AGENCIES: **BVI Tourist Board** (☎ 284/494–3134), **BVI Hotel and Commerce Assoc.** (☎ 284/494–2947), **St. Croix Chamber of Commerce** (☎ 340/773–1435), **St. Croix Hotel and Tourism Association** (☎ 340/773–7117), **St. Thomas/St. John Chamber of Commerce** (☎ 340/776–0100), **St. Thomas/St. John Hotel Association** (☎ 340/774–6835), and **USVI Licensing and Consumer Affairs Department** (☎ 340/774–3130).

CRUISE TRAVEL

St. Thomas is the USBVI's most popular cruise destination, but ships also call at St. Croix, St. John, and Tortola. You'll find numerous activities available through your ship, including trips to beaches, sailing and kayaking adventures, and shopping excursions. The tours allow you to see a lot in a little time. Don't be afraid, however, to strike out on your own. Taxis can whisk you to downtown shopping areas, or you can walk—a great opportunity to see the sights at a slower pace.

➤ CRUISE LINES: **American Canadian Caribbean Line** (✉ Box 368, Warren, RI 02885, ☎ 401/247–0955 or 800/556–7450), **Carnival Cruise Lines** (✉ Carnival Pl., 3655 N.W. 87th Ave., Miami, FL 33178, ☎ 305/599–2600), **Celebrity Cruises** (✉ 5200 Blue Lagoon Dr., Miami, FL 33126, ☎ 800/437–3111), **Clipper Cruise Line** (✉ 7711 Bonhomme Ave., St. Louis, MO 63105, ☎ 800/325–0010), **Club Med** (✉ 40 W. 57th St., New York, NY 10019, ☎ 800/258–2633), **Commodore Cruise Line** (✉ 800 Douglas Rd., Coral Gables, FL 33134, ☎ 305/529–3000), **Costa Cruise Lines** (✉ World Trade Center, 80 S.W. 8th St., Miami, FL 33130, ☎ 800/462–6782), **Crystal Cruises** (✉ 2121 Ave. of the Stars, Los Angeles, CA 90067, ☎ 800/446–6620), **Cunard Line** (✉ 555 5th Ave., New York, NY 10017, ☎ 800/221–4770), **Holland America Line** (✉ 300 Elliott Ave. W, Seattle, WA 98119, ☎ 800/426–0327), **Norwegian Cruise Line** (✉ 95 Merrick Way, Coral Gables, FL 33134, ☎ 800/327–7030), **Premier Cruise Line** (✉ Box 517, Cape Canaveral, FL 32920, ☎ 800/473–3262), **Princess Cruises** (✉ 10100 Santa Monica Blvd., Los Angeles, CA

90067, ☎ 310/553–1770), **Radisson Seven Seas Cruises** (✉ 600 Corporate Dr., Suite 410, Fort Lauderdale, FL 33334, ☎ 800/333–3333), **Royal Caribbean Cruise Line** (✉ 1050 Caribbean Way, Miami, FL 33132, ☎ 800/327–6700), **Royal Olympic Cruises** (✉ 1 Rockefeller Plaza, Suite 315, New York, NY 10020, ☎ 800/872–6400), **Seabourn Cruise Line** (✉ 55 Francisco St., San Francisco, CA 94133, ☎ 800/351–9595), **Silversea Cruises** (✉ 110 E. Broward Blvd., Fort Lauderdale, FL 33301, ☎ 305/522–4477 or 800/722–6655), **Windjammer Barefoot Cruises** (✉ 1759 Bay Rd., Miami Beach, FL 33139, ☎ 800/327–2602), **Windstar Cruises** (✉ 300 Elliott Ave. W, Seattle, WA 98119, ☎ 800/258–7245).

CUSTOMS & DUTIES

When shopping, **keep receipts** for all purchases. Upon reentering the country, **be ready to show customs officials what you've bought.** If you feel a duty is incorrect or object to the way your clearance was handled, note the inspector's badge number and ask to see a supervisor. If the problem isn't resolved, write to the appropriate authorities, beginning with the port director at your point of entry.

IN THE USBVI

Visitors to the USVI arriving from the continental United States or Puerto Rico don't need to pass through customs. Those arriving from any other point of origin do. Items of a personal nature may be brought in to the USVI duty-free; any items of significant commercial value may be subject to a 6% duty.

All visitors to the BVI must pass through customs. Items of a personal nature may be brought in to the BVI duty-free; any items of significant commercial value may be subject to a duty, which varies by the item.

IN AUSTRALIA

Australia residents who are 18 or older may bring home $A400 worth of souvenirs and gifts (including jewelry), 250 cigarettes or 250 grams of tobacco, and 1,125 ml of alcohol (including wine, beer, and spirits). Residents under 18 may bring back $A200 worth of goods. Prohibited items include meat products. Seeds, plants, and fruits need to be declared upon arrival.

➤ INFORMATION: **Australian Customs Service** (Regional Director, ✉ Box 8, Sydney, NSW 2001, ☎ 02/9213–2000, ℻ 02/9213–4000).

IN CANADA

Canadian residents who have been out of Canada for at least 7 days may bring home C$500 worth of goods duty-free. If you've been away less than 7 days but more than 48 hours, the duty-free allowance drops to C$200; if your trip lasts 24–48 hours, the allowance is C$50. You may not pool allowances with family members. Goods claimed under the C$500 exemption may follow you by mail; those claimed under the lesser exemptions must accompany you. Alcohol and tobacco products may be included in the 7-day and 48-hour exemptions but not in the 24-hour exemption. If you meet the age requirements of the province or territory through which you reenter Canada, you may bring in, duty-free, 1.14 liters (40 imperial ounces) of wine or liquor *or* 24 12-ounce cans or bottles of beer or ale. If you are 16 or older you may bring in, duty-free, 200 cigarettes and 50 cigars. Check ahead of time with Revenue Canada or the Department of Agriculture for policies regarding meat products, seeds, plants, and fruits.

You may send an unlimited number of gifts worth up to C$60 each duty-free to Canada. Label the package UNSOLICITED GIFT—VALUE UNDER $60. Alcohol and tobacco are excluded.

➤ INFORMATION: **Revenue Canada** (✉ 2265 St. Laurent Blvd. S, Ottawa, Ontario K1G 4K3, ☎ 613/993–0534; 800/461–9999 in Canada).

IN NEW ZEALAND

Homeward-bound residents 17 or older may bring back $700 worth of souvenirs and gifts. Your duty-free allowance also includes 4.5 liters of wine or beer; one 1,125-ml bottle of spirits; and either 200 cigarettes, 250 grams of tobacco, 50 cigars, or a combination of the three up to 250 grams. Prohibited items include meat products, seeds, plants, and fruits.

THE GOLD GUIDE / SMART TRAVEL TIPS

➤ INFORMATION: **New Zealand Customs** (Custom House, ✉ 50 Anzac Ave., Box 29, Auckland, New Zealand, ☎ 09/359–6655, FAX 09/359–6732).

IN THE U.K.

From countries outside the EU, including the Virgin Islands, you may bring home, duty-free, 200 cigarettes or 50 cigars; 1 liter of spirits or 2 liters of fortified or sparkling wine or liqueurs; 2 liters of still table wine; 60 ml of perfume; 250 ml of toilet water; plus £136 worth of other goods, including gifts and souvenirs. If returning from outside the EU, prohibited items include meat products, seeds, plants, and fruits.

➤ INFORMATION: **HM Customs and Excise** (✉ Dorset House, Stamford St., Bromley Kent BR1 1XX, ☎ 020/7202–4227).

IN THE U.S.

U.S. residents who have been out of the country for at least 48 hours and who have not used the $600 allowance or any part of it in the past 30 days may bring home $600 worth of foreign goods duty-free. This allowance, higher than the standard $400 exemption, applies to the two dozen countries in the Caribbean Basin Initiative (CBI). If you visit a CBI country and a non-CBI country, such as Martinique, you may still bring in $600 worth of goods duty-free, but no more than $400 may be from the non-CBI country. If you're returning from the USVI, the duty-free allowance is $1,200. If your travel included the USVI and another country—say, the Dominican Republic—the $1,200 allowance still applies, but at least $600 worth of goods must be from the USVI.

U.S. residents 21 and older may bring back 1 liter of alcohol duty-free. In addition, regardless of your age, you are allowed 200 cigarettes and 100 non-Cuban cigars. Antiques, which the U.S. Customs Service defines as objects more than 100 years old, enter duty-free, as do original works of art done entirely by hand, including paintings, drawings, and sculptures.

You may also send packages home duty-free: up to $200 worth of goods for personal use, with a limit of one parcel per addressee per day (and no alcohol or tobacco products or perfume worth more than $5); label the package PERSONAL USE and attach a list of its contents and their retail value. Do not label the package UNSOLICITED GIFT or your duty-free exemption will drop to $100. Mailed items do not affect your duty-free allowance on your return.

➤ INFORMATION: **U.S. Customs Service** (inquiries, ✉ 1300 Pennsylvania Ave. NW, Washington, DC 20229, ☎ 202/927–6724; complaints, ✉ Office of Regulations and Rulings, 1300 Pennsylvania Ave. NW, Washington, DC 20229; registration of equipment, ✉ Resource Management, 1300 Pennsylvania Ave. NW, Washington, DC 20229, ☎ 202/927–0540).

DINING

Throughout the book, the restaurants we list are the cream of the crop in each price category. For price charts and details on island specialties and dress codes, *see* the Dining sections in individual island chapters.

RESERVATIONS & DRESS

Reservations are always a good idea: we mention them only when they're essential or aren't accepted. Book as far ahead as you can, and reconfirm as soon as you arrive. In individual reviews, we mention dress only when men are required to wear a jacket or a jacket and tie.

DISABILITIES & ACCESSIBILITY

The USBVI are sometimes difficult destinations for travelers with disabilities. The islands are hilly, and the pavement uneven in many places. Some hotels have ramps and moderately accessible facilities, but **make arrangements in advance** to ensure that ground-floor rooms are available. Taxis or specially adapted rental cars are the most practical option for sightseeing. The Virgin Island Coalition of Citizens with Disabilities offers information on USVI Dial-A-Ride services and special parking permits.

Hotels and resorts will usually accommodate requests for ground-floor rooms, but it's wise to **inquire ahead** as to whether access to the beach, pool, lobby, and dining room requires the use of stairs and whether alternative ramps or elevators are available.

➤ LOCAL RESOURCES: **The Virgin Island Coalition of Citizens with Disabilities** (☎ 340/776–1277).

LODGING

When discussing accessibility with an operator or reservations agent **ask hard questions.** Are there any stairs, inside *or* out? Are there grab bars next to the toilet *and* in the shower/tub? How wide is the doorway to the room? To the bathroom? For the most extensive facilities meeting the latest legal specifications **opt for newer accommodations.**

➤ BEST CHOICE IN THE BVI: **Prospect Reef Resort** (☎ 284/494–3311 or 800/356–8937) on Tortola.

➤ BEST CHOICES IN THE USVI: **Caneel Bay Resort** (☎ 340/776–6111 or 800/928–8889) on St. John, **Hibiscus Beach Hotel** (☎ 340/773–4042 or 800/442–0121) on St. Croix, **Marriott Frenchman's Reef and Morning Star Beach Resorts** (☎ 340/776–8500 or 800/524–2000) on St. Thomas, **Renaissance Grand Beach Resort** (☎ 340/775–1510 or 800/468–3571) on St. Thomas.

TRANSPORTATION

Taxis—generally large safari vans with ample room for a wheelchair—are probably the best option for visitors with mobility problems. They're plentiful and relatively inexpensive. Although they aren't fitted with ramps or lifts, drivers are generally happy to provide assistance. All ferries running between the islands can be fitted with roll-up ramps.

➤ COMPLAINTS: **Aviation Consumer Protection Division** (☞ Air Travel, *above*) for airline-related problems, **Civil Rights Office** (✉ U.S. Department of Transportation, Departmental Office of Civil Rights, S-30, 400 7th St. SW, Room 10215, Washington, DC 20590, ☎ 202/366–4648, FAX 202/366–9371) for problems with surface transportation, **Disability Rights Section** (✉ U.S. Department of Justice, Civil Rights Division, Box 66738, Washington, DC 20035-6738,

☎ 202/514–0301; 800/514–0301; 202/514–0301 TTY; 800/514–0301 TTY, FAX 202/307–1198) for general complaints.

TRAVEL AGENCIES

In the United States, although the Americans with Disabilities Act requires that travel firms serve the needs of all travelers, some agencies specialize in working with people with disabilities.

➤ TRAVELERS WITH MOBILITY PROBLEMS: **Access Adventures** (✉ 206 Chestnut Ridge Rd., Rochester, NY 14624, ☎ 716/889–9096), run by a former physical-rehabilitation counselor; **Accessible Vans of the Rockies, Activity and Travel Agency** (✉ 2040 W. Hamilton Pl., Sheridan, CO 80110, ☎ 303/806–5047 or 888/837–0065, FAX 303/781–2329); **Care-Vacations** (✉ 5-5110 50th Ave., Leduc, Alberta T9E 6V4, ☎ 780/986–6404 or 780/986–8332), which has group tours and is especially helpful with cruise vacations; **Flying Wheels Travel** (✉ 143 W. Bridge St., Box 382, Owatonna, MN 55060, ☎ 507/451–5005 or 800/535–6790, FAX 507/451–1685); **Hinsdale Travel Service** (✉ 201 E. Ogden Ave., Suite 100, Hinsdale, IL 60521, ☎ 630/325–1335); **Tomorrow's Level of Care** (✉ Box 470299, Brooklyn, NY 11247, ☎ 718/756–0794 or 800/932–2012), for nursing services and medical equipment.

DISCOUNTS & DEALS

Be a smart shopper and **compare all your options** before making decisions. A plane ticket bought with a promotional coupon from travel clubs, coupon books, and direct-mail offers may not be cheaper than the least expensive fare from a discount ticket agency. And always keep in mind that what you get is just as important as what you save.

DISCOUNT RESERVATIONS

To save money **look into discount-reservations services** with toll-free numbers, which use their buying power to get a better price on hotels, airline tickets, even car rentals. When booking a room, always **call the hotel's local toll-free number** (if one is available) rather than the central reservations number—you'll often get a better price. Always ask about special packages or corporate rates.

➤ AIRLINE TICKETS: ☎ 800/FLY–4–LESS. ☎ 800/FLY–ASAP.

➤ HOTEL ROOMS: **RMC Travel** (☎ 800/245–5738).

PACKAGE DEALS

Don't confuse packages and guided tours. When you buy a package, you travel on your own, just as though you had planned the trip yourself. Fly/drive packages, which combine airfare and car rental, are often a good deal.

ECOTOURISM

St. John has the Virgin Islands National Park, which helps to keep a lid on development, and a coterie of environmental activists, who help to keep the island green. None of the BVI is very developed, and Tortola and other islands have national parks.

GAY & LESBIAN TRAVEL

Gay and lesbian travelers are welcome in the USBVI, but some unfriendly attitudes still exist. It's wise to avoid public displays of affection in local bars, where the men aren't shy about making their views known. Ask at your hotel for advice on places to go. St. Thomas has a thriving gay community, and you'll be made very welcome.

➤ GAY- AND LESBIAN-FRIENDLY TRAVEL AGENCIES: **Different Roads Travel** (⊠ 8383 Wilshire Blvd., Suite 902, Beverly Hills, CA 90211, ☎ 323/651–5557 or 800/429–8747, FAX 323/651–3678); **Kennedy Travel** (⊠ 314 Jericho Turnpike, Floral Park, NY 11001, ☎ 516/352–4888 or 800/237–7433, FAX 516/354–8849); **Now Voyager** (⊠ 4406 18th St., San Francisco, CA 94114, ☎ 415/626–1169 or 800/255–6951, FAX 415/626–8626); **Skylink Travel and Tour** (⊠ 1006 Mendocino Ave., Santa Rosa, CA 95401, ☎ 707/546–9888 or 800/225–5759, FAX 707/546–9891), which serves lesbian travelers; and **Yellowbrick Road** (⊠ 1500 W. Balmoral Ave., Chicago, IL 60640, ☎ 773/561–1800 or 800/642–2488, FAX 773/561–4497).

HEALTH

FOOD & DRINK

While you might find some unpleasant tasting tap water, food and water in the USBVI is safe. If you do get a mild case of diarrhea it should respond to Imodium (known generically as loperamide) or Pepto-Bismol (not as strong), both of which can be purchased over the counter. Drink plenty of purified water or tea—chamomile is a good folk remedy. In severe cases, rehydrate yourself with a salt-sugar solution (½ teaspoon salt and 4 tablespoons sugar per quart of water). Also note that ciguatera, a toxin found in some reef fish (particularly kingfish), can be a problem at local restaurants.

MEDICAL PLANS

No one plans to get sick while traveling, but it happens, so **consider signing up with a medical-assistance company.** Members get doctor referrals, emergency evacuation or repatriation, hot lines for medical consultation, cash for emergencies, and other assistance.

➤ MEDICAL-ASSISTANCE COMPANIES: **International SOS Assistance** (⊠ 8 Neshaminy Interplex, Suite 207, Trevose, PA 19053, ☎ 215/245–4707 or 800/523–6586, FAX 215/244–9617; ⊠ 12 Chemin Riantbosson, 1217 Meyrin 1, Geneva, Switzerland, ☎ 4122/785–6464, FAX 4122/785–6424; ⊠ 331 N. Bridge Rd., 17-00, Odeon Towers, Singapore 188720, ☎ 65/338–7800, FAX 65/338–7611).

PESTS & OTHER HAZARDS

Mosquitoes can be a problem here, particularly after a spate of showers. Off! insect repellent is readily available, but you may want to bring something stronger. Also a nuisance are the little varmints from the sandflea family known as no-see-ums. You don't realize you're being had for dinner until it's too late, and these bites stay, and itch, and itch, and itch. No-see-ums start getting hungry around 3 PM and are out in force by sunset. They're always more numerous in shady and wooded areas (such as the campgrounds on St. John). **Take a towel along for sitting on the beach, and keep reapplying insect**

repellent. If you can't find any repellent and are desperate, blot a cloth with vodka or gin and dab the itch.

SUN PROTECTION

Even if you've never been sunburned in your life, believe the warnings and **use a sunscreen** in the USBVI. If you're dark-skinned, start with at least an SPF 15 and keep it on. If you're fair-skinned, use a sunscreen with a higher SPF and stay out of the sun during the midday. Rays are most intense between 11 and 2, so move under a sea-grape tree (although you can still burn here) or, better yet, take a shady lunch break. You can also burn in this part of the world when it's cloudy, so putting sunscreen on every day no matter what the weather is the best strategy.

SWIMMING & DIVING

In the water, **watch for black spiny sea urchins** on the bottom; stepping on their spines can really hurt. The good news is that they're usually found in reef areas where you'll be snorkeling, so you aren't likely to step on one by accident. **Familiarize yourself with the various types of coral** before you go out. The fire coral, which can give you a bad burn if you scrape against it, is particularly nasty. **If you do get burned, apply ammonia** to the spot as soon as possible. Scuba divers take note: **Do not fly within 24 hours of scuba diving.**

INSURANCE

The most useful travel insurance plan is a comprehensive policy that includes coverage for trip cancellation and interruption, default, trip delay, and medical expenses (with a waiver for preexisting conditions).

Without insurance you'll lose all or most of your money if you cancel your trip, regardless of the reason. Default insurance covers you if your tour operator, airline, or cruise line goes out of business. Trip-delay covers expenses that arise because of bad weather or mechanical delays. Study the fine print when comparing policies.

If you're traveling internationally, a key component of travel insurance is coverage for medical bills incurred if you get sick on the road. Such expenses are not generally covered by Medicare or private policies. U.K. residents can buy a travel-insurance policy valid for most vacations taken during the year in which it's purchased (but check pre-existing-condition coverage). British and Australian citizens need extra medical coverage when traveling overseas.

Always **buy travel policies directly from the insurance company**; if you buy it from a cruise line, airline, or tour operator that goes out of business you probably won't be covered for the agency or operator's default, a major risk. Before you make any purchase **review your existing health and home-owner's policies** to find what they cover away from home.

➤ TRAVEL INSURERS: In the U.S. **Access America** (✉ 6600 W. Broad St., Richmond, VA 23230, ☎ 804/285–3300 or 800/284–8300), **Travel Guard International** (✉ 1145 Clark St., Stevens Point, WI 54481, ☎ 715/345–0505 or 800/826–1300). In Canada **Voyager Insurance** (✉ 44 Peel Center Dr., Brampton, Ontario L6T 4M8, ☎ 905/791–8700; 800/668–4342 in Canada).

➤ INSURANCE INFORMATION: In the United Kingdom the **Association of British Insurers** (✉ 51–55 Gresham St., London EC2V 7HQ, ☎ 020/7600–3333, FAX 020/7696–8999). In Australia the **Insurance Council of Australia** (☎ 03/9614–1077, FAX 03/9614–7924).

LODGING

Decide whether you want to pay the extra price for a room overlooking the ocean or pool. At slightly less expensive properties, the difference may be as little as $10–$20 per room; at luxury resorts, however, it could be as much as $100 per room. Also **find out how close the property is to a beach;** at some hotels you can walk barefoot from your room onto the sand; others are across a road or a 10-minute drive away.

Nighttime entertainment is often alfresco in the USBVI, so if you go to sleep early or are a light sleeper, ask for a room away from the dance floor. Air-conditioning isn't a necessity on all islands, many of which are cooled by trade winds, but it can be a plus if you enjoy an afternoon snooze or are bothered by humidity. Breezes are best in second-floor rooms, particularly corner rooms. If you like to sleep without air-conditioning, make sure that windows can be opened and have screens. If you're staying away from the water, make sure the room has a ceiling fan, and that it works. That said, you should note that in even the most luxurious resorts there are times when things simply *don't* work; it's a fact of Caribbean life. No matter how diligent the upkeep, humidity and salt air take their toll, and cracked tiles and chipped paint are common everywhere.

The lodgings we list are the cream of the crop in each price category. We always list available facilities, but we don't specify whether they cost extra: When pricing accommodations, always ask what's included. All hotels listed have rooms with private baths unless otherwise noted.

Assume that hotels operate on the **European Plan** (EP, with no meals) unless we specify that they are **all-inclusive** (including all meals and most activities) or use the **Breakfast Plan** (BP, with a full breakfast daily), **Continental Plan** (CP, with a Continental breakfast daily), or **Modified American Plan** (MAP, with breakfast and dinner daily). For price charts and details on types of accommodations, *see* the Lodging sections in individual island chapters.

APARTMENT & VILLA RENTALS

If you want a home base that's roomy enough for a family and comes with cooking facilities **consider a furnished rental.** These can save you money, especially if you're traveling with a group. Home-exchange directories sometimes list rentals as well as exchanges.

➤ INTERNATIONAL AGENTS: **At Home Abroad** (✉ 405 E. 56th St., Suite 6H, New York, NY 10022, ☎ 212/421–9165, FAX 212/752–1591), **Europa-Let/Tropical Inn-Let** (✉ 92 N. Main St., Ashland, OR 97520, ☎ 541/482–5806 or 800/462–4486, FAX 541/482–0660), **Hideaways International** (✉

767 Islington St., Portsmouth, NH 03801, ☎ 603/430–4433 or 800/843–4433, FAX 603/430–4444; membership $99), **Hometours International** (✉ Box 11503, Knoxville, TN 37939, ☎ 423/690–8484 or 800/367–4668), **Rent-a-Home International** (✉ 7200 34th Ave. NW, Seattle, WA 98117, ☎ 206/789–9377, FAX 206/789–9379), **Vacation Home Rentals Worldwide** (✉ 235 Kensington Ave., Norwood, NJ 07648, ☎ 201/767–9393 or 800/633–3284, FAX 201/767–5510), **Villas and Apartments Abroad** (✉ 420 Madison Ave., Suite 1003, New York, NY 10017, ☎ 212/759–1025 or 800/433–3020, FAX 212/755–8316), **Villas International** (✉ 950 Northgate Dr., Suite 206, San Rafael, CA 94903, ☎ 415/499–9490 or 800/221–2260, FAX 415/499–9491).

CAMPING

Camping on the USBVI is limited to established campgrounds. Except for the national park service's Cinnamon Bay Campground on St. John, all are privately operated. None have hot showers, game rooms, or swimming pools such as you'd find at mainland private campgrounds. Instead, your entertainment comes on the beach and along hiking trails.

➤ CAMPGROUNDS: **Cinnamon Bay Campground** (☎ 800/539–9998), **Maho Bay Camps** (☎ 800/392–9004).

HOTELS

Several large hoteliers have establishments in the USVI.

➤ TOLL-FREE NUMBERS: **Best Western** (☎ 800/528–1234), **Marriott** (☎ 800/228–9290), **Renaissance Hotels & Resorts** (☎ 800/468–3571), **Ritz-Carlton** (☎ 800/341–3333), **Westin Hotels & Resorts** (☎ 800/228–3000), **Wyndham Hotels & Resorts** (☎ 800/822–4200).

MAIL & SHIPPING

"Whimsical" might best describe Caribbean addresses. Streets change name for no apparent reason, maps and signage aren't always reliable, and many buildings have no numbers. Addresses throughout this guide include cross streets, landmarks, and other directionals. But to find your destination, you may have to ask a local—and be prepared for such directions as "Take a right at the fish market, then a left where you see the cow pasture."

Airmail between the USBVI and cities in the United States or Canada takes 7–14 days; surface mail can take 4–6 weeks. Airmail to the United Kingdom takes 2–3 weeks; to Australia and New Zealand, 3–4 weeks. For island-specific information on post office locations, postal rates, and opening hours, *see* Telephones and Mail *in* A to Z sections of individual island chapters.

MEDIA

NEWSPAPERS & MAGAZINES

The New York Times and *USA Today* are available mid-morning at most major hotels. Local daily newspapers in the USVI include the *Daily News,* the *Independent,* and the *Avis.* On St. John, the *Tradewinds* comes out weekly, and the *St. John Times* is published monthly. The *Beacon* comes out twice a week and the *Island Sun* weekly in the BVI.

RADIO & TELEVISION

Many islanders depend on the radio to stay up to date. WSTA at 1340 AM and WVWI at 1000 AM on St. Thomas and WSTX at 970 AM or 100.3 FM on St. Croix are popular. In the BVI, tune in to ZBVI (pronounced Zed BVI) at 780 AM. Cable television is available nearly everywhere.

MONEY MATTERS

The U.S. dollar is the currency on both the BVI and the USVI. Admission prices throughout this guide are given for adults. Substantially reduced fees are almost always available for children, students, and senior citizens. For island-specific information on banks, currency, service charges, taxes, and tipping, *see* the A to Z sections in the individual island chapters.

ATMS

Chase Bank has ATMs at all its locations on both the USVI and the BVI. You'll also find ATMs at Banco Popular branches throughout the USVI.

➤ ATM LOCATIONS: **MasterCard Cirrus** (☎ 800/424–7787; www.mastercard.com/atm), **Visa Plus** (☎ 800/843–7587; www.visa.com/atm).

CREDIT CARDS

Most USBVI merchants accept credit cards. Villa renters should be forewarned that villa managers may be the exception. And that quaint little restaurant tucked off the beaten path may prefer cash only.

Throughout this guide, the following abbreviations are used: **AE**, American Express; **D**, Discover; **DC**, Diner's Club; **MC**, Master Card; and **V**, Visa.

TRAVELER'S CHECKS

Do you need traveler's checks? It depends on where you're headed. If you're going to rural areas and small towns, go with cash; traveler's checks are best used in cities. Lost or stolen checks can usually be replaced within 24 hours. To ensure a speedy refund, buy your own traveler's checks—don't let someone else pay for them: irregularities like this can cause delays. The person who bought the checks should make the call to request a refund.

PACKING

Make sure you can handle your luggage. There are no carts at USBVI airports, and porters can be scarce. Small interisland planes have very limited carry-on space. Suitcases that fit under seats in major carriers just won't fit on these tiny planes. So **check your luggage** and **pack only small, essential items (medicine, bathing suit, etc.) in your carry-on.** Regional carriers let you tote your luggage to the plane, where the pilot or first mate will stow it away. If you're worried about losing your bags, this is a good practice to follow.

You won't need a suit and tie or a cocktail dress, but at the fancier resorts men will need a jacket (but not a tie), particularly in high season. Women will need summery dresses or pant suits. Casual clothes are appropriate almost everywhere. Natural materials that breathe work best in these warm climates, and there are few dry cleaners around so bring washable clothing. At many places you'll spend the day in your bathing suit, wear a coverup to lunch, and then slip into something casual for dinner. If you plan to hike, be sure to bring along some sturdy shoes. You also may want to **bring a lightweight sweater or long-sleeve T-shirt** for breezy nights (or overly air-conditioned restaurants) or for the ferry ride home after a day in the sun.

One clothing tip that will go a long way in tourist-local relations: **Men, keep your shirts on, and women, get your tan on the beach, not in town.** You'll receive a much kinder reception from the prim Virgin Islanders if you're fully, albeit casually, dressed.

To avoid paying shockingly high drugstore prices in the Virgin Islands, **buy creams, lotions, insect repellents, sunscreens, and sunburn remedies before you leave home.** For the same reason, **buy your film at home.**

In your carry-on luggage **bring an extra pair of eyeglasses or contact lenses** and **enough of any medication you take** to last the entire trip. You may also want your doctor to write a spare prescription using the drug's generic name, since brand names may vary from country to country. In luggage to be checked, **never pack prescription drugs or valuables.** To avoid customs delays, carry medications in their original packaging. And don't forget to copy down and carry addresses of offices that handle refunds of lost traveler's checks.

CHECKING LUGGAGE

How many carry-on bags you can bring with you is up to the airline. Most allow two, but not always, so **make sure that everything you carry aboard will fit under your seat,** and get to the gate early. Note that if you have a seat at the back of the plane, you'll probably board first, while the overhead bins are still empty.

If you're flying internationally, note that baggage allowances may be determined not by piece but by weight—generally 88 pounds (40 kilograms) in first class, 66 pounds (30 kilograms) in business class, and 44 pounds (20 kilograms) in economy.

Airline liability for baggage is limited to $1,250 per person on flights within the United States. On international flights it amounts to $9.07 per pound or $20 per kilogram for checked baggage (roughly $640 per 70-pound bag) and $400 per passenger for unchecked baggage. You can buy additional coverage at check-in for about $10 per $1,000 of coverage, but it excludes a rather extensive list of items, shown on your airline ticket.

Before departure **itemize your bags' contents** and their worth, and label the bags with your name, address, and phone number. (If you use your home address, cover it so that potential thieves can't see it readily.) Inside each bag **pack a copy of your itinerary.** At check-in **make sure that each bag is correctly tagged** with the destination airport's three-letter code. If your bags arrive damaged or fail to arrive at all, file a written report with the airline before leaving the airport.

PASSPORTS & VISAS

When traveling internationally **carry a passport even if you don't need one** (it's always the best form of ID), and **make two photocopies of the data page** (one for someone at home and another for you, carried separately from your passport). If you lose your passport, promptly call the nearest embassy or consulate and the local police.

ENTERING THE USBVI

Upon entering the USVI, U.S. and Canadian citizens are required to present some proof of citizenship, if not a passport then a birth certificate, citizenship certificate, voter registration card, or driver's license. Australian, New Zealand, and U.K. citizens must present a passport. Upon entering the BVI, Australian, Canadian, New Zealand, U.K., and U.S. citizens must have a valid passport.

PASSPORT OFFICES

The best time to apply for a passport or to renew is during the fall and winter. Before any trip, check your passport's expiration date, and, if necessary, renew it as soon as possible.

➤ AUSTRALIAN CITIZENS: **Australian Passport Office** (☎ 131–232).

➤ CANADIAN CITIZENS: **Passport Office** (☎ 819/994–3500 or 800/ 567–6868).

➤ NEW ZEALAND CITIZENS: **New Zealand Passport Office** (☎ 04/494–0700 for information on how to apply; 04/474–8000 or 0800/225–050 in New Zealand for information on applications already submitted).

➤ U.K. CITIZENS: **London Passport Office** (☎ 0990/210–410) for fees and documentation requirements and to request an emergency passport.

➤ U.S. CITIZENS: **National Passport Information Center** (☎ 900/225–5674; calls are 35¢ per minute for automated service, $1.05 per minute for operator service).

REST ROOMS

You'll find public rest rooms in all restaurants as well as at visitors centers near shopping areas. Some beaches, particularly those that get a lot of traffic, have modern amenities.

SAFETY

In the USVI, ask hotel staff members about the wisdom of venturing off the beaten path. Although it may seem like a nice night for a stroll back to your hotel from that downtown restaurant, it's better to take a taxi than face an incident. Although local police go to great lengths to ensure your safety, crime does happen. The BVI has seen less crime than its neighbors to the west, but again, better safe than sorry.

Follow the same precautions you would anywhere. Look around before using the ATM machine. Keep tabs on your pocketbook; put it on your lap—not the back of your chair—in restaurants. Stow valuable jewelry or other items in the hotel safe when you leave your room; hotel and villa burglaries do occur infrequently. Deserted beaches on St. John and the BVI are usually safe, but think twice about stopping at that luscious strand of lonely sand on St. Croix and St. Thomas. Hotel or public beaches are your best bets. Never leave your belongings unattended at the beach or on the seats of your rental car.

WOMEN IN THE USBVI

It's perfectly safe for women to travel alone to the USBVI, and you won't lack for dance partners at local night spots. Use common sense, and don't fall prey to age-old lines delivered with a charming Caribbean accent.

SENIOR-CITIZEN TRAVEL

In the off-season, many hotels on the USVI and BVI may offer substantial rate reductions. While they're usually not for senior citizens alone, it never hurts to ask.

To qualify for age-related discounts **mention your senior-citizen status up front** when booking hotel reservations (not when checking out) and before you're seated in restaurants (not when paying the bill). When renting a car ask about promotional car-rental discounts, which can be cheaper than senior-citizen rates.

➤ EDUCATIONAL PROGRAMS: **Elderhostel** (✉ 75 Federal St., 3rd fl., Boston, MA 02110, ☎ 877/426–8056, FAX 877/426–2166).

SHOPPING

St. Thomas, and to a lesser extent St. Croix and St. John, are a duty-free shopper's paradise. Liquor, jewelry, and electronic items all shout for your attention when you browse through the shopping areas. Check prices before you leave home. You may do better on electronics at stateside outlet stores. Don't expect to bargain with the merchants.

KEY DESTINATIONS

The prime St. Thomas shopping districts are historic downtown Charlotte Amalie and the Havensight Mall next to the cruise-ship pier. On St. Croix, Christiansted and Frederiksted both have many shops. St. John's Cruz Bay has two charming malls with a string of shops in between. For shopping on Tortola, head to Road Town. You'll find shops adjacent to marinas and in hotels on both the USVI and BVI.

SMART SOUVENIRS

Although duty-free goods may tempt you, the real finds are tucked away in small shops where the owner has scoured the ends of the earth, and the Virgin Islands, to stock his or her store. Look for jams and jellies made in the USBVI, local artwork in various styles, and hand-crafted jewelry in all price ranges.

WATCH OUT

USBVI shopkeepers are honest as a whole, but there's always a bad banana or two in the bunch. If you're buying a big-ticket item, ask for a guarantee. Be particularly careful when shopping the vendor's plaza on St. Thomas: once in a while, someone tries to pass off fake designer goods as the real thing.

STUDENTS IN THE USBVI

Students are especially fond of the BVI in general and of St. John in the USVI. Camping on these islands cuts costs considerably. In addition, inter-island ferry trips are affordable, so students can often island-hop their way from St. Thomas, which has a major airport, to St. John and on to the BVI.

➤ STUDENT IDs & SERVICES: **Council on International Educational Exchange** (CIEE, ✉ 205 E. 42nd St., 14th fl., New York, NY 10017, ☎ 212/822–2600 or 888/268–6245, FAX 212/822–2699) for mail orders only, in the U.S. **Travel Cuts** (✉ 187 College St., Toronto, Ontario M5T 1P7, ☎ 416/979–2406 or 800/667–2887) in Canada.

TELEPHONES

Phone and fax service to and from the USBVI is up-to-date and efficient. Phone cards are used throughout the islands; you can buy them (in several denominations) at many retail shops and convenience stores. They must be used in special card phones, which are also widely available. For island-specific information on phones, *see* the A to Z sections *in* individual island chapters.

COUNTRY & AREA CODES

The area code for the USVI is 340; for the BVI, 284.

DIRECTORY & OPERATOR INFORMATION

In the USVI, dial 913 to reach the operator. In the BVI, dial 119. In both locations, dial 0 for advice on how to place your call.

INTERNATIONAL CALLS

Calling the United States and Canada from the USBVI is just like making a long distance call within the United States: dial 1, plus the area code. To reach Europe, Australia, and New Zealand dial 011 followed by the country code.

LOCAL CALLS

Local calls from USBVI pay phones run 25¢, although some privately owned phones are now charging 35¢. Calls from the USVI to the BVI and vice versa are charged as international toll calls.

LONG-DISTANCE SERVICES

AT&T, MCI, and Sprint access codes make calling long distance relatively convenient, but you may find the local access number blocked in many hotel rooms. First ask the hotel operator to connect you. If the hotel operator balks ask for an international operator, or dial the international operator yourself. One way to improve your odds of getting connected to your long-distance carrier is to travel with more than one company's calling card (a hotel may block Sprint, for example, but not MCI). If all else fails call from a pay phone.

➤ ACCESS CODES: **AT&T** (☎ 800/225–5288), **MCI** (☎ 800/888–8000), **Sprint** (☎ 800/366–2255).

TOURS & PACKAGES

On a prepackaged tour or independent vacation everything is prearranged so you'll spend less time planning—and often get it all at a good price.

BOOKING WITH AN AGENT

Travel agents are excellent resources. But it's good to collect brochures from several agencies because some agents' suggestions may be influenced by relationships with tour and package firms that reward them for volume sales. If you have a special interest **find an agent with expertise in that area;** the American Society of Travel Agents, or ASTA (☞ Travel Agencies, *below*), has a database of specialists worldwide.

Make sure your agent knows the accommodations and other services of the place they're recommending. Ask about the hotel's location; room sizes; beds; and whether it has a pool, room service, or programs for children, if you care about these. Has your agent been there in person or sent others whom you can contact?

Do some homework on your own, too: Local tourist boards can provide information about lesser-known and small-niche operators, some of which may sell only direct.

BUYER BEWARE

Each year consumers are stranded or lose their money when tour operators—even large ones with excellent reputations—go out of business. So **check out the operator.** Ask several travel agents about its reputation, and try to **book with a company that has a consumer-protection program.** (Look for information in the company's brochure.) In the United States, members of the National Tour Association (NTA) and the United States Tour Operators Association (USTOA) are required to set aside funds to cover your payments and travel arrangements in case the company defaults. It's also a good idea to choose a company that participates in the ASTA's Tour Operator Program (TOP); ASTA will act as mediator in any disputes between you and your tour operator.

Remember that the more your package or tour includes the better you can predict the ultimate cost of your vacation. Make sure you know exactly what is covered, and **beware of hidden costs.** Are taxes, tips, and transfers included? Entertainment and excursions? These can add up.

➤ TOUR-OPERATOR RECOMMENDATIONS: **ASTA** (☞ Travel Agencies, *below*), **NTA** (✉ 546 E. Main St., Lexington, KY 40508, ☎ 606/226–4444 or 800/682–8886), **USTOA** (✉ 342 Madison Ave., Suite 1522, New York, NY 10173, ☎ 212/599–6599 or 800/468–7862, ℻ 212/599–6744).

PACKAGES

Independent vacation packages are available from major tour operators and airlines. The companies listed below offer vacation packages in a broad price range.

➤ AIR/HOTEL: **Delta Vacations** (☎ 800/872–7786, ℻ 954/357–4687), **US Airways Vacations** (☎ 800/455–0123).

➤ FROM THE U.K.: **British Virgin Islands Holidays** (✉ 11–19 Hockerill St., Bishop's Stortford, Herts. CM23 5DH, ☎ 01279/656111), **Caribbean Connection** (✉ Concorde House, Forest St., Chester CH1 1QR, ☎ 01244/341131), **Caribtours** (✉ 161 Fulham Rd., London SW3 6SN, ☎ 020/7581–3517), **Harlequin Worldwide** (✉ 2 North Rd., South Ockendon, Essex RM15 6QJ, ☎ 01708/850300), **Hayes and Jarvis Ltd.** (✉ Hayes House, 152 King St., London W6 0QU, ☎ 020/8222–7811).

THEME TRIPS

➤ SAILING SCHOOLS: **Annapolis Sailing School** (✉ Box 3334, 601 6th St., Annapolis, MD 21403, ☎ 410/267–7205 or 800/638–9192), **Offshore Sailing School** (✉ 16731-110 McGregor Blvd., Fort Myers, FL 33908, ☎ 941/454–1700 or 800/221–4326, ℻ 941/454–1191).

➤ SCUBA DIVING: **Rothschild Dive Safaris** (✉ 900 West End Ave., #1B, New York, NY 10025-3525, ☎ 800/359–0747, ℻ 212/749–6172).

➤ YACHT CHARTERS: **Alden Yacht Charters** (✉ 1909 Alden Landing, Portsmouth, RI 02871, ☎ 401/683–4200 or 800/662–2628, ℻ 401/683–3668), **Huntley Yacht Vacations** (✉ 210 Preston Rd., Wernersville, PA 19565, ☎ 610/678–2628 or 800/322–9224, ℻ 610/670–1767), **Lynn Jachney Charters** (✉ Box 302, Marblehead, MA 01945, ☎ 617/639–0787 or 800/223–2050, ℻ 617/639–0216), **The Moorings** (✉ 19345 U.S. Hwy. 19 N, 4th floor, Clearwater, FL 34624-3193, ☎ 813/530–5424 or 800/535–7289, ℻ 813/530–9474), **Nicholson Yacht Charters** (✉ 78 Bolton St., Cambridge, MA 02140-3321, ☎ 617/661–0555 or 800/662–6066, ℻ 617/661–0554), **Ocean Voyages** (✉ 1709 Bridgeway, Sausalito, CA 94965, ☎ 415/332–4681 or 800/299–4444, ℻ 415/332–7460), **Russell Yacht Charters** (✉ 404 Hulls Hwy., #175, Southport, CT 06490, ☎ 203/255–2783 or 800/635–8895), **SailAway Yacht Charters** (✉ 15605 S.W. 92nd Ave., Miami, FL 33157-1972, ☎ 305/253–7245 or 800/724–5292, ℻ 305/251–4408).

THE GOLD GUIDE / SMART TRAVEL TIPS

TRAVEL AGENCIES

A good travel agent puts your needs first. Look for an agency that has been in business at least five years, emphasizes customer service, and has someone on staff who specializes in your destination. In addition **make sure the agency belongs to a professional trade organization.** The Amercian Society of Travel Agents (ASTA), with 27,000 agents in some 170 countries, is the largest and most influential in the field. Operating under the motto "Integrity in Travel," it maintains and enforces a strict code of ethics and will step in to help mediate any agent-client disputes if necessary. ASTA also maintains a Web site that includes a directory of agents. (Note that if a travel agency is also acting as your tour operator, *see* Buyer Beware *in* Tours & Packages, *above*.)

➤ LOCAL AGENT REFERRALS: **American Society of Travel Agents (ASTA,** ☎ 800/965–2782 24-hr hot line, ℻ 703/684–8319, www.astanet.com), **Association of British Travel Agents (ABTA;** ✉ 55–57 Newman St., London W1P 4AH, ☎ 020/7637–2444, ℻ 020/7637–0713), **Association of Canadian Travel Agents (ACTA;** ✉ 1729 Bank St., Suite 201, Ottawa, Ontario K1V 7Z5, ☎ 613/521–0474, ℻ 613/521–0805), **Australian Federation of Travel Agents (AFTA;** ✉ Level 3, 309 Pitt St., Sydney 2000, ☎ 02/9264–3299, ℻ 02/9264–1085), **Travel Agents' Association of New Zealand (TAANZ;** ✉ Box 1888, Wellington 10033, ☎ 04/499–0104, ℻ 04/499–0786).

VISITOR INFORMATION

For general information on the islands, contact these tourist offices before you go. (For details on island offices, *see* the A to Z sections of individual island chapters.)

➤ USVI: **United States Virgin Islands Department of Tourism** (✉ 500 N. Michigan Ave., Chicago, IL 60611, ☎ 312/670–8784, ℻ 312/670–8789; ✉ 3460 Wilshire Blvd., Suite 412, Los Angeles, CA 90010, ☎ 213/739–0138, ℻ 213/739–2005; ✉ 2655 Le Jeune Rd., Suite 907, Coral Gables, FL 33134, ☎ 305/442–7200, ℻ 305/ 445–9044; ✉ 630 5th Ave., New York, NY 10111, ☎ 212/332–2222, ℻ 212/332–2223; ✉ 444 Capitol St., Washington, DC 20006, ☎ 202/624–3590, ℻ 202/624–3594; ✉ 1300 Ashford Ave., Condado, Santurce, Puerto Rico 00907, ☎ 787/724–3816, ℻ 787/724–7223; ✉ 33 Bloor St. W., Toronto, Ontario M5V 1C2 Canada, ☎ 416/233–1414; ✉ Molasses House, Clove Hitch Quay, Plantation Wharf, York Pl., London SW11 3TN, United Kingdom, ☎ 020/7978–5262, ℻ 020/7924–3171).

➤ BVI: **British Virgin Islands Tourist Board** (✉ 630 5th Ave., New York, NY 10111, ☎ 212/696–0400 or 800/835–8530, ℻ 212/949–8254), **British Virgin Islands Tourism Bureau** (✉ 1804 Union St., San Francisco, CA 94123, ☎ 415/775–0344 or 800/232–7770, ℻ 415/775–2554; ✉ 110 St. Martins La., London WC2N 4DY United Kingdom, ☎ 020/7240–4259, ℻ 020/7240–4270).

➤ U.S. GOVERNMENT ADVISORIES: **U.S. Department of State** (✉ Overseas Citizens Services Office, Room 4811 N.S., 2201 C St. NW, Washington, DC 20520; ☎ 202/647–5225 for interactive hot line; 301/946–4400 for computer bulletin board; ℻ 202/647–3000 for interactive hot line); enclose a self-addressed, stamped, business-size envelope.

WEB SITES

On the USVI Department of Tourism's Web site (www.usvi.net) you need only pick a palm tree to access information on St. Croix, St. Thomas, or St. John. In addition to the usual lodging, dining, and shopping categories, the BVI Tourism Bureau's site (www.bviwelcome.com) has a separate "At Sea" category, a nod to the popularity of water sports on these islands. And of course every Caribbean traveler should bookmark the Caribbean Tourism Organization's comprehensive site (www.caribtourism.com).

WHEN TO GO

Traditionally, high season in the USBVI has been in the winter, from about December 15 to the week after the USVI Carnival, usually the last week in April. This is the most fashionable, the most expensive, and the most popular time for cruising or lolling on the beaches, far from the icy north, so most hotels fill up. **Make your reservations at least two or three months in advance** for the very best places. There's usually a lull in the middle to the end of January, when it can be easier to get last-minute reservations and sometimes even slightly lower rates.

Summer is one of the prettiest times of the year; the sea is even calmer, it's cheaper, and things generally move at a slower pace (except for the first two weeks of August on Tortola when the BVI celebrates Carnival).

CLIMATE

Weather in the USBVI is a year-round wonder. The average daily temperature is about 80°F, and there isn't much variation from the coolest to the warmest months. Rainfall averages 40–44 inches per year. But in the tropics, rainstorms tend to be sudden and brief, often erupting early in the morning and at dusk.

In May and June what's known as the Sahara Dust sometimes moves through. That's dust that literally blows across the oceans from the African desert, making for hazy spring days and spectacular sunsets.

Toward the end of summer, of course, hurricane season begins in earnest, with the first tropical wave passing by in June. Islanders pay close attention to the tropical waves as they form and travel up from Africa. In an odd paradox, tropical storms passing by leave behind the sunniest and clearest days you'll ever see. (And that's saying something in the land of zero air pollution.)

➤ FORECASTS: **Weather Channel Connection** (☎ 900/932–8437), 95¢ per minute from a Touch-Tone phone.

What follows are average daily maximum and minimum temperatures for the Virgin Islands.

Climate in the Virgin Islands

Jan.	86F	25C	May	88F	31C	Sept.	92F	33C
	74	23		75	24		76	24
Feb.	86F	25C	June	88F	31C	Oct.	92F	33C
	74	23		75	24		76	24
Mar.	87F	30C	July	95F	35C	Nov.	86F	25C
	71	22		77	25		72	22
Apr.	87F	30C	Aug.	95F	35C	Dec.	86F	25C
	71	22		77	25		72	22

1 DESTINATION: THE VIRGIN ISLANDS

SOMETHING FOR EVERYONE

SEPARATED BY ONLY a narrow channel of shimmering water patrolled by flotillas of pelicans and pleasure craft, the United States and British Virgin Island groups are nevertheless a world apart. It isn't just the obvious: a tale of two traditions and governments. Indeed, clearing customs is usually a formality (although it's taken very seriously), and the U.S. dollar is the official currency on both sides of the "border." Rather, it's the individual look and feel that set them apart, the atmosphere they determinedly cultivate—and the differing breeds of visitors this attracts—an atmosphere perhaps too glibly defined as American verve versus British reserve.

Though the islands are closely grouped, the vegetation and terrain vary widely. The USVI are largely lush and tropical. On St. John, where two-thirds of the land is under U.S. National Park Service protection, there are more than 250 species of trees, vines, shrubs, flowers, and other plant life. Each of the three major USVI—St. John, St. Thomas, and St. Croix—is really a collection of ecosystems, ranging from tropical seacoast to mountain, rain forest to desert. The flowering trees are particularly superb: frangipani, flamboyant, hibiscus, and lignum vitae blanket the hills and rolling fields with a dainty blue, pink, yellow, and white quilt.

In contrast, the BVI's largest island, Tortola, lost lots of its vegetation to the farmer's field. This gives it a very different look than that of the heavily forested St. John, just a 2-mi boat ride away. Its high peaks culminate with see-forever views at Sage Mountain National Park. Virgin Gorda is fringed with monumental boulders whose exact origins are still shrouded in mystery. These are the "cactus tropics," dotted with agave and other spiny plants and enlivened by the vibrant colors of an occasional wild hibiscus or bougainvillea tree.

Both island groups are steeped in history. The USVI are graced with the rich architectural legacy of the original Danish settlers, including the picturesque ruins of their sugar plantations. Christiansted and Frederiksted, the two main towns on St. Croix, feature delightful red-roof gingerbreads in coral and canary yellow, fronted by shaded galleries and stately colonnades. The old sugar estates on St. Croix are the islands' best preserved and most elegant. Caribbean ghost towns unto themselves, they're crawling and cracked with undergrowth, the haunting grandeur of their double stairways eloquently attesting to St. Croix's former prosperity.

If their architectural remains aren't as spectacular, the BVI have an incomparable *air* of history. In the 17th and 18th centuries the islands' numerous cays, rocks, secret coves, and treacherous reefs formed the perfect headquarters for raiding corsairs and privateers, among them the infamous Edward "Blackbeard" Teach, Captain Kidd, and Sir Francis Drake. The nautical spirit lives on, and today these pirate hideaways attract legions of "yachties." The calm, iridescent waters of the BVI are among the world's most popular sailing destinations. In fact, the islands, forested by masts and flecked with sails, are perhaps best experienced by boat—what better way to explore every rainbow-colored coral reef or gleaming scimitar of white sand (replete with beach bar)? The favorite sport may well be motoring to a private cove, waving if it's occupied, and cruising to the next.

But ultimately the greatest differences between the USVI and the BVI are the ways in which they've been developed. Step off the plane in St. Thomas and you know you're in a consumer society where bigger is better. Posters hawking products and fast-food franchises dominate the lush surroundings. Charlotte Amalie, the bustling capital, pulsates with legendary duty-free shopping and by far the most active nightlife in the area. You'll discover more pristine pockets on pastoral St. Croix, which by comparison resembles a friendly small town. The odd isle out in the USVI equation is tranquil, sleepy St. John, the closest American island to the BVI in distance and temperament. But even here the development and pace often exceed that of its British cousins.

With so many options for the tourist dollar, competition among USVI properties is fierce. The constant upgrading of facilities, added amenities, and attractive package rates translate into tremendous values. If you want all the comforts, conveniences (and convenience stores) of home—with tropical sun and exotic accent—head for the USVI.

Although tourism is as much the number-one industry on the BVI as it is on the USVI, you'd never know it. On these quiet, unhurried islands, there are few major developments and no high-rises or traffic lights. Cruise ships do visit regularly, but far fewer stop here than at the USVI. Though there are repeated promises (viewed more as threats by locals) from the tourist office to deepen the harbor and lengthen the airport runways (now scheduled to happen by 2003), there's a tacit understanding that it's precisely their comparatively undeveloped state that makes the BVI such desirable vacation spots.

By many tourism standards, the BVI are *not* a bargain. The hotels tend to be small and exclusive; many were built by industrial barons and shipping magnates as hideaways for themselves and friends. But true luxury is often understated. It isn't necessarily blow-dryers and satellite TVs in every room. Rather, it's the privacy, the relaxed, easygoing pace, the personalized service, and the ambience.

Expatriates on both sets of islands often delight in taking potshots at their neighbors. You'll find many passionate devotees and repeat visitors who wouldn't dream of crossing the border. USVI detractors point to the swarming crowds and comparatively high crime rate on St. Thomas and St. Croix. BVI critics cite the boring lifestyle and the difficulty of getting top-notch goods even on Tortola. The USVI have been disparaged as "entry-level Caribbean" and "Detroit with palm trees." Their aficionados will counter, "There's a reason the British Home Office once called the BVI 'the least important part of the Empire.' "

The rivalry only demonstrates how popular the islands are with their respective fans. Luckily, whichever you prefer, there's always the advantage of proximity. In the Virgin Islands you can truly have the best of both worlds.

— Jordan Simon

A freelance writer who has traveled throughout the Caribbean, Jordan Simon has written for *Elle, Travel & Leisure, Modern Bride,* and *Fodor's Caribbean.*

WHAT'S WHERE

The U.S. Virgin Islands
ST. THOMAS➤ Because it's the transportation hub of the Virgin Islands, many visitors at least land on hilly St. Thomas. Those who stay longer may have come for its legendary shopping or the wide variety of water sports, activities, and accommodations. The bustling port of Charlotte Amalie is the main town; about ¼ mi off its shores is Water Island, which was made the fourth Virgin Island in 1996 when the U.S. Department of the Interior transferred it to the territorial government. Up-and-coming Red Hook sits on St. Thomas's eastern tip. The island's western end is relatively wild, and hotels and resorts rim its southern and eastern shores.

ST. CROIX➤ The largest of the USVI, St. Croix is 40 mi south of St. Thomas. Plantation ruins, reminiscent of the days when it was a great producer of sugar, dot the island. Its northwest is covered by a lush rain forest, its drier East End spotted with cacti. The restored Danish port of Christiansted and the more Victorian-looking Frederiksted are its main towns; Buck Island, off the northeast shore, attracts many day visitors.

ST. JOHN➤ Only 3 mi from St. Thomas but still a world apart, St. John is the least developed of the USVI. Although two-thirds of its tropical hills remain protected as national parkland, a bit of hustle and bustle has come to Cruz Bay, the main town. Accommodations range from world-class luxury resorts to top-notch vacation villas to back-to-basics campgrounds.

The British Virgin Islands
TORTOLA➤ A day might not be enough to tour this island—all 10 sq mi of it—not because there's so much to see and do

but because you're meant to relax while you're here. Time stands still even in Road Town, the biggest community, where the hands of the central square's clock occasionally move, but never tell the right time. The harbor, however, is busy with sailboats—this is the charter-boat capital of the world. Tortola's roads dip and curve and lead to lovely, secluded accommodations.

VIRGIN GORDA➤ Progressing from laid-back to more laid-back, mountainous and arid Virgin Gorda fits right in. Its main road sticks to the center of the island, connecting the odd-shaped north and south appendages; sailing is the preferred mode of transportation. Spanish Town, the most noteworthy settlement, is on the southern wing, as are The Baths. Here smooth, giant boulders are scattered about the beach and form delightful sea grottoes just offshore.

OTHER ISLANDS➤ **Jost Van Dyke,** a sparsely populated island northwest of Tortola, has a disproportionate number of surprisingly lively bars and is a favorite haunt of yachties. Hilly **Peter Island** also attracts sailors with its wonderful anchorages. Flat **Anegada** lurks 20 mi northeast of Virgin Gorda. It rises just 28 ft above sea level, but its reef stretches out underwater, practically inviting wrecks. The scores of shipwrecks that encircle the island attract divers and a bounty of fish.

PLEASURES AND PASTIMES

Beaches

With their warm, clear days, unspoiled sandy strands, and beautiful turquoise water, the Virgin Islands are a beach bum's paradise. Even if you're not a connoisseur, a day or two on the sand is central to a complete vacation here.

Your accommodation may border a beach or provide transportation to one nearby, but you have other options. You could spend one day at a lively, touristy beach that has plenty of water-sports facilities and is backed by a bar and another at an isolated cove that offers nothing but seclusion. Of course, these beaches are just jumping-off points to the underwater world.

In the USVI, public access to beach waters is guaranteed but land access to them isn't, effectively restricting some areas to resort guests. On St. Thomas, Magens Bay is among the prettiest (but also the liveliest) public beaches, and Hull Bay is the only place to surf. St. Croix's west-end beaches are popular, and the calm waters of Isaac Bay, on the more isolated East End, can give you a stretch all to yourself. Beautiful Trunk Bay, St. John, gets a lot of day-trip cruise-ship passengers; Salt Pond Bay is remote and mostly undeveloped.

Nowhere in the BVI will you find crowds to match those at the most popular USVI beaches, but Cane Garden Bay on Tortola probably comes the closest. Apple Bay and Josiah's Bay, also on Tortola, are good for surfing, and Long Bay (West) is quieter. Virgin Gorda's beaches are easiest to get to from the water but are also approachable from land. Swimming among the rock formations at The Baths is a priority for many visitors, but this area can be crowded. On the smaller BVI, the lovely beaches are most likely sparsely populated by those who have dropped anchor and made their way in.

Historic Sites

Columbus, pirates, European colonizers, and plantation farmers and their slaves are among the people who have left their marks on these islands, all of which are benefiting the tourism industry, a relatively recent development.

In Charlotte Amalie, St. Thomas, Fort Christian (1672), Blackbeard's Castle (1679), the Synagogue of Beracha Veshalom Vegmiluth Hasidim (1833), and the Danish Consulate (1830) are some noteworthy sights that give glimpses into the town's past. St. Croix's countryside is dotted with ruins of plantation great houses and sugar mills. St. John, too, has several plantations in varying degrees of decay.

Die-hard sightseers will find less to keep them busy in the British Virgin Islands. Numbering among the historic sights, however, are Tortola's Mt. Healthy National Park, an old plantation site, and Copper Mine Point, the ruins of a 400-year-old mine on Virgin Gorda.

Nightlife

Although you'll never be too far from a Jimmy Buffett tune, the nightlife establishments in the Virgin Islands do their share to provide something for everyone. Yachties congregate, not surprisingly, at the waterfront bars, where live guitar music may accompany the rum drinks. BVI watering holes, especially those on Jost Van Dyke, are most likely to be true beach bars. Steel-drum, calypso, and reggae music—as well as broken-bottle dancing—are common in shows at larger hotels. Musicians also often play impromptu in the street, and if you look around you may come across a piano bar or a jazz band.

Shopping

Charlotte Amalie, St. Thomas, is *the* place to shop. As the Virgin Islands' main commercial center, it has the best selection of just about everything. Bargain hunters drool over the duty-free allowances and the lack of sales tax; liquor, china, crystal, and jewelry are especially popular buys. But you should also seek out artwork, crafts, and spices that are sold locally throughout the islands.

Water Sports

Whether you charter a boat or head out on a day-sail, traveling by boat is a relaxing and efficient way to see the islands. Wrecks and reefs make the islands as interesting underwater as above. For pointers on how to plan a trip that involves sailing, scuba diving, or snorkeling, *see* "Exploring the Waters of the Virgin Islands" *in* Chapter 4.

NEW AND NOTEWORTHY

ST. THOMAS➤ Two more airlines are offering direct service to Cyril E. King Airport. At press time, **Caledonian Airways** announced that it would soon begin offering charter service between London and St. Thomas. Flights were slated to be available once every two weeks in May, June, and September and once a week July–August. **United Airlines** also announced plans to offer year-round, twice-weekly,

non-stop service from Chicago's O'Hare International Airport and Washington D.C.'s Dulles International Airport.

ST. CROIX➤ **Casinos** are in the wind. The legislature in 1995 approved six casino hotels in hopes of jump-starting the island's economy. When they'll begin building is anyone's guess, but at press time insiders expected action in 1999.

The **road to Point Udall** is newly paved, making it easier to reach the easternmost point in the United States.

ST. JOHN➤ The **Virgin Islands National Park** now charges a $4 admission fee to enter the Annaberg Plantation and Trunk Bay. (The fee gets you into both sights.)

The **Vitran public bus** can now take you all the way from Cruz Bay through Coral Bay to Salt Pond. It's a bargain at only $1 a ride.

FODOR'S CHOICE

Beaches

★ **Magens Bay, St. Thomas,** a long, lovely loop of white sand.

★ **Palm-fringed Dead Man's Bay, Peter Island,** conducive to romance.

★ **Smuggler's Cove, Tortola,** for its good snorkeling and view of Jost Van Dyke.

★ **Spring Bay or The Baths, Virgin Gorda,** where you can swim among unique rock formations—essential to a Virgin Gorda vacation.

★ **Trunk Bay, St. John,** beautiful, if at times crowded. Its snorkeling trail is a big draw.

Comforts

★ **Biras Creek Hotel, Virgin Gorda.** The setting and service here are exceptional. $$$$

★ **Caneel Bay Resort, St. John.** Civilized and luxurious, Caneel Bay draws the same visitors year after year. $$$$

★ **Ritz-Carlton, St. Thomas.** Built like an Italian villa, there's elegance everywhere, from the marbled-floor reception area to a pool that seems to flow right into the sea. *$$$$*

★ **Sunterra Carambola Beach Resort, St. Croix.** Room decor is tasteful but not overdone, and all rooms look out on a garden or an exquisite ecru beach. *$$$$*

★ **Long Bay Beach Resort, Tortola.** Accommodations range from hillside rooms and to beachside cabanas on stilts—all positioned to take advantage of the spectacular setting. *$$$–$$$$*

★ **Hotel 1829, St. Thomas.** Romance and classic elegance abound at this historic, Spanish-style inn. *$–$$$$*

Flavors

★ **Le Chateau de Bordeaux, St. John,** set in what's basically a glorified tree house, draws on different culinary traditions. The chef produces such delicacies as rosemary-perfumed lamb with a honey-Dijon-nut crust. *$$$–$$$$*

★ **Top Hat, St. Croix.** The delicious Danish fare and the delightful Danish owners are reminders of the time when Denmark ruled St. Croix. *$$$–$$$$*

★ **Virgilio's, St. Thomas.** This intimate, elegant hideaway serves the best northern Italian food on the island, right down to its cappuccino. *$$$–$$$$*

★ **Brandywine Bay, Tortola.** The Tuscan food and the romantic setting here are both big draws. *$$$–$$$$*

★ **Skyworld, Tortola.** Here, stunning views accompany outstanding cuisine and service. *$$$–$$$$*

Music, Nightlife, Bars

★ **Any bar on Jost Van Dyke.** You can't go wrong on this island, which does its best to entertain the charter-yacht crowd.

★ **Bath and Turtle, Virgin Gorda.** Good island bands play on Wednesday and Sunday evenings.

★ **Blue Moon, St. Croix.** You'll find great live jazz every Friday night.

★ **Bomba's Surfside Shack, Tortola,** is one of the island's liveliest spots.

★ **Quito's Gazebo, Tortola.** The surf is the perfect accompaniment to whatever's playing: ballads, reggae, or Quito Rhymer's love songs.

Scenic Views

★ **Annaberg Plantation, St. John,** provides a glimpse into the island's history and gorgeous views of the BVI and the sound that runs from St. Thomas eastward.

★ **The beautiful parade of cruise ships** out of Charlotte Amalie, St. Thomas, harbor.

★ **Sailing into Red Hook (St. Thomas) from St. John at sunset,** perfectly positioned for a mellow evening in town.

★ **Sunsets from the Skyworld observation tower, Tortola,** are especially colorful.

2 UNITED STATES VIRGIN ISLANDS

From St. Thomas's dazzling duty-free shops to St. Croix's historic sugar plantation ruins to the natural splendor of St. John's national parkland, the USVI offer three distinct ways to enjoy Caribbean ambience all under the American flag.

MORNINGS AT THE SQUIRREL CAGE coffee shop on St. Thomas aren't much different from those in coffee shops back home. A cop stops by to joke with the waitress and collect his first cup of coffee; a high-heeled secretary runs in for the paper and some toast; a store clerk lingers over a cup of tea to discuss politics with the cook. But is the coffee shop back home in a bright pink hole-in-the-wall of a 19th-century building, steps from a park abloom with frangipani—in January? Are bush tea and johnnycake served alongside oatmeal and omelets?

Updated by
Carol Bareuther
and Lynda Lohr

It's the combination of the familiar and the exotic found in St. Thomas, St. Croix, and St. John—the United States Virgin Islands (USVI)—that defines this "American Paradise" and explains much of its appeal. The effort to be all things to all people—while remaining true to the best of itself—has created a sometimes paradoxical blend of island serenity and American practicality in this U.S. territory 1,000 mi (1,600 km) from the southern tip of the U.S. mainland.

The images you'd expect from a tropical paradise are here: stretches of beach arc into the distance, and white sails skim across water so blue and clear it stuns the senses. Red-roof houses color the green hillsides as do the orange of the flamboyant tree, the red of the hibiscus, the magenta of the bougainvillea, and the blue stone ruins of old sugar mills. Towns of pastel-tone European-style villas, decorated by filigree wrought-iron terraces, line narrow streets that climb from the harbor. Amid all the images, you can find moments—sometimes whole days— of exquisite tranquillity: an egret standing in a pond at dawn, palm trees backlit by a full moon, sunrises and sunsets that send your spirit soaring with the frigate bird flying overhead.

Chances are that on one of the three islands you'll find your own idea of paradise. Check into a beachfront condo on the East End of St. Thomas, eat burgers, and watch football at a beachfront bar and grill. Or stay at an 18th-century plantation great house on St. Croix, dine on Danish delicacies, and go horseback riding at sunrise. Rent a tent or a cottage in the pristine national park on St. John, take a hike, kayak off the coast, read a book, or just listen to the sounds of the forest at night. Or dive deep into "island time" and learn the art of "limin' " (hanging out, Caribbean-style) on all three islands.

Idyllic though they may be, these bits of volcanic rock in the middle of the Caribbean Sea haven't entirely escaped such modern-day worries of overdevelopment as trash, crime, and traffic. The isolation and limited space of the islands have, in fact, accentuated these problems. What, for example, do you do with 76 million cans and bottles imported annually when the nearest recycling plant is across 1,000 mi (1,600 km) of ocean? Despite these dilemmas, wildlife has found refuge here. The brown pelican is on the endangered list worldwide but is a common sight in the USVI. The endangered native boa tree is protected, as is the hawksbill turtle, whose females lumber onto the beaches to lay their eggs.

Preserving its own culture while progressing as a tourist destination is another problem. The islands have been inhabited by Taino Indians (on St. John and St. Thomas); Carib Indians (on St. Croix); Danish settlers and Spanish pirates; traders and invaders from all the European powers; Africans brought in as slaves; migrants from other Caribbean islands; and, finally, Americans, first as administrators, then as businesspeople and tourists. All these influences are creating a more homogeneous culture, and with each passing year the USVI lose more of their rich, spicy, Caribbean personality.

Sailing into the Caribbean on his second voyage in 1493, Christopher Columbus came upon St. Croix before the group of islands including St. Thomas, St. John, and the British Virgin Islands (BVI). He named St. Croix "Santa Cruz" (called Ay Ay by the Carib Indians already living there) but moved on quickly after he encountered the fierce residents. As he approached St. Thomas and St. John, he was impressed enough with the shapely silhouettes of the numerous islands and cays (including the BVI) to name them after Ursula and her 11,000 virgins, but he found the islands barren and moved on to explore Puerto Rico.

Over the next century, as it became clear that Spain couldn't defend the entire Caribbean, other European powers began to settle the islands. In the 1600s the French were joined by the Dutch and the English on St. Croix, and St. Thomas had a mixture of European residents in the early 1700s. By 1695 St. Croix was under the control of the French, but the colonists had moved on to what is today Haiti. The island lay virtually dormant until 1733, when the Danish government bought it—along with St. Thomas and St. John—from the Danish West India Company. At that time settlers from St. Thomas and St. John moved to St. Croix to cultivate the island's gentler terrain. St. Croix developed a plantation economy, but St. Thomas's soil and terrain were ill suited to agriculture. There the harbor became an internationally known seaport because of its size and ease of entry; it's still hailed as one of the most beautiful harbors in the world.

Plantations depended on slave labor, of which there was a plentiful supply in the Danish West Indies. As early as 1665 agreements between the Brandenburger Company (which needed a base in the West Indies from which to ship the slaves it had imported from Africa) and the West India Company (which needed the kind of quick cash it could collect in duties, fees, and rents from the slave trade) established St. Thomas as a primary slave market.

It's from the slaves who worked the plantations that the majority of Virgin Islanders are descended. More than likely the sales clerk who sells you a watch and the waitress serving your rum punch trace their lineage back to ancestors captured in Africa some 300 years ago and brought to the West Indies, where they were sold on the block, priced according to their comeliness and strength. Most were captured along Africa's Gold Coast, from the tribes of Asante, Ibo, Mandika, Amina, and Woloff. They brought with them African rhythms in music and language, herbal medicine, and such crafts as basketry and wood carving. The West Indian–African culture comes to full bloom at Carnival time, when playing *mas* (with abandon) takes precedence over all else.

Yet you can still see the influence of the early Danish settlers here, too. It's reflected in the language and architecture; in common surnames such as Petersen, Jeppesen, and Lawaetz; and in street names such as Kongen's Gade (King Street) and Kronprindsen's Gade (Prince Street). The town of Charlotte Amalie was named after a Danish queen. The Lutheran Church is the state church of Denmark, and Frederick Lutheran Church on St. Thomas dates from 1666. Other peoples have left their marks on the USVI as well. Jewish settlers came to the territory as early as 1665; they were shipowners, chandlers, and brokers in the slave trade. Today their descendants coexist with nearly 1,500 Arabs—95% of whom are Palestinian. You'll also find many East Indians, who are active members of the business community. Immigrants from Puerto Rico and the Dominican Republic make up close to half

United States Virgin Islands

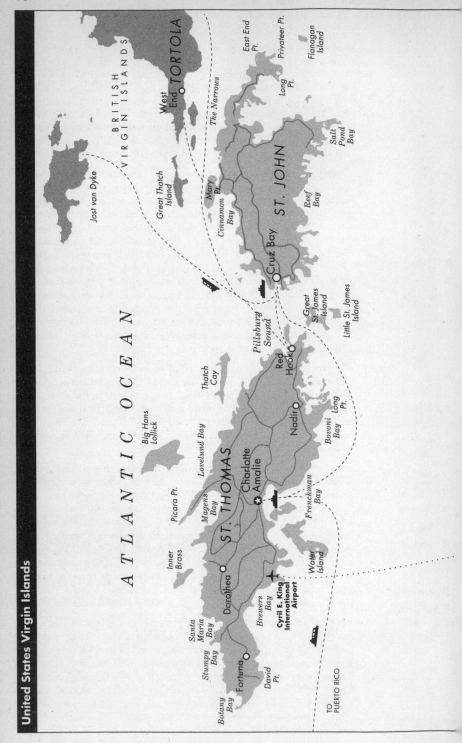

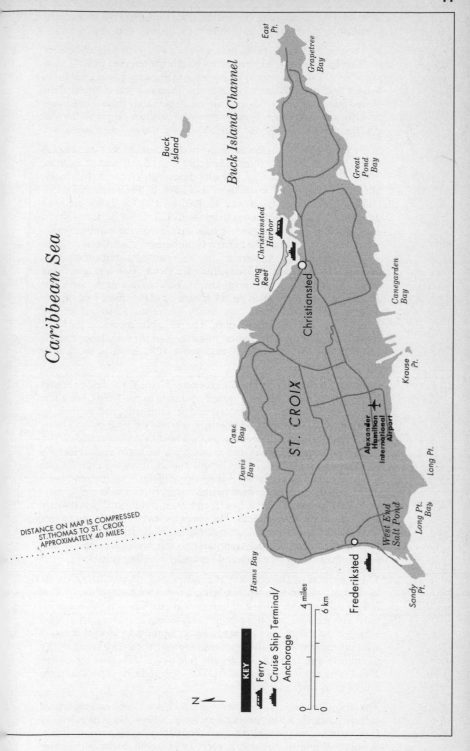

11

Caribbean Sea

Buck Island Channel

East Pt.

Grapetree Bay

Buck Island

Great Pond Bay

Christiansted Harbor

Long Reef

Canegarden Bay

Christiansted

ST. CROIX

Krause Pt.

Cane Bay

Alexander Hamilton International Airport

Davis Bay

Long Pt.

West End Salt Pond

Long Pt. Bay

Hams Bay

DISTANCE ON MAP IS COMPRESSED
ST. THOMAS TO ST. CROIX
APPROXIMATELY 40 MILES

Frederiksted

Sandy Pt.

KEY
Ferry
Cruise Ship Terminal/
Anchorage

4 miles

6 km

N

of St. Croix's population. Transplants from Caribbean countries to the south continue to arrive, seeking better economic opportunities.

St. Thomas, St. Croix, and St. John were known collectively as the Danish West Indies until the United States bought the territory in 1917, during World War I, prompted by fears that Germany would establish a U-boat base in the Western Hemisphere. The name was changed to the United States Virgin Islands, and, almost immediately thereafter, British-held Tortola and Virgin Gorda—previously known simply as the Virgin Islands—hastily inserted "British" on the front of their name.

In the 1960s, Pineapple Beach Resort (today Renaissance Grand Beach Resort) was built on St. Thomas, and the Caneel Bay Resort on St. John, built in 1956, was expanded; and with direct flights from the U.S. mainland, the islands' tourism industry was born. In 1960 the total population of all three islands was 32,000. By 1970 it had more than doubled to 75,000, as workers from the BVI, Antigua, St. Kitts–Nevis, and other Caribbean countries immigrated to man the building boom. When the boom waned the Eastern Caribbeaners stayed, bringing additional diversity to the territory but also putting a tremendous burden on its infrastructure. Today there are about 50,000 people living on the 32-square-mi (83-square-km) St. Thomas (about the same size as Manhattan), 51,000 on the 84 square mi (216 square km) of pastoral St. Croix, and about 5,000 on 20-square-mi (52-square-km) St. John, ⅔ of which is a national park. The per capita income in the USVI is the highest in the West Indies. Just over ¼ of the total labor force is employed by the government, and about 10% work in tourism or tourism-related jobs.

Agriculture hasn't been a major economic factor since the last sugarcane plantation on St. Croix ceased operating in the 1960s, but a few farmers on St. Croix, St. Thomas, and St. John still produce some of the mangoes, pineapples, and herbs you'll find on your plate. The islands' cuisine reflects a dependency on a land that gives grudgingly of its bounty. Root vegetables such as sweet potato, hardy vegetables such as okra, and stick-to-your-ribs breads and stuffings were staples 200 years ago, and their influence is still evident in the *fungi* (cornmeal and okra), johnnycake (deep-fried dough snack, often made with a mixture of cornmeal and white flour), and sweet-potato stuffings that are ever-present on menus today. The fruits are sweet (slaves got energy to cut sugarcane from a sugar-water drink made from sugar apples). Beverages include not only rum but coconut water, fruit juices, and *maubi,* made from tree bark and reputedly a virility enhancer.

The backbone of the economy is tourism, but at the heart of the islands is an independent, separate being: a rollicking hodgepodge of West Indian culture with a sense of humor that puts sex and politics in almost every conversation. Lacking a major-league sports team, Virgin Islanders follow the activities and antics of their 15 elected senators with the rabidity of Washingtonians following their Redskins. Loyalty to country and faith in God are the rule in the USVI, not the exception. Prayer is a way of life, and ROTC is one of the most popular high-school extracurricular activities.

The struggle to preserve the predominantly black Caribbean–influenced culture is heating up in America's paradise. Native Virgin Islanders say they want access to more than just the beach when big money brings in big development. Senators in early 1996 agreed that majority ownership of two of the casino hotels to be built in St. Croix will be reserved for natives. But the three islands are far from united as to exactly how they will balance economic growth and the protection of their number-one resource—scenic beauty. The ongoing conflict between progress and preservation here is no mere philosophical exercise, and attempts at resolutions display yet another aspect of the islands' unique blend of character.

ST. THOMAS

Updated by
Carol
Bareuther

If you fly to the 32-square-mi (83-square-km) island of St. Thomas, you land at its western end; if you arrive by cruise ship, you come into one of the world's most beautiful harbors. Either way, one of your first sights is the town of Charlotte Amalie. From the harbor, you see an idyllic-looking village that spreads into the lower hills. If you were expecting a quiet village, its inhabitants hanging out under palm trees, you've missed that era by about 300 years. While other islands in the USVI developed plantation economies, St. Thomas cultivated its harbor, and it became a thriving seaport soon after it was settled by the Danish in the 1600s.

The success of the naturally perfect harbor was enhanced by the fact that the Danes—who ruled St. Thomas with only a couple of short interruptions from 1666 to 1917—avoided involvement in some 100 years' worth of European wars. Denmark was the only European country with colonies in the Caribbean to stay neutral during the war of the Spanish succession in the early 1700s. Thus, products of the Dutch, English, and French islands—sugar, cotton, and indigo—were traded through Charlotte Amalie, along with the regular shipments of slaves. When the Spanish wars ended, trade fell off, but by the end of the 1700s, Europe was at war again, Denmark again remained neutral, and St. Thomas continued to prosper. Even into the 1800s, while the economies of St. Croix and St. John foundered with the market for sugarcane, St. Thomas's economy remained strong. This prosperity led to the development of shipyards for repairing boats, a well-organized banking system, and a large merchant class. In 1845 Charlotte Amalie had 101 large importing houses owned by Englishmen, Frenchmen, Germans, Haitians, Spaniards, Americans, Sephardim, and Danes.

Charlotte Amalie is still one of the most active cruise-ship ports in the world. On almost any day at least one and sometimes as many as eight cruise ships are tied to the dock or anchored outside the harbor. Gently rocking in the shadows of these giant floating hotels are just about every other kind of vessel imaginable: sleek sailing mono- and multihulls that will take you on a sunset cruise complete with rum punch and a Jimmy Buffett soundtrack; private megayachts that spirit busy execs away; and the 39-ft *Stars & Stripes,* which was sailed by Dennis Conner in the 1992 America's Cup Defender series and has been resurrected as the V. I. Challenge's training vessel for its America's Cup 2000 bid in New Zealand. Huge container ships pull up in Sub Base, just west of the harbor, bringing in everything from cornflakes to tires. Anchored right along the waterfront are the picturesque down-island sloops of the type that has plied the waters between the Greater Antilles and the Leeward Islands for hundreds of years. The sloops still deliver produce, but today they also return down-island with refrigerators, VCRs, and disposable diapers.

The waterfront road through Charlotte Amalie was once part of the harbor. Before it was filled to build the highway, the beach came right up to the back door of the warehouses that now line the thoroughfare. Two hundred years ago, those warehouses contained indigo, tobacco, and cotton. Today the stone buildings house silk, crystal, linens, and leather. Exotic fragrances are still traded, but by island beauty queens in air-conditioned perfume palaces instead of through open market stalls.

Pirates of old used St. Thomas as a base from which to raid merchant ships of any and every nation, though they were particularly fond of the gold- and silver-laden treasure ships heading from Mexico, Cuba, and Puerto Rico to Spain. There are still pirates around, but today's versions use St. Thomas as a drop-off for their contraband: illegal immigrants and drugs.

The island's western end is the least developed: with the exception of some private homes, it's still relatively wild. If you stay on the quiet north side, you'll go up the mountain along roads lined with giant ferns and philodendron, banana trees, and flamboyant trees that thrive in the cooler, wetter climate. The lush vegetation muffles the sound of all but the birds, and it's here you'll find many private villas for rent. In the drier areas to the south and east, the roads are lined with colossal cacti and succulents, punctuated by the bright colors of the hardy bougainvillea and hibiscus. The southeastern and far eastern ends of the island are flat, and this is where you'll find the beachfront hotels and condominiums. At the eastern tip is Red Hook, a friendly little village anchored by the marine community nestled at Red Hook harbor.

Lodging

Of the USVI, St. Thomas has the most rooms and the greatest variety of accommodations. You can let yourself be pampered at a luxurious south shore, east end, or west end resort—albeit at a price of $300 to more than $900 per night, not including meals. If your means are more modest, you will find fine hotels (often with rooms that have a kitchen and a living area) in lovely settings throughout the island. There are also guest houses and inns with great views (if not a beach at your door) and great service at about half the cost of the beachfront pleasure palaces. Many of these are east and north of Charlotte Amalie, in the Frenchtown area or overlooking hills—ideal if you plan to get out and mingle with the locals. There are also inexpensive lodgings (most right in town) that are perfect if you just want a clean room to return to after a day of exploring or beach-bumming.

Families often stay at an East End condominium complex. Although condos are somewhat pricey (winter rates average $240 per night for a two-bedroom unit, which usually sleeps six), they have full kitchens, and you can definitely save money by cooking for yourself—especially if you bring your own nonperishable foodstuffs. (Virtually everything on St. Thomas is imported, and restaurants and shops pass shipping costs on to you.) Though you may spend some time laboring in the kitchen, many condos ease your burden with daily maid service and on-site restaurants; a few also have resort amenities, including pools and tennis courts. The East End is convenient to St. John; it's home to the boating crowd and some good restaurants. The prices below reflect rates in high season, which runs from December 15 to April 15. Rates are 25% to 50% lower the rest of the year.

CATEGORY	COST*
$$$$	over $200
$$$	$150–200
$$	$100–150
$	under $100

All prices are for a standard double room, excluding 8% tax.

Hotels

$$$–$$$$ ⊞ **Best Western Emerald Beach Resort.** On a white-sand beach, just across from the airport, this miniresort has the feel of its much larger East End cousins. Each room in the four pink three-story buildings has its own terrace or balcony, palms, and colorful flowers that frame an ocean view. Rooms are decorated in modern tropical prints and rattan. A plus: the resort is popular with businesspeople, so the pool and beach are rarely crowded. A minus: the noise from nearby jets taking off and landing can be heard intermittently over a three-hour period each afternoon. ⊠ *8070 Lindbergh Bay 00802,* ☎ *340/777–8800 or 800/233–4936 (direct to hotel),* FAX *340/776–3426. 90 rooms. Restaurant, air-conditioning, pool, beach. AE, D, MC, V. EP.*

$$$–$$$$ ⊞ **Bluebeard Castle.** Though not exactly a castle, this large red-roof complex offers kingly modern comforts on a steep hill above town. All rooms are air-conditioned and have terraces. The hotel is a short ride from the shops of Charlotte Amalie and Havensight Mall—there's free transportation to Magens Bay Beach and to town. ⊠ *Bluebeard's Hill (Box 7480) 00801,* ☎ *340/774–1600 or 800/524–6599 (direct to hotel),* FAX *340/774–5134. 170 rooms. 3 restaurants, bar, air-conditioning, pool, 2 tennis courts, exercise room. AE, D, DC, MC, V. EP.*

$$–$$$ ⊞ **L'Hotel Boynes.** On a hill just above the harbor, this intimate inn stands like a monument to a time gone by. Each of the rooms in the 200-year-old stone and ballast-brick building has its own character— ranging from the sophisticated Red Room, with its mahogany four-poster bed and Persian carpets, to the fanciful Whimsy Room, where the bed is built into an old Danish oven. On Friday and Saturday nights, you can sip cocktails while watching spectacular sunsets from the terrace, then enjoy live piano music, poetry readings, and mingling with the local working crowd. Transportation to Magens Bay is included in the rate. ⊠ *Blackbeard's Hill 00802,* ☎ *340/774–5511 or 800/377– 2905 (direct to hotel),* FAX *340/774–8509. 8 rooms. Bar, air conditioning, in-room VCRs, pool. AE, MC, V. CP.*

$$–$$$ ⊞ **Villa Santana.** Built by General Santa Anna of Mexico, the villa (circa
★ 1857) still provides a panoramic view of the harbor and plenty of West Indian charm. This landmark, close to town, has six villa-style rooms. Dark wicker furniture, plaster and stone walls, shuttered windows, cathedral ceilings, and interesting nooks contribute to the feeling of romance and history. All units have full kitchens, TVs, and either four-poster or cradle beds; ceiling fans and natural trade winds keep things cool. Villas La Torre and La Mansion are split-level quarters with spiral staircases. ⊠ *2D Denmark Hill 00802,* ☎ *340/776–1311,* FAX *340/776– 1311. 6 rooms. Kitchenettes, pool, croquet. AE. EP.*

$–$$$$ ⊞ **Hotel 1829.** This historic Spanish-style inn is popular with visiting
★ government officials and people with business at Government House down the street. Rooms, on several levels (no elevator), range from elegant and roomy to quite small but are priced accordingly, so there's one for every budget. Author Graham Greene is said to have stayed here, and it's easy to imagine him musing over a drink in the small, dark bar. The second-floor botanical gardens and open-air champagne bar make a romantic spot for sunset viewing before dinner in the gourmet ☞ Hotel 1829 restaurant. Rooms count phones and TVs in their list of amenities. There's a tiny, tiny pool for cooling off, and the shops of Charlotte Amalie are close by. ⊠ *Government Hill (Box 1567, 00804),* ☎ *340/776–1829 or 800/524–2002 (direct to hotel),* FAX *340/776–4313. 14 rooms. Restaurant, air-conditioning, refrigerators, pool. AE, D, MC, V.*

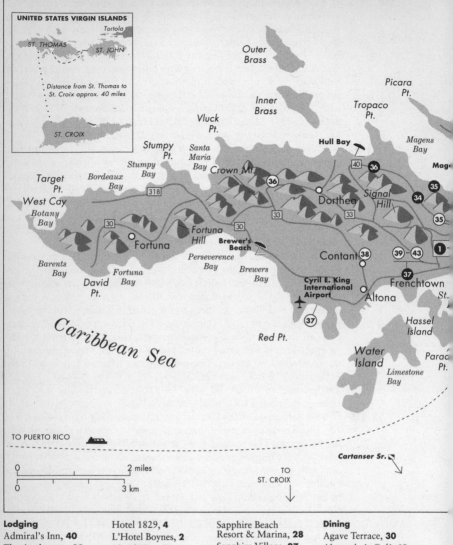

Lodging

Admiral's Inn, **40**

The Anchorage, **20**

Best Western
Emerald Beach
Resort, **37**

Blazing Villas, **33**

Bluebeard
Castle, **1**

Bolongo Bay Beach
Club & Villas, **15**

Elysian Beach
Resort, **25**

Hotel 1829, **4**

L'Hotel Boynes, **2**

Island View Guest
House, **38**

Marriott
Frenchman's Reef and
Morning Star Beach
Resorts, **14**

Renaissance Grand
Beach Resort, **33**

Ritz-Carlton,
St. Thomas, **26**

Sapphire Beach
Resort & Marina, **28**

Sapphire Village, **27**

Sea Horse
Cottages, **21**

Secret Harbour Beach
Resort and Villas, **19**

Villa Santana, **3**

Wyndham Sugar Bay
Beach Club &
Resort, **29**

Dining

Agave Terrace, **30**

Alexander's Café, **42**

Beni Iguana's, **7**

Café LuLu, **10**

Cafe Wahoo, **24**

The Chart House, **41**

Craig & Sally's, **43**

Duffy's Love
Shack, **22**

Eunice's Terrace, **32**

Ferrari's, **36**

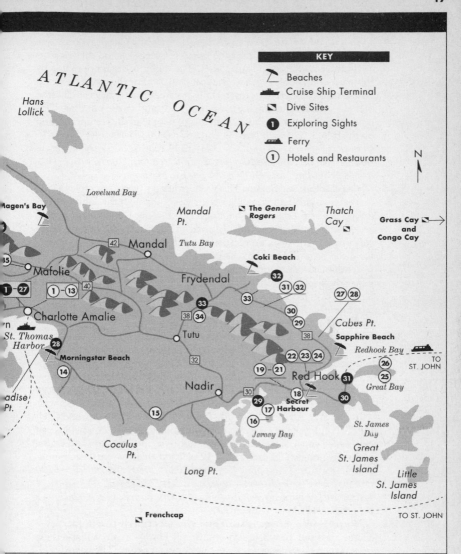

ATLANTIC OCEAN

Hans Lollick

KEY

- ⚓ Beaches
- 🚢 Cruise Ship Terminal
- ◥ Dive Sites
- **①** Exploring Sights
- 🚢 Ferry
- ① Hotels and Restaurants

N

Lovelund Bay

Magen's Bay

Mandal Pt.

◥ The *General Rogers*

Thatch Cay

Grass Cay and Congo Cay ◥→

42 Mandal

Tutu Bay

Coki Beach

Mafolie

Frydendal

32

31 32

27 28

35

1 27

1 13 40

33

33

30

29

Cabes Pt.

Charlotte Amalie

38 34

38

Sapphire Beach

Tutu

Redhook Bay

TO ST. JOHN

St. Thomas Harbor

28

32

Red Hook

22 23 24

26

Morningstar Beach

Nadir

19 21

31

25 Great Bay

14

30

29

18

Secret Harbour

17

30

paradise Pt.

15

16

St. James Bay

Jersey Bay

Coculus Pt.

Long Pt.

Great St. James Island

Little St. James Island

◥ Frenchcap

TO ST. JOHN

Finn McCool's Restaurant and Pub, **16**
Gladys' Cafe, **8**
Greenhouse Bar and Restaurant, **5**
Hard Rock Cafe, **6**
Hervé, **9**
Hotel 1829, **4**
Jerry's Beachfront Restaurant, **18**
Polli's, **34**

Raffles, **17**
Romanos, **31**
Sib's Mountain Bar and Restaurant, **35**
Tavern on the Waterfront, **11**
Tickles Dockside Pub, **23**
Victor's New Hide-Out, **39**
Virgilio's, **13**
Zorba's Sagapo, **12**

Exploring
Compass Point Marina, **29**
Coral World Marine Park, **32**
Drake's Seat, **35**
Estate St. Peter Greathouse & Botanical Gardens, **36**
Frenchtown, **37**
Mountain Top, **34**
Paradise Point Tramway, **28**

Red Hook, **31**
Tillett Gardens, **33**
Virgin Islands National Park Headquarters, **30**

EAST END

$$$$ ⊡ **Renaissance Grand Beach Resort.** The zigzag architectural angles
★ spell luxury, from this resort's marble atrium lobby to the one-bedroom
suites with whirlpool baths. The beach is excellent, and there's a fitness center with Nautilus machines. The lobby is often populated by
those lucky business types whose companies favor the resort as a con-
vention-and-conference center. Daily organized activities for children
include iguana hunts, T-shirt painting, and sand-castle building. This
tends to be a very busy hotel, with lots of people in the restaurants and
on the beach. ⊠ *Smith Bay Rd. (Box 8267) 00801,* ☏ *340/775–1510
or 800/468–3571,* 𝖥𝖠𝖷 *340/775–3757. 204 rooms, 86 suites. 2 restaurants, snack bar, air-conditioning, 2 pools, 6 tennis courts, beach, children's programs. AE, D, DC, MC, V. EP, MAP.*

$$$$ ⊡ **Ritz-Carlton, St. Thomas.** This premier luxury resort resembles a villa
★ in Venice and offers stunning ocean views through the lobby's glass
doors. Guest rooms, in six buildings that fan out from the main villa,
are spacious and tropically furnished—they just might tempt you to
stay inside. When you do venture out, you'll find elegance everywhere,
from the beautiful pool to the gourmet restaurant and the casual alfresco lunch area. A multilingual staff and 24-hour room service enhance the sophisticated atmosphere. ⊠ *6900 Great Bay Estate 00802,*
☏ *340/775–3333 or 800/241–3333,* 𝖥𝖠𝖷 *340/775–4444. 152 rooms.
3 restaurants, 3 bars, air-conditioning, room service, pool, 3 tennis courts,
health club, beach. AE, D, DC, MC, V. EP.*

$$$$ ⊡ **Sapphire Beach Resort & Marina.** On a clear day the lush green mountains of the neighboring BVI seem close enough to touch from this Meri-
Star resort on one of St. Thomas's prettiest beaches (there's also excellent
snorkeling on the reefs to each side of it). This is a quiet retreat where
you can nap while swinging in one of the hammocks strung between
the palm trees in your front yard; but on Sunday the place rocks with
a beach party. All units have fully equipped kitchens, phones, and satellite TV. Children may join the Kids Klub, where 4- to 12-year-olds can
enjoy such supervised activities as sandcastle building, arts and crafts,
and sing-alongs. Children under 12 sleep in their parents' accommodations for free. ⊠ *Sapphire Bay (Box 8088) 00801,* ☏ *340/775–6100
or 800/524–2090 (direct to hotel),* 𝖥𝖠𝖷 *340/775–2403. 155 suites. 4
restaurants, 2 bars, air-conditioning, 4 tennis courts, beach, children's
programs. AE, MC, V. EP, MAP.*

$$$$ ⊡ **Secret Harbour Beach Resort and Villas.** Formerly two properties—
Secret Harbour Beach Resort and Secret Harbourview Villas—these
resorts merged in 1998 to create one compact resort. The beige buildings, which contain low-rise studios and suites, are set hillside and beachside on an inviting sandy cove with marvelous sunsets. All units have
air-conditioning and maid service. From early April to the end of December, children under age 12 stay free, making this a family-friendly
resort all summer. ⊠ *6280 Estate Nazareth 00802-1104,* ☏ *340/775–
6550 or 800/524–2250 (direct to hotel),* 𝖥𝖠𝖷 *340/775–1501. 84 suites,
7 studios. 2 restaurants, bar, air-conditioning, pool, 2 tennis courts,
exercise room, beach, dive shop. AE, MC, V. CP.*

$$$$ ⊡ **Wyndham Sugar Bay Beach Club & Resort.** From afar, this large cluster of bulky white buildings looks overwhelming, but the hotel has a
lot to offer. Most rooms overlook water; some have views of the BVI.
All are spacious and comfortable and have balconies, hair dryers, and
coffeemakers. The beach is small, but there's a giant pool with waterfalls.
The rates cover meals and beverages; use of the fitness center, tennis
courts, and beach facilities; and a daily activities program. ⊠ *6500 Estate Smith Bay 00802,* ☏ *340/777–7100 or 800/927–7100 (direct to
hotel),* 𝖥𝖠𝖷 *340/777–7200. 300 rooms. Restaurant, bar, air-condition-*

ing, 3 pools, 2 tennis courts, health club, beach, snorkeling, windsurfing. AE, D, DC, MC, V. All-inclusive.

$$$–$$$$ ▦ **Elysian Beach Resort.** The coral-color villas here are situated down along the hillside all the way to the edge of Cowpet Bay. Rooms are decorated in muted tropical floral prints and have terraces, TVs, and phones; some have full kitchens. Activity centers on a kidney-shape pool with a waterfall and thatch-roof pool bar. The Palm Court restaurant has a strong local following for the Sunday buffet brunch. ⊠ Estate Nazareth (Box 51), Red Hook 00802, ☎ 340/775–1000 or 800/753–2554 (direct to hotel), ℻ 340/776–0910. 175 rooms. 2 restaurants, 2 bars, air-conditioning, fans, pool, tennis court, health club, beach. AE, MC, V. CP.

FRENCHTOWN

$–$$ ▦ **Admiral's Inn.** This charming inn stretches down a hillside on the
★ point of land known as Frenchtown, just west of Charlotte Amalie. All rooms have wonderful views of either the town and the harbor or the ocean; the four ocean-view rooms have balconies and refrigerators. All units have rattan furniture; cream- or teal-color bedspreads; vertical blinds; coral, teal, and cream carpeting; and large, tiled vanity areas. The rocky shoreline is perfect for snorkeling, and the freshwater pool (there's bar service here) is surrounded by a large wooden deck that's ideal for sunning. ⊠ Villa Olga 00802, ☎ 340/774–1376 or 800/544–0493 (direct to hotel), ℻ 340/774–8010. 12 rooms. Restaurant, bar, pool. AE, D, MC, V. CP.

SOUTH SHORE

$$$$ ▦ **Bolongo Bay Beach Club & Villas.** This 75-room, beachfront resort also includes the 20-room Bolongo Villas next door and the six-room Bolongo Bayside Inn across the street. All rooms—which include minisuites and one- and two-bedroom units—have efficiency kitchens and balconies and are just steps from a strand of white beach. The resort offers a choice of all inclusive or semi-inclusive plans, which means you can pay less if you opt for fewer activities. The all-inclusive rate covers all meals and drinks, the use of tennis courts, and many water-sports activities—including an all-day sail and half-day snorkel trip on one of the resort's yachts. There's a three-night minimum for the all-inclusive plan. ⊠ 50 Estate Bolongo 00802, ☎ 340/775–1800 or 800/524–4746 (direct to hotel), ℻ 340/775–3208. 101 units. 2 restaurants, 2 bars, air-conditioning, 3 pools, 2 tennis courts, health club, volleyball, beach, dive shop, dock, snorkeling, windsurfing, boating, jet skiing. AE, D, DC, MC, V. All-inclusive.

$$$$ ▦ **Marriott Frenchman's Reef and Morning Star Beach Resorts.** Sprawl-
★ ing, luxurious, and on a prime harbor promontory east of Charlotte Amalie, these two full-service superhotels were renovated extensively in 1997. Frenchman's Reef was given 128 suites—each with glorious ocean and harbor views. Morning Star rooms are more elegant and are in buildings nestled surfside along the fine white sand of Morning Star Beach. Guests at both resorts can work out at the Reef Health Club & Spa, which offers state-of-the-art cardiovascular and strength training equipment, therapeutic massages, and skin care therapies. Dining is alfresco on American or gourmet Caribbean fare, or oceanfront at the Tavern on the Beach; there's also a lavish buffet served, overlooking the sparkling lights of Charlotte Amalie and the harbor. Live entertainment and dancing, scheduled activities for all ages, and a shuttle boat to town make having fun easy. ⊠ Estate Bakkeroe (Box 7100) 00801, ☎ 340/776–8500 or 800/524–2000 (direct to hotel), ℻ 340/776–3054. 373 rooms, 128 suites. 6 restaurants, 6 bars, snack bar, air-conditioning, 2 pools, spa, 4 tennis courts, health club, beach. AE, D, DC, MC, V. EP.

Guest House
CHARLOTTE AMALIE

$–$$ 🏨 **Island View Guest House.** Nestled in tropical foliage 545 ft up on the face of Crown Mountain, this simply furnished bed-and-breakfast offers sweeping views of Charlotte Amalie harbor from the pool and shaded terraces. Continental breakfast is served daily; however, six rooms have kitchenettes. All rooms have phones, ceiling fans, TVs, and baths. The friendly office staff can arrange tours. ✉ *Estate Contant (Box 1903) 00801,* ☎ *340/774–4270 or 800/524–2023 (direct to hotel),* FAX *340/ 774–6167. 15 rooms. Fans, pool. MC, AE, V. CP.*

Villas and Condominiums
EAST END

$$$$ 🏨 **The Anchorage.** Next to the St. Thomas Yacht Club and facing Cowpet Bay, these two- and three-bedroom villas are right on the beach. They have washing machines and dryers, and the complex has two lighted tennis courts, a freshwater pool, and an informal dining room. ✉ *Estate Nazareth (Ocean Property Management, Box 8529) 00801,* ☎ *340/775–2600 or 800/874–7897 (direct to hotel),* FAX *340/775–5901. 30 rooms. Dining room, air-conditioning, pool, 2 tennis courts. AE, D, MC, V. EP.*

$$$–$$$$ 🏨 **Blazing Villas.** On the Renaissance Grand Beach Resort property,
★   these cool pastel yellow, pink, green, and blue villas have their own private garden patios and can be combined with other villas to create a four-bedroom, four-bath unit. All quarters have refrigerators, microwaves, and phones. You can use all the adjoining resort's facilities. ✉ *Smith Bay Rd. (Box 502697) 00805,* ☎ *340/776–0760 or 800/382– 2002 (direct to hotel),* FAX *340/776–3603. 19 rooms. 2 restaurants, snack bar, air-conditioning, refrigerators, 2 pools, 6 tennis courts, beach. AE, MC, V. EP.*

$$$–$$$$ 🏨 **Sapphire Village.** A stay in these high-rise units may take you back to the swinging-singles days of apartment-house living, since many of the units are rented out long-term to refugees from northern winters. The best units overlook the marina and St. John; the beach is in sight and just a short walk down the hill. ✉ *Sapphire Bay (Ocean Property Management, Box 852) 00801,* ☎ *340/775–2600 or 800/874–7897 (direct to hotel),* FAX *340/775–5901. 35 units. Restaurant, pub, air-conditioning, 2 pools. AE, D, MC, V. EP.*

$–$$$ 🏨 **Sea Horse Cottages.** These simple cottages, at the eastern end of the island on Nazareth Bay, look across to St. Croix, 40 mi (65 km) south. Although there's no beach, steps go directly into the sea from a swimming platform. All rooms have kitchens and ceiling fans. ✉ *Estate Nazareth (Box 302312) 00803,* ☎ *340/775–9231. 11 units, from studios to 2-bedrooms. Fans, kitchenettes, pool. No credit cards. EP.*

Private Homes
You can arrange private-home rentals through various agents, including **Calypso Realty** (✉ Box 12178, 00801, ☎ 340/774–1620 or 800/ 747–4858) and **McLaughlin-Anderson Villas** (✉ 100 Blackbeard's Hill, Suite 3, 00802, ☎ 340/776–0635 or 800/537–6246). Both specialize in luxury-end villas; write for brochures with photos of the properties they represent. Some residences are suitable for travelers with disabilities.

Dining

The beauty of St. Thomas and its sister islands has attracted a cadre of professionally trained chefs who know their way around fresh fish and local fruits. You can dine on everything from terrific, cheap local dishes such as goat water (a spicy stew) and fungi, to imports such as hot pastrami sandwiches and raspberries in crème fraîche.

In large hotels you'll pay prices similar to those in New York City or Paris. Fancy restaurants may have a token chicken dish under $20, but otherwise, main courses are pricey. You can, however, find good inexpensive Caribbean restaurants. To snack on some local fare, order a johnnycake or a thick slice of dumb bread (a dense round loaf often cut into triangles and filled with cheddar cheese) from any of the mobile food vans parked all over the island. Familiar fast-food franchises also abound.

If your accommodations have a kitchen and you plan to cook, you'll find good variety in St. Thomas's mainland-style supermarkets. Note, however, that grocery prices are about 20% higher than those on the mainland United States. As for drinking, outside the hotels, a beer in a bar will cost between $2 and $3 and a piña colada $4 or more.

What to Wear

Dining on St. Thomas is relaxed and informal. Few restaurants require a jacket and tie. Still, at dinner in the snazzier places, shorts and T-shirts are highly inappropriate; men would do well to wear slacks and a shirt with buttons. Dress codes on St. Thomas rarely require women to wear skirts, but you'll never go wrong with something flowing.

CATEGORY	COST*
$$$$	over $35
$$$	$25–$35
$$	$15–$25
$	under $15

*average cost of a three-course dinner, per person, excluding drinks and service; there's no sales tax in the USVI

Charlotte Amalie

AMERICAN

$$–$$$ ✕ **Greenhouse Bar and Restaurant.** Watch the waterfront wake up at this large, bustling, open air restaurant, whose waitstaff looks like a bunch of all-American college kids on spring break. Breakfast and lunch (burgers, salads, and sandwiches) are good values. Dinner specials include peel-'n'-eat shrimp, Maine lobster, and prime rib. You can work it all off dancing to the Wednesday night band, which plays until the crowd clears. ⊠ *Waterfront Hwy. at Storetvaer Gade,* ☎ *340/774–7998. AE, D, MC, V.*

$–$$$ ✕ **Hard Rock Cafe.** A hot spot from the day it opened, this waterfront restaurant is pretty much like its namesakes around the world. Rock-and-roll memorabilia abound, and the menu offers hamburgers, sandwiches, salads, and great desserts. Doors are open from 11 AM until 2 AM; there's always a wait for a table during prime meal times. ⊠ *International Plaza on the Waterfront,* ☎ *340/777–5555. AE, MC, V.*

ASIAN

$–$$ ✕ **Beni Iguana's.** Here sushi is served as "edible art" in a charming Danish courtyard setting. Among the offerings are cucumber and avocado or scallop with scallion rolls, specialty big rolls such as the Kung Fooee (shiitake, cucumber, daikon, and flying fish roe), and tuna or salmon sashimi. A pictorial menu board makes ordering by the piece, plate, or combination platter much easier. ⊠ *Grand Hotel Court,* ☎ *340/777–8744. No credit cards. Closed Sun.*

CARIBBEAN/CREOLE

$$–$$$ ✕ **Gladys' Cafe.** Even if the local specialties—conch in butter sauce,
★ salt fish and dumplings, hearty red bean soup—didn't make this a recommended café, it would be worth coming for Gladys's smile. While you're here, pick up some of her special hot sauce for $6 a bottle. ⊠ *Royal Dane Mall,* ☎ *340/774–6604. AE. Closed Sun. No dinner.*

CONTINENTAL

$$$-$$$$ ✕ **Hotel 1829.** You'll dine by candlelight flickering over stone walls
★ and pink table linens at this restaurant on the terrace of the ☞ **Hotel**
1829. The menu and award-winning wine list (325 varieties; 15 avail-
able by the glass) are extensive, from Caribbean rock lobster to rack
of lamb. Many items—including a warm spinach salad—are prepared
table-side, and the restaurant is justly famous for its dessert soufflés:
chocolate, Grand Marnier, raspberry, or coconut, to name a few. ⊠
Government Hill near Main St., ☎ *340/776–1829. Reservations es-*
sential. AE, D, MC, V. Closed Sun.

ECLECTIC

$$$-$$$$ ✕ **Hervé.** French-trained Hervé Chassin's long experience in the St.
Thomas restaurant industry has led to a menu that offers a delightful
mix of Caribbean and Continental cuisine. In the warm glow of can-
dlelight—at tables impeccably set with linen cloths, silver settings, and
fine crystal—you can start off with crispy conch fritters served with a
spicy-sweet mango chutney, and then choose from such entrées as
fresh tuna encrusted with sesame seeds or succulent roast duck with a
ginger and tamarind sauce. The raspberry cheesecake is to die for. ⊠
Government Hill, ☎ *340/777–9703. AE, MC, V. Closed Sun.*

$$-$$$$ ✕ **Café LuLu.** From the heights of Blackbeard's Castle you can enjoy
a 180-degree sweeping harbor view and the romantic ambience of the
historic stone-walled dining room while sampling dishes that combine
the essence of Caribbean, Asian, and Mediterranean cuisines. Crispy
plantain-coated sea bass and a fork-tender filet mignon filled with goat
cheese may be two of the selections on the monthly changing menu.
For Sunday brunch, the orange-mango mimosas and wasabi-spiced
Bloody Marys are musts. ⊠ *Blackbeard's Hill,* ☎ *340/714–1641.*
Reservations essential. AE, D, MC, V. No lunch.

$$-$$$$ ✕ **Tavern on the Waterfront.** White linen tablecloths, silver and crys-
tal table settings, and a rich mahogany decor set the scene for an ele-
gant meal at this second-floor restaurant. You can sit in air-conditioned
comfort overlooking the harbor. The menu offers flavors from every
corner of the globe. Try the soft-shell crabs with mango salsa or the
tuna sushi for lunch. Dinner offerings include the 2-pound Caribbean
lobster house specialty. Wednesday is Latin night, and Friday features
authentic Mediterranean cuisine. ⊠ *Waterfront, at Royal Dane Mall,*
☎ *340/776–4328. AE, MC, V. Closed Sun.*

GREEK

$$-$$$ ✕ **Zorba's Sagapo.** Tired of shopping? Summon up a little more en-
★ ergy and head up Government Hill to Zorba's. Sit and have a cold beer
or bracing iced tea in the dining room of this 19th-century building,
and then fork into Greek salads and appetizers, moussaka, and an ex-
cellent vegetarian plate. Fridays feature a "Wine Down" happy hour,
popular with the local professional crowd. Next door, Zorba's owner
Jimmy Boukas serves healthy baked goods-to-go at Jimmy's patis-
serie. ⊠ *Government Hill,* ☎ *340/776–0444. Dinner reservations es-*
sential. AE, MC, V.

ITALIAN

$$$-$$$$ ✕ **Virgilio's.** For the best Northern Italian cuisine on the island, don't
★ miss this intimate, elegant hideaway whose two dining rooms face each
other across a quiet side street. Eclectic art covers the two-story-high
brick walls. Come here for more than 40 homemade pastas comple-
mented by superb sauces—*cappellini* (very thin spaghetti) with fresh
tomatoes and garlic, say, or spaghetti peasant-style (in a rich tomato
sauce with mushrooms and prosciutto). Try Virgilio's own mango
flambé with crepes or a steaming cup of cappuccino for dessert. Maître

d' Matthew Richardson is on hand day and night, welcoming customers and helping the gracious staff. ⊠ *16 and 18 Main St.,* ☎ *340/776–4920. Reservations essential. AE, MC, V. Closed Sun.*

East End

AMERICAN

$–$$ ✕ **Tickles Dockside Pub.** Both the Crown Bay and East End locations of this casual, alfresco restaurant have a devout following of locals who live and work on boats docked nearby. Enjoy sandwiches, ribs, and chicken (served with sweet-potato French fries) while you watch the iguanas beg for table scraps—and bring your camera. ⊠ *American Yacht Harbor, Red Hook, Bldg. D,* ☎ *340/775–9425;* ⊠ *Crown Bay Marina, Charlotte Amalie,* ☎ *340/776–1595. MC, V.*

CARIBBEAN/CREOLE

$–$$ ✕ **Eunice's Terrace.** Eunice is an excellent West Indian cook, who is justly famous for introducing visitors to native-style cuisine. Her roomy, two-story restaurant has a bar and a menu of native dishes, including callaloo (a spicy stew thick with spinach-like greens and seafood), conch fritters, fried fish, local sweet potatoes, *fungi* (a polenta-like cornmeal dish with okra), and green banana. Be sure to pick up one of Eunice's gift-wrapped rum cakes to go for $4 apiece. ⊠ *Rte. 38 near Renaissance Grand Beach Resort and Coral World, Smith Bay,* ☎ *340/775–3975. AE, MC, V.*

ECLECTIC

$–$$$ ✕ **Duffy's Love Shack.** If the floating bubbles don't attract you to this zany eatery, the lime green shutters, loud rock music, and fun-loving waitstaff sure will. It is billed as the "ultimate tropical drink shack," and the bartenders shake up such exotic concoctions as the Love Shack Volcano—a 50-ounce flaming extravaganza. Dining selections are just as trendy. Try the tequila-lime shrimp or jerk chicken Caesar. Thursday nights feature theme parties complete with prizes and giveaways. ⊠ *Red Hook Plaza parking lot,* ☎ *340/779–2080. No credit cards.*

$–$$$ ✕ **Raffles.** In a homelike dining room, set in a quaint marina, owner-
★ chef Sandra Englesburger puts on a one-woman culinary show. Her from-scratch creations include an English shepherd's pie, mahimahi in a rich lobster sauce, and a two-day Peking duck. Entrées on the prix-fixe ($10), three-course menu change nightly. For dessert, try Peter's Paradise—a dark chocolate sphere filled with white chocolate mousse and fruit. ⊠ *41-6-1 Compass Point Marina,* ☎ *340/775–6004. Reservations essential. AE, MC, V. Closed Mon. No lunch.*

IRISH

$$–$$$ ✕ **Finn McCool's Restaurant and Pub.** You'll find traditional Irish stew
★ and shepherd's pie in this restaurant with a warm decor (lots of wood) and a big friendly bar. If you like seafood, try the Irish salmon or the crab cakes and fried oysters. There's live music on weekends, and every St. Patrick's Day sees a parade led by restaurateur Frank Brittingham (corned beef and cabbage and green beer are served afterward). ⊠ *41-6-3 Compass Point Marina,* ☎ *340/775–6194. MC, V.*

ITALIAN

$$$–$$$$ ✕ **Romanos.** Inside this huge, old, stucco house is a delightful surprise:
★ a spare yet elegant setting and superb Northern Italian cuisine. Owner Tony hasn't advertised since the restaurant opened in 1988, and it's always packed. Try the pastas, either with a classic sauce or one of Tony's unique creations, such as a cream sauce with mushrooms, prosciutto, pine nuts, and Parmesan. ⊠ *97 Smith Bay,* ☎ *340/775–0045. Reservations essential. MC, V. Closed Sun. No lunch.*

\$\$–\$\$\$\$ ✕ **Jerry's Beachfront Restaurant.** This quintessential beach bar serves
★ such rib-sticking Italian specialties as mussels marinara, veal Parmesan, and chicken marsala. Owner Jerry DeFreitas's conch bisque (made from a secret recipe) adds island spice to the menu and is definitely worth sampling. Save room for a jumbo banana split, piled high with Haägen-Dazs ice cream. Monday is all-you-can-eat shrimp night for \$18.95. At Sunday brunch you'll find such items as veggie-filled omelets and fruit-topped pancakes. ⊠ *Anchorage Condominiums, Red Hook,* ☎ *340/779–2462. MC, V.*

SEAFOOD

\$\$\$–\$\$\$\$ ✕ **Agave Terrace.** At this dimly lit, open-air pavilion restaurant, fresh fish is served as steaks or fillets, and the catch of the day is listed on the blackboard. Come early and have a drink at the Lookout Lounge, which has breathtaking views of the BVI. The food enjoys as good a reputation as the view. ⊠ *Colony Point Pleasant Resort, Smith Bay,* ☎ *340/775–4142. AE, MC, V. No lunch.*

\$\$–\$\$\$\$ ✕ **Cafe Wahoo.** The fish is so fresh at this open-air eatery that you may see it coming in from one of the boats tied up at the dock just steps away. For starters, try the medallion of yellowfin tuna seviche marinated in lime, onion, and white wine. Entrées include a grilled fillet of wahoo with pineapple and cucumber sauce and sea bass poached in spiced carrot essence and topped with caviar. Steak, poultry, and pasta lovers will find something to please on the menu, too. ⊠ *Piccola Marina, Red Hook,* ☎ *340/775–6350. AE, MC, V. No lunch.*

TEX-MEX

\$–\$\$\$ ✕ **Polli's.** You'll feel as if you're sitting deep within a tropical jungle at this open-air restaurant, where a live parrot squawks a greeting to incoming diners. The menu is Tex-Mex complete with jalapeño poppers (deep-fried cheese-stuffed hot peppers), chicken- or seafood-stuffed fajitas, and margarita pie for dessert. All entrées come vegetarian-style upon request, with soy replacing the meat. ⊠ *Tillett Gardens,* ☎ *340/775–4550. AE, MC, V.*

Frenchtown

AUSTRIAN

\$\$\$ ✕ **Alexander's Café.** This place is a favorite with the people in the restaurant business on St. Thomas—always a sign of quality. Alexander is
★ Austrian, and the schnitzels are delicious and reasonably priced; pasta specials are fresh and tasty. Save room for strudel. Next door is Alexander's Bar & Grill, serving food from the same kitchen but in a more casual setting and at lower prices. ⊠ *24A Honduras,* ☎ *340/776–4211. Reservations essential. AE, D, MC, V. Closed Sun.*

CARIBBEAN/CREOLE

\$\$–\$\$\$ ✕ **Victor's New Hide-Out.** Although it's a little hard to find—it's up the hill between the Nisky Shopping Center and the airport—this landmark restaurant is worth the search. Native food—steamed fish, marinated pork chops, and local lobster—and native music are offered in a casual, friendly, West Indian atmosphere. ⊠ *Sub Base,* ☎ *340/776–9379. AE, MC, V.*

ECLECTIC

\$\$–\$\$\$\$ ✕ **The Chart House.** In an old great house at the tip of the Frenchtown peninsula, this restaurant offers superb views along with fresh fish and teriyaki dishes, lobster, Hawaiian chicken, and a large salad bar. ⊠ *Villa Olga,* ☎ *340/774–4262. AE, D, DC, MC, V.*

\$\$–\$\$\$ ✕ **Craig & Sally's.** In the heart of Frenchtown, Sally Darash whips up
★ such eclectic starters as grilled shrimp and melon kabobs and entrées such as polenta-crusted yellowtail snapper with artichoke and olive sauce.

Save room for dessert—the white-chocolate cheesecake is truly special. Husband Craig makes sure more than a dozen wines are available by the glass and many more by the bottle. ⊠ *22 Honduras,* ☎ *340/777–9949. AE, MC, V. Closed Mon.–Tues. No lunch Sat.–Sun.*

Northside

AMERICAN

$$–$$$ ✕ **Sib's Mountain Bar and Restaurant.** Here you'll find live music, football, burgers, barbecued ribs and chicken, and beer. This friendly two-fisted drinking bar, with a restaurant on the back porch, is a good place for a casual dinner after a day at the beach. Kids of all ages can doodle on the paper tablecloths with the colorful crayons left on every table. ⊠ *Mafolie Hill,* ☎ *340/774–8967. AE, MC, V.*

ITALIAN

$$–$$$$ ✕ **Ferrari's.** St. Thomas residents have consistently voted this the "best
★ value" restaurant in the *USVI Daily News* poll. The menu has such staples as antipasto, veal marsala, lasagna, pizzas, and garlic bread. Sit at a table or have a seat at the bar from 4:30 until 11. ⊠ *33 Crown Mountain Rd.,* ☎ *340/774–6800. AE, MC, V. No lunch.*

Beaches

All 44 St. Thomas beaches are open to the public, although you can only reach some of them by walking through a resort. Hotel guests frequently have access to lounge chairs and floats that are off-limits to nonguests; for this reason, you may feel more comfortable at one of the beaches not associated with a resort, such as Magens Bay (which charges an entrance fee to cover beach maintenance) or Coki. Whichever one you choose, remember to remove your valuables from the car, and keep them out of sight when you go swimming.

Brewer's Beach, on Route 30 near the airport, is a long stretch of powdery white sand. Trucks that sell lunch, snacks, and drinks often park along the road bordering the beach.

Coki Beach, next to Coral World (turn north off Route 38), is a popular snorkeling spot for cruise-ship passengers; it's common to find a group of them among the reefs on the east and west ends of the beach. This is also a good place to dash in for a swim or just do some people-watching from shore. Don't leave valuables unattended in your car or on the beach.

Hull Bay beach, on the north shore (Route 37), faces Inner and Outer Brass cays and attracts fishermen and beachcombers. With its rougher Atlantic surf and relative isolation, Hull Bay is one of the best surfing spots on the island. Take a break from the rigors of sightseeing at the Hull Bay Hideaway, a laid-back beach bar where a local band plays rock and roll on Sunday afternoons.

Magens Bay, on Route 35, is usually lively because of its spectacular crescent of white sand, more than ½ mi (¾ km) long, and its calm waters, which are protected by two peninsulas. It's often listed among the world's most beautiful beaches. (If you arrive between 8 AM and 6 PM, you'll have to pay an entrance fee of $1 per car and an additional $1 per person.) The bottom is flat and sandy, so this is a place for sunning and swimming rather than snorkeling. On weekends and holidays, the sounds of groups partying under the sheds fills the air. There's also an outdoor bar, bathhouses, a nature trail (unmarked and often overgrown), and a snack bar. East of the beach is Udder Delight, a one-room shop of the St. Thomas Dairies that serves a USVI tradition—a milk shake with a splash of Cruzan rum. Kids can enjoy virgin shakes, with a touch of soursop, mango, or banana flavoring.

Morning Star Beach, close to Charlotte Amalie, is where many young locals body surf or play volleyball. The pretty curve of beach fronts Marriott's Frenchman's Reef Hotel. Snorkeling is good near the rocks when the current doesn't affect visibility.

Sapphire Beach has a fine view of St. John and other islands. The snorkeling is excellent at the reef to the right or east, near Pettyklip Point. Sapphire Beach Resort rents water-sports gear.

Secret Harbour's condo resort doesn't at all detract from the attractiveness of its covelike beach. Not only is this East End spot pretty, it also has superb snorkeling—head out to the left, near the rocks.

Outdoor Activities and Sports

Participant Sports

BICYCLING

Hills are steep and roads don't have shoulders, but you'll never ride too far from a beautiful beach and cool swim. **Mountain Bike Tours of Water Island** (✉ Box 308262, 00803, ☎ 340/714–2186) is a cycling adventure to the USVI's "newest" Virgin. You'll take a 10-minute ferry ride from Crown Bay Marina to the island before jumping on a Cannondale M-200 18-speed mountain bike for a 3-hour tour over rolling hills on mostly paved roads. Helmets, water, a guide, and ferry fare are covered in the $60 cost. **St. Thomas Mountain Bike Adventure** (✉ Box 7037, 00801, ☎ 340/776–1727) takes you on a 1½-hour cycle out past Magens Bay to Peterborg Point, using Trek 830 21-speed mountain bikes. There are lots of photo opportunities: flora, fauna, and a lesser-seen side of Magens's picturesque half-moon beach. Helmets, water, and a guide are provided; the cost is $35.

BOATING AND SAILING

Calm seas, crystal-clear waters, and close-by islands (perfect for picnicking, snorkeling, and exploring) make St. Thomas a favorite jumping-off spot for day- or weeklong sails or power boat adventures. With well over 100 vessels to choose from, St. Thomas is the charter-boat mecca of the USVI. You can go through a broker to book a private sailing vessel with a crew or contact a charter company directly.

Blue Water Cruises (✉ Box 1345, Camden, ME 04843, ☎ 800/524–2020) is a brokerage with an excellent worldwide reputation. Charter-boat companies include **Island Yachts** (✉ 6100 Red Hook Quarter, 18B, ☎ 340/775–6666 or 800/524–2019) in Red Hook, **Regency Yacht Vacations** (✉ 5200 Long Bay Rd., ☎ 340/776–5950 or 800/524–7676) at the Yacht Haven Marina, and **VIP Yacht Charters** (✉ 6118 Estate Frydenhoj 58, ☎ 340/776–1510 or 800/524–2015), near Red Hook.

Nauti Nymph (✉ 6501 Red Hook Plaza, Suite 201, ☎ FAX 340/775–5066 or 800/734–7345) has a large selection of powerboats for rent. Rates range from $215 to $350 a day and include snorkel gear.

FISHING

Fishing from St. Thomas is synonymous with blue marlin angling—especially from June through October. Four 1,000-pound plus blues, including three world records, have been caught on the famous North Drop, about 20 mi (32 km) north of St. Thomas. If you're not into marlin fishing, try hooking up sailfish in the winter, dolphinfish (also called mahimahi) come spring, and wahoo in the fall.

To book a boat, contact the **American Yacht Harbor** (✉ 6100 Red Hook Plaza, ☎ 340/775–6454), **Charter Boat Center** (✉ 6300 Red Hook Plaza, ☎ 340/775–7990 or 800/866–5714), or **Sapphire Beach Marina** (✉ Sapphire Bay, ☎ 340/775–6100). Or, to find the trip that will best suit you, walk down the docks at either American Yacht Harbor or Sapphire Beach Marina and chat with the captains.

GOLF

The **Mahogany Run Golf Course** (⊠ Rte. 42, ☎ 340/777–5000) is open daily and often hosts informal tournaments on weekends. A spectacular view of the BVI and challenging 3-hole "Devil's Triangle" attracts avid golfers to this Tom Fazio–designed, par-70, 18-hole course.

HORSEBACK RIDING

Half Moon Stables (☎ 340/777–6088) offers hour-long guided rides along a secluded trail that winds through lush, green hills to a pebble-covered beach on the East End. Horses and ponys are available, and so are Western or English saddles. The cost is $45.

PARASAILING

The Caribbean waters are so clear here that the outlines of coral reefs are visible from high in the sky. Parasailers sit in a harness attached to a parachute that lifts off from the boat deck until they're sailing up in the air. **Caribbean Parasail and Watersports** (⊠ 6501 Red Hook Plaza, ☎ 340/775–9360) makes parasailing pick-ups from every beachfront resort on St. Thomas. They also rent such water toys as jet skis, kayaks, and floating battery-powered chairs.

SCUBA DIVING AND SNORKELING

Dive sites feature wrecks such as the **Cartanser Sr.,** a 35-ft-deep, beautifully encrusted, World War II cargo ship, and the **General Rogers,** a 65-ft-deep Coast Guard cutter with a gigantic resident barracuda. Reef dives offer hidden caves and archways at **Cow and Calf Rocks,** coral-covered pinnacles at **Frenchcap,** and tunnels where you can explore undersea from the Caribbean to the Atlantic at **Thatch Cay, Grass Cay,** and **Congo Cay.** Many resorts and charter yachts offer dive packages. A one-tank dive starts at $40; two-tank dives are $55 or more. There are plenty of snorkeling possibilities, too. Nick Aquilar's *At A Glance Snorkeller's Guide To St. Thomas,* available at local souvenir shops, describes 15 idyllic spots in detail.

Aqua Action (⊠ 6501 Red Hook Plaza, ☎ 340/775–6285) is a full-service, PADI, five-star shop that offers all levels of instruction at Secret Harbour Beach Resort. **Chris Sawyer Diving Center** (☎ 340/775–7320 or 800/882–2965), at Compass Point Marina, is a PADI five-star outfit that specializes in dives to the 310-ft-long RMS *Rhone* in the BVI. It also has a NAUI certification center that offers instruction up to dive master. **Seahorse Dive Boats** (⊠ Crown Bay Marina, Suite 505, ☎ 340/774–2001) is another PADI five-star facility that does both day and night dives to wrecks and reefs.

SEA EXCURSIONS

Landlubbers and seafarers alike will enjoy the wind in their hair and salt spray in the air while exploring the waters surrounding St. Thomas. Several businesses can effortlessly book you on a half-day, inshore light-tackle fishing trip; a snorkel-and-sail to a deserted cay; or an excursion over to the BVI. Contact the **Adventure Center** (⊠ Marriott Frenchman's Reef Hotel, Estate Bakkeroe, ☎ 340/774–2990), **Charter Boat Center** (☞ Fishing, *above*), **Limnos Charters** (⊠ 6100 Red Hook Plaza, ☎ 340/775–3203), or **Treasure Isle Cruises** (⊠ 6616 Estate Nadir 30-31, ☎ 340/775–9500).

SEA KAYAKING

Fish dart, birds sing, and iguanas lounge on the limbs of dense mangroves deep within a marine sanctuary on St. Thomas's southeast shore. **Virgin Islands Ecotours** (⊠ 2 Estate Nadir, on Rte. 32, ☎ 340/

779–2155) offers 2½-hour, guided trips on two-man sit-atop ocean kayaks; there are stops for swimming and snorkeling. Many of the resorts on St. Thomas's eastern end have kayaks, too.

STARGAZING

Without the light pollution so prevalent in more densely populated areas, the heavens appear supernaturally bright. On a **Star Charters Astronomy Adventure** (✉ Nisky Mail Center, No. 693, ☎ 340/774–9211), you can peer into the Caribbean's largest optical telescope—an 18-inch Newtonian Reflector—and learn both the science and lore of the stars through a well-informed celestial guide.

SUBMARINING

Dive 90 ft under the sea to one of St. Thomas's most beautiful reefs without getting wet. **Atlantis Submarines** (✉ Havensight Shopping Mall, Bldg. VI, ☎ 340/776–5650) are 46-passenger, air-conditioned conduits to a watery world teeming with brightly colored fish, vibrant sea fans, and an occasional shark. A guide narrates the two-hour journey, while a diver makes a mid-tour appearance for a fish-feeding show. The cost is $72. No children under 36 inches tall are allowed.

TENNIS

The Caribbean sun is hot, so be sure to hit the courts before 10 AM or after 5 PM (many of the courts are lighted). You can indulge in a set or two even if you're staying in a guest house without courts, since most hotels rent time to nonguests. For reservations, call **Bluebeard Castle Hotel** (✉ Bluebeard's Hill, ☎ 340/774–1600, ext. 196), **Mahogany Run Tennis Club** (✉ Rte. 42, ☎ 340/775–5000), **Marriott Frenchman's Reef Tennis Courts** (✉ Estate Bakkeroe, ☎ 340/776–8500, ext. 444), **Renaissance Grand Beach Resort** (✉ Smith Bay Rd., ☎ 340/775–1510), **Ritz-Carlton, St. Thomas** (✉ 6900 Great Bay Estate, ☎ 340/775–3333), **Sapphire Beach Resort** (✉ Sapphire Bay, ☎ 340/775–6100, ext. 2131), or **Wyndham Sugar Bay** (✉ 6500 Estate Smith Bay, ☎ 340/777–7100). There are two public courts at **Sub Base** (next to the Water and Power Authority), open on a first-come, first-served basis. The lights are on here until 8 PM.

WINDSURFING

Expect some spills, anticipate the thrills, and try your luck clipping through the seas on a surfboard with a sail. Most beachfront resorts rent Windsurfers and offer 1-hour lessons for about $50. One of the island's best known independent outfits is **West Indies Windsurfing** (✉ Vessup Beach, No. 9 Nazareth, ☎ 340/775–6530), which helped organize the U.S. Windsurfing Association National Championships on St. Thomas in 1997.

Spectator Sport

HORSE RACING

The **Clinton Phipps Racetrack** (✉ Rte. 30 at Nadir 42, ☎ 340/775–4555) schedules races—especially on local holidays—with sanctioned betting. Be prepared for large crowds; this is a popular sport.

Shopping

St. Thomas lives up to its self-described billing as a shopper's paradise. Even if shopping isn't your idea of how to spend a vacation, you still may want to slip in on a quiet day (check the cruise-ship listings—Monday and Saturday are usually the least crowded) to browse. Among the best buys are liquor, linens, imported china, crystal (most stores ship), and jewelry. The amount of jewelry available makes this one of the few items for which comparison shopping is worth the effort. Local crafts include shell jewelry, carved calabash bowls, straw brooms, woven baskets, and dolls. Creations by local doll maker Gwendolyn Harley—like her costumed West Indian market woman—have been goodwill ambassadors bought by visitors from as far away as Asia. Spice mixes, hot sauces, and tropical jams and jellies are other native products worth purchasing.

There's no sales tax in the USVI, and shoppers can take advantage of the $1,200 duty-free allowance per family member (remember to save your receipts). Although you'll find the occasional salesclerk who will make a deal, bartering is not the norm here.

Areas and Malls

The prime shopping area in **Charlotte Amalie** is between Post Office and Market squares; it consists of three parallel streets that run east–west (Waterfront Highway, Main Street, and Back Street) and the alleyways that connect them. Particularly attractive are the historic **Royal Dane Mall, A. H. Riise Alley,** and pastel-painted **International Plaza**—quaint alleys between Main Street and the Waterfront.

Vendors Plaza, on the waterfront side of Emancipation Gardens, is a central location for outdoor folks who sell handmade earrings, necklaces, and bracelets; straw baskets and handbags; T-shirts; fabrics; African artifacts; local foods; and fresh tropical fruit smoothies.

West of town, the pink-stucco **Nisky Center,** on Harwood Highway about ½ mi (¾ km) east of the airport, is more of a hometown shopping center than a tourist area, but there's a bank, a pharmacy, clothing stores, a record shop, and a Radio Shack.

Havensight Mall, next to the cruise-ship dock, may not be as charming as downtown Charlotte Amalie, but it does have more than 60 shops. You'll find an excellent bookstore, a bank, a pharmacy, a gourmet grocery, and smaller branches of many downtown stores. Steps away, there are also a few shops at **Port of $ale.**

East of town, **Tillett Gardens** (⊠ Estate Tutu, ☎ 340/775–1405) is an oasis of artistic endeavor across from the Tutu Park Shopping Center (☞ *below*). The late Jim Tillett and then-wife Rhoda converted this old Danish farm into an artist's retreat in 1959. Today you can watch craftspeople and artisans produce silk-screen fabrics, pottery, candles, watercolors, gold jewelry, stained glass, and other handicrafts. Local herb-infused honeys and olive oils are also available. Something special is often happening in the gardens as well: the "Classics in the Gardens" program is a classical music series presented under the stars, and "Arts Alive" is a visual-arts and crafts festival held four times yearly.

Tutu Park Shopping Center, across from Tillett Gardens, is the island's one and only enclosed mall. The 47 stores and food court are anchored by a KMart and a grocery store. Archaeologists have discovered evidence that ancient Arawak Indians once lived near the mall grounds.

Red Hook has **American Yacht Harbor,** a waterfront shopping area with a dive shop, a tackle store, an art gallery, a bar, and a few restaurants. Don't forget **St. John** (☞ Shopping *in* St. John, *below*). A ferry ride (an hour from Charlotte Amalie or 20 minutes from Red Hook) will take you to the charming shops of **Mongoose Junction** and **Wharfside Village,** which specialize in unique, often island-made items.

Specialty Items

ART

A. H. Riise Caribbean Print Gallery. Historic and contemporary prints, posters, and photo note cards depicting West Indian life are sold here. ⊠ *37 Main St., at Riise's Alley,* ☎ *340/776–2303.*

Camille Pissarro Art Gallery. This second-floor gallery, in the birthplace of St. Thomas's famous artist, offers a fine collection of original paintings and prints by local and regional artists. ⊠ *14 Main St.,* ☎ *340/ 774–4621.*

Jonna White Gallery. Here, etchings of exotic images and tropical scenes (done on hand-made papers) are available unframed or framed. Shipping to the U.S. mainland is free. ⊠ *Waterfront Hwy. next to Palm Passage,* ☎ *340/776–7779.*

Mango Tango. Works by popular local artists—originals, prints, and note cards—are displayed (there's a one-person show at least one weekend a month) and sold here. You'll also find the island's largest humidor and a brand-name cigar gallery. ⊠ *Al Cohen's Plaza, atop Raphune Hill, ½ mi (¾ km) east of Charlotte Amalie,* ☎ *340/777–3060.*

BOOKS AND MAGAZINES

Dockside Bookshop. This place is packed with books for children, travelers, cooks, and historians, as well as a good selection of paperback mysteries, best-sellers, art books, calendars, and prints. It also carries a selection of books written in and about the Caribbean and the Virgin Islands. ⊠ *Havensight Mall,* ☎ *340/774–4937.*

Education Station Books. The emphasis at this full-service bookstore is on Caribbean literature and African-American and African history. There's also a large cookbook selection, a music section featuring jazz and world beat tapes from Africa, and prints by local artists. In addition, you can buy and sell used books of all types here. Visit Education Station Ltd., just next door, for children's titles. ⊠ *Wheatley Center, intersection of Rtes. 35 and 38,* ☎ *340/776–5433.*

Island Newsstand. This place has the largest selection of magazines and newspapers on St. Thomas. Expect to pay about 20% above stateside prices. ⊠ *Grand Hotel Court, Charlotte Amalie,* ☎ *340/774–0043.*

CAMERAS AND ELECTRONICS

Boolchand's. A variety of brand-name cameras, audio and video equipment, and binoculars is sold here. ⊠ *31 Main St.,* ☎ *340/776–0794;* ⊠ *Havensight Mall,* ☎ *340/776–0302.*

Royal Caribbean. Shop here for cameras, camcorders, stereos, watches, and clocks. ⊠ *33 Main St.,* ☎ *340/776–8166;* ⊠ *Havensight Mall,* ☎ *340/776–8890.*

CHINA AND CRYSTAL

A. H. Riise Gift Shops. A. H. Riise carries Waterford, Royal Crown, and Royal Doulton at good prices. A five-piece place setting of Royal Crown Derby's Old Imari goes for less than $500. The branch at Riise's Alley also sells jewelry, pearls, perfumes, and watches, including an outstanding Rolex selection (Riise's is the exclusive retailer for Rolex in the USVI). ⊠ *37 Main St., at Riise's Alley,* ☎ *340/776–2303;* ⊠ *Havensight Mall,* ☎ *340/776–7713.*

The English Shop. This store offers figurines, cutlery, and china and crystal from major European and Japanese manufacturers, including Spode, Limoges, Royal Doulton, Portmeirion, Noritaki, and Wedgwood. You can choose what you like from the catalogs here, and shopkeepers will order and factory-ship it for you. (Be sure to keep your receipts in case something goes awry.) ⊠ *Havensight Mall,* ☎ *340/776–3776.*

Island Galleria. This second-floor store displays china and crystal glasses, decanters, bowls, and vases in several patterns. Famous names here are Swarovski, Wedgwood, Royal Doulton, and Balleek. They ship purchases. ⊠ *3B Main St.,* ☎ *340/777–5892.*

Little Switzerland. All of this establishment's shops carry crystal from Baccarat, Waterford, Orrefors, and Riedel; china from Villeroy & Boch and Wedgwood, among others; and fine Swiss watches. There's also an assortment of cut-crystal animals, china and porcelain figurines, and many other affordable collectibles. They also do a booming mail-order business; ask for a catalog. ⊠ *Tolbod Gade, across from Emancipation Garden,* ☎ *340/776–2010;* ⊠ *3B Main St.,* ☎ *340/776–2010;* ⊠ *5 Main St., inside A. H. Riise Gift Mart,* ☎ *340/776–2010;* ⊠ *Dockside at Havensight Mall,* ☎ *340/776–2010.*

CLOTHES

Cosmopolitan. At this sophisticated clothing emporium, look for such top lines as Paul and Shark, Bally, Timberland, Sperry Topsider, Givenchy, and Nautica. ⊠ *Drake's Passage at the Waterfront,* ☎ *340/776–2040.*

Java Wraps. Now you, too, can wear the snazzy Indonesian batik creations that the USVI's female athletes modeled at the opening ceremonies of the 1996 Summer Olympic Games in Atlanta. Snazzy swimwear; unisex floral-print shirts; cover-ups; and leisure attire for men, women, and children are the attractions at this shop. ⊠ *Waterfront Hwy. at Royal Dane Mall,* ☎ *340/714–1219.*

Local Color. Here St. John artist Sloop Jones exhibits colorful, hand-painted island designs on cool dresses, T-shirts, and sweaters. You'll also find wearable art by other local artists; unique jewelry; sundresses, shorts, and shirts in bright Jams World–brand prints; and big-brim straw hats dipped in fuchsia, turquoise, and other tropical colors. ⊠ *Hibiscus Alley,* ☎ *340/774–3727.*

Lover's Lane. With the motto "Couples that play together, stay together," this romantic second-floor shop sells sensuous lingerie, sexy menswear, and provocative swimwear. ⊠ *Waterfront Hwy. at Raadets Gade,* ☎ *340/777–9616.*

Nicole Miller Boutique. This world-renowned New York designer has created an exclusive motif for the USVI: a map of the islands, a cruise ship, and tropical sunset. Find this print, and Miller's full line of other designs, on ties, scarves, boxer shorts, sarong skirts and dresses at this chic boutique. ⊠ *24 Main St. at Palm Passage,* ☎ *340/774–8286.*

Pusser's Tropical & Nautical Co. Store. Here, tropical sports and travel clothing for men, women, and children all have a nautical-inspired theme. Look for bottles of Pusser's rum at the sales counter. ⊠ *Waterfront Hwy. at Riise's Alley,* ☎ *340/777–9281;* ⊠ *across from Havensight Mall,* ☎ *340/774–9680.*

Tommy Hilfiger. Stop by this shop for classic American jeans and sportswear as well as trendy bags, belts, ties, socks, caps, and wallets. ⊠ *Waterfront Hwy. at Trompeter Gade,* ☎ *340/777–1189.*

V.I. America's Cup Challenge. Support the VI's bid to win the 2000 Cup from New Zealand by wearing team clothing—T-shirts, polo shirts, hats, caps, visors, and more. ⊠ *Hibiscus Alley,* ☎ *340/774–9090.*

FOODSTUFFS

A Chew Or Two. Everything at this confectionery tastes as good as it smells. A wide assortment of Godiva chocolates shares space with Caribbean rum balls, tropical-flavor saltwater taffy, colorful jelly beans, homemade fudge, oversize chocolate-chip cookies, and Trinidadian coffees. ⊠ *Trompeter Gade,* ☎ *340/774–6675.*

Cost-U-Less. This store sells everything from soup to nuts, but in giant sizes and case lots. The meat and seafood department, however, has smaller family-size portions. ⊠ *1 mi (1½ km) east of Charlotte Amalie* *on Route 38 (¼ mi/½ km west of the Route 39 intersection),* ☎ *340/ 777–3588.*

Fruit Bowl. For fruits and vegetables, this is the place. ⊠ *Wheatley Center,* ☎ *340/774–8565.*

Gourmet Gallery. Visiting millionaires buy their caviar here. There's also an excellent and reasonably priced wine selection, as well as specialty ingredients for everything from tacos to curries to chow mein. A full-service deli offers imported meats and cheeses, and in-store prepared foods perfect for a gourmet picnic. ⊠ *Crown Bay Marina,* ☎ *340/776–8555;* ⊠ *Havensight Mall,* ☎ *340/774–4948.*

Marina Market. You won't find a better fresh-meat and seafood department in any other place on the island. ⊠ *Across from Red Hook ferry,* ☎ *340/779–2411.*

Plaza Extra. This supermarket has a large selection of Middle Eastern foods. ⊠ *Tutu Park Shopping Center,* ☎ *340/775–5646.*

Pueblo Supermarkets. Find stateside brands of most products at these large supermarkets, but at higher prices due to the cost of shipping. ⊠ *Four Winds Plaza, across from Tillett Gardens,* ☎ *340/775–4655;* ⊠ *Sub Base, 1 mi (1½ km) north of Havensight Mall,* ☎ *340/774–4200;* ⊠ *Estate Thomas, 1 mi (1½ km) north of Havensight Mall,* ☎ *340/ 774–2695.*

HANDICRAFTS

Caribbean Marketplace. This is a great place to buy handicrafts from the Caribbean and elsewhere. Also look for Sunny Caribee spices, soaps, coffee and teas from Tortola, and coffee from Trinidad. ⊠ *Havensight Mall,* ☎ *340/776–5400.*

Caribbean Safari. For straw hats—in all sizes, shapes, and styles—this is a must-shop stop. You'll also find jewelry fashioned with larimar (a blue-hued Caribbean gemstone) and island-style Christmas ornaments. ⊠ *Back St., at Raadets Gade,* ☎ *340/777–8795.*

Down Island Traders. These traders deal in hand-painted calabash bowls; finely printed Caribbean note cards; jams, jellies, spices, hot sauces and herbs; herbal teas made of lemongrass, passion fruit, and mango; coffee from Jamaica; and a variety of handicrafts from throughout the Caribbean. ⊠ *Waterfront Hwy. at Post Office Alley,* ☎ *340/776– 4641.*

Native Arts and Crafts Cooperative. More than 40 local artists—including school children, senior citizens, and people with disabilities— create an ever-changing array of handcrafted items: African-style jewelry, quilts, calabash bowls, dolls, carved-wood figures, woven baskets, straw brooms, note cards, and cookbooks. ⊠ *Tolbod Gade, across from Emancipation Garden and next to visitors center,* ☎ *340/ 777–1153.*

Pampered Pirate. This busy store carries island-made dolls, Christmas ornaments, prints, and paintings along with other gift items. ⊠ *4 Norre Gade,* ☎ *340/775–5450.*

JEWELRY

Amsterdam Sauer. Many fine one-of-a-kind designs are displayed and sold here. ⊠ *14 Main St.,* ☎ *340/774–2222;* ⊠ *Havensight Mall,* ☎ *340/776–3828;* ⊠ *Ritz-Carlton Resort, 6900 Great Bay Estate,* ☎ *340/ 779–2308.*

Blue Carib Gems. At family-owned and -run Blue Carib Gems, watch Alan O'Hara, Sr., polish Caribbean amber and larimar, agate, and other gems and mount them into gold and silver settings. Visit Alan, Jr., at the Wharfside Village branch on St. John. ⊠ *2–3 Back St.,* ☎ *340/774–8525.*

Cardow's. An enormous "chain bar"—with gold chains in several lengths, widths, sizes and styles—awaits you here, along with diamonds, emeralds, and other precious gems. You're guaranteed 30%–

50% savings off U.S. retail prices or your money will be refunded within 30 days of purchase. ⊠ *33 Main St.,* ☎ *340/776–1140;* ⊠ *Havensight Mall,* ☎ *340/774–0530 or 340/774–5905;* ⊠ *Marriott Frenchman's Reef Resort, Estate Bakkeroe,* ☎ *340/774–0434.*

Colombian Emeralds. Well-known in the Caribbean, this store offers set and unset emeralds as well as gems of every description. ⊠ *30 Main St.,* ☎ *340/774–3400;* ⊠ *Havensight Mall,* ☎ *340/774–2442.*

Diamonds International. Choose a diamond, emerald, or tanzanite gem and a mounting, and you'll have your dream ring set in an hour. Famous for having the largest inventory of diamonds on the island, this shop welcomes trade-ins, has a U.S. service center, and offers free diamond earrings with every purchase. ⊠ *31 Main St.,* ☎ *340/774–3707;* ⊠ *3 Drakes Passage,* ☎ *340/775–2010;* ⊠ *7AB Drakes Passage,* ☎ *340/774–1516.*

H. Stern. The World Collection of jewels set in modern, fashionable designs and the exclusive Sapphire Watch have earned this store a stellar name. ⊠ *12 Main St.,* ☎ *340/776–1939;* ⊠ *32AB Main St.,* ☎ *340/776–1146;* ⊠ *Havensight Mall,* ☎ *340/776–1223;* ⊠ *Marriott Frenchman's Reef Resort, Estate Bakkeroe,* ☎ *340/776–3550.*

LEATHER GOODS

Coach Boutique. A whole wall of high-fashion handbags leads deeper into the store where lightweight Tumi luggage of nylon or leather is so strong you can sit on it. There are also sporty canvas Kipling bags, all under $100. ⊠ *34 Main St.,* ☎ *340/777–1469.*

Leather Shop. You'll find mostly big names at big prices here (Fendi and Bottega Veneta are prevalent), but if you look hard enough you'll find some reasonably priced, high-quality purses, wallets, and briefcases. ⊠ *24 Main St.,* ☎ *340/776–3995.*

Purses and Things. This "house of handbags" has a wide selection of sizes and great prices (you can buy a five-in-one leather clutch for only $20). Bargains are equally good on eelskin goods. ⊠ *International Plaza,* ☎ *340/777–9713.*

Zora's. Fine leather sandals made to order are the specialty here. There's also selection of made-only-in-the-Virgin-Islands backpacks, purses, and briefcases in durable, brightly colored canvas. ⊠ *Norre Gade across from Roosevelt Park,* ☎ *340/774–2559.*

LINENS

Fabric In Motion. Fine Italian linens share space with Liberty's of London silky cottons, colorful batiks, cotton prints, ribbons, and accessories at this small shop. There are also paintings, quilts, and dolls made by local craftspeople. ⊠ *Storetvaer Gade,* ☎ *340/774–2006.*

Mr. Tablecloth. The friendly staff here will help you choose from the floor-to-ceiling array of linens, from Tuscany lace tablecloths to Irish linen pillowcases. The prices will please you. ⊠ *6–7 Main St.,* ☎ *340/774–4343.*

LIQUOR AND TOBACCO

A. H. Riise Liquors. This Riise venture offers a large selection of tobacco (including imported cigars), as well as cordials, wines, and other liquors (rare vintage cognacs, Armagnacs, ports, and Madeiras). It also stocks fruits in brandy and barware from England. ⊠ *37 Main St., at Riise's Alley,* ☎ *340/776–2303;* ⊠ *Havensight Mall,* ☎ *340/776–7713.*

Al Cohen's Discount Liquor. The wine selection at this warehouse-style store is very large. ⊠ *Across from Havensight Mall, Long Bay Rd.,* ☎ *340/774–3690.*

MUSIC

Modern Music. Shop for the latest stateside and Caribbean CD and cassette releases, plus oldies, classical, and New Age music. ⊠ *Across from*

Havensight Mall, ☎ *340/774–3100;* ✉ *Nisky Center,* ☎ *340/777–8787;*
✉ *Four Winds Plaza,* ☎ *340/775–3310.*

Parrot Fish Records and Tapes. A stock of standard stateside tapes and
CDs, plus a good selection of Caribbean artists, including local groups,
can be found here. For a catalog of calypso, *soca* (up-tempo calypso
music), steel band, and reggae music, write to Parrot Fish, Box 9206,
St. Thomas 00801. ✉ *Back St.,* ☎ *340/776–4514.*

PERFUME

Tropicana Perfume Shoppes. Tropicana has the largest selection of fragrances for men and women in all of the VI. ✉ *2 Main St.,* ☎ *340/
774–0010.*

SUNGLASSES

Davante. Find an enormous eyewear collection tucked into this glit-
tering, glamorous store. Filling prescriptions is no problem. ✉ *A. H.
Riise Mall,* ☎ *340/714–1220.*

Sun Glass Hut. Take your pick from among such name-brand eyewear
as Biagiotti, Serengetti, Carrera, and others. ✉ *15 Main St.,* ☎ *340/
777–5585;* ✉ *37 Main St.,* ☎ *340/774–9030;* ✉ *Havensight Mall,* ☎
340/777–7563.

TOYS

Grandpa's Korner Emporium. Birds sing, dogs bark, and fish swim in
this animated toyland. Adults have as much fun trying out the wares
as do kids. ✉ *International Plaza,* ☎ *340/777–4944;* ✉ *Tutu Park Shopping Center,* ☎ *340/777–7533.*

Nightlife and the Arts

On any given night, especially in season, you'll find steel-pan orches-
tras, rock-and-roll bands, piano music, jazz, broken-bottle dancing (dancing atop broken glass), disco, and karaoke. Pick up a copy of the free,
bright-yellow *St. Thomas This Week* magazine when you arrive (you'll
see it at the airport, in stores, and in hotel lobbies); the back pages list
who's playing where. The Thursday edition of the *Daily News* carries
complete listings for the upcoming weekend.

Nightlife

BARS

Athena's. Dance to Latin, jazz, R&B, and contemporary tunes against
a backdrop mural that depicts the Acropolis in Athens and Mt. Olym-
pus. Sidle up to the bar and mingle with island business and political
celebrities. The action runs from 5 PM until the wee hours, Thursday–
Sunday. ✉ *32 Raadets Gade,* ☎ *340/714–1909.*

The Greenhouse. This place is slowly making a transition from a waterfront
bar to something like the Caribbean equivalent of the T.G.I. Friday's chain
in the United States. It strives to meet all tastes, starting with a breakfast that's popular with locals; burgers and taco salad for lunch; and then
prime rib and lobster specials for dinner. Once the Greenhouse puts away
the salt-and-pepper shakers at 10 PM, it becomes a rock-and-roll club
with a DJ or live reggae bands raising the weary to their feet six nights
a week. ✉ *Waterfront Hwy. at Storetvaer Gade,* ☎ *340/774–7998.*

Iggies. Sing along karaoke style to the sounds of the surf or the latest
hits at this beachside lounge. There's often a DJ on weekends, when
a buffet barbecue precedes the 9 PM music fest. Dance inside, or kick
up your heels under the stars. ✉ *50 Estate Bolongo,* ☎ *340/775–1800.*

JoJo's. Dance to music ranging from Top 40 to salsa and calypso in
this second-floor nightclub. Oil candles illuminating dark wood paneling, small tables and booths, and a long oak bar with plenty of stools

make this an upscale and intimate place to meet and mingle. ✉ *24 Honduras, Frenchtown,* ☎ *340/714–1694.*

You'll find a piano bar nightly at **Andiamo at the Martini Cafe** (✉ 70 Honduras, Frenchtown, ☎ 340/776–7916) and on weekends at **L'Hotel Boynes** (✉ Blackbeard's Hill, ☎ 340/774–5511). **Cafe LuLu** (✉ Blackbeard's Hill, ☎ 340/714–1641) features guitar and jazz on Friday and Saturday nights, respectively. **Zorba's Sagapo** (✉ Government Hill, ☎ 340/776–0444) fills in with guitar tunes on Saturday and Sunday.

Island-style steel pan bands play at the **Agave Terrace** (✉ Point Pleasant Resort, Smith Bay, ☎ 340/775–4142) on Tuesday, Thursday, and Saturday; **Eunice's Terrace** (✉ Rte. 38, near Renaissance Grand Beach Resort and Coral World, Smith Bay, ☎ 340/775–3975) on Wednesday, Friday, and Sunday; and at the **Ritz-Carlton** (✉ 6900 Great Bay Estate, ☎ 340/775–3333) on Monday.

The Arts

MUSEUMS

The Virgin Islands Museum. In Ft. Christian (☞ Exploring St. Thomas, *below*), the VI's oldest standing structure, see exhibits on USVI history, natural history, and turn-of-the-century furnishings. Local artists display their works monthly in the gallery. A gift shop sells local crafts, books, and other souvenir items. ✉ *Waterfront Hwy. just east of shopping district,* ☎ *340/776–4566.* ⌐ *Free.* ☉ *Weekdays 8:30–4:30.*

Weibel Museum. In this museum next to the synagogue (☞ Exploring St. Thomas, *below*), 300 years of Jewish history on St. Thomas are showcased. The small gift shop sells a commemorative coin in gold or silver celebrating the anniversary of the Hebrew Congregation's establishment on the island in 1796. ✉ *15 Crystal Gade,* ☎ *340/774–4312.* ⌐ *Free.* ☉ *Weekdays 9–4.*

THEATER

Reichhold Center for the Arts. This open-air amphitheater has its more expensive seats covered by a roof. Schedules vary, so check the paper to see what's on when you're in town. Throughout the year, there's an entertaining mix of local plays, dance exhibitions, and music of all types. ✉ *Rte. 30, across from Brewers Beach,* ☎ *340/693–1559.*

Exploring St. Thomas

St. Thomas is only 13 mi (21 km) long and less than 4 mi (6½ km) wide, but it's an extremely hilly island, and even an 8- or 10-mi (13- or 16-km) trip could take several hours. Don't let that discourage you, though, because the ridge of mountains that runs from east to west through the middle and separates the Caribbean and Atlantic sides of the island has spectacular vistas and is a lot of fun to explore.

Charlotte Amalie

When exploring Charlotte Amalie, look beyond the pricey shops, T-shirt vendors, and bustling crowds for a glimpse of the island's history. The city served as the capital of Denmark's outpost in the Caribbean until 1917, an aspect of the island often lost in the glitz of the shopping district. As part of the Charlotte Amalie 2000 historic preservation and beautification project, sponsored by the St. Thomas–St. John Chamber of Commerce, you can "adopt" a brick for $50 and have your name engraved on it. The bricks will help pave the sidewalk area in front of the U.S. Post Office at the head of Main Street. When driving into town, park in the public lot next to Ft. Christian.

Emancipation Gardens, right next to the fort, is a good place to start a walking tour. Tackle the hilly part of town first: head north up Government Hill to the historic buildings that house government offices and have incredible views. Several regal churches line the route that runs west back to the town proper and the old-time market. Virtually all the alleyways that intersect Main Street lead to eateries that serve frosty tropical drinks, sandwiches and burgers, and West Indian fare. You'll find public rest rooms in this area, too. Allow an hour for a quick view of the sights, two hours if you plan to tour Government House.

A note about the street names: In deference to the island's heritage, the streets downtown are labeled by their Danish names. Locals will use both the Danish name and the English name (such as Dronningens Gade and Norre Gade for Main Street), but most people refer to things by where they're located ("a block toward the Waterfront off Main Street," or "next to the Little Switzerland Shop"). It's best to ask for directions by shop names or landmarks.

Numbers in the margin correspond to points of interest on the Charlotte Amalie map.

SIGHTS TO SEE

⑰ All Saints Anglican Church. Built in 1848 from stone quarried on the island, the church has thick, arched window frames lined with the yellow brick that came to the islands as ballast aboard merchant ships. The merchants left the brick on the waterfront when they filled their boats with molasses, sugar, mahogany, and rum for the return voyage. The church was built in celebration of the end of slavery in the USVI. ⊠ *Domini Gade,* ☎ *340/774–0217.* ☉ *Mon.–Sat. 6–3.*

㉓ Cathedral of St. Peter and St. Paul. This building was consecrated as a parish church in 1848 and serves as the seat of the territory's Roman Catholic diocese. The ceiling and walls are covered with murals painted in 1899 by two Belgian artists, Father Leo Servais and Brother Ildephonsus. The San Juan–marble altar and side walls were added in the 1960s. ⊠ *Lower Main St.,* ☎ *340/774–0201.* ☉ *Mon.–Sat. 8–5.*

⑲ Danish Consulate Building. Built in 1830, this structure housed the Danish Consulate until the Danish West India Company sold its properties to the local government in 1992. It now serves as home to the territory's governor. ⊠ *Take stairs north at corner of Bjerge Gade and Crystal Gade to Denmark Hill.*

⑯ Dutch Reformed Church. This church has an austere loveliness that's amazing considering all it has been through—founded in 1744, it burned down in 1804, and was rebuilt in 1844; it was then blown down by Hurricane Marilyn in 1995 and rebuilt in 1997. The unembellished cream-color hall gives you a sense of peace—albeit monochromatically. The only other color is the forest green of the shutters and the carpet. ⊠ *Nye Gade and Crystal Gade,* ☎ *340/776–8255.* ☉ *Weekdays 9–5. Call ahead; doors are sometimes locked.*

❼ Educators Park. A peaceful place amid the town's hustle and bustle, the park has memorials to three famous Virgin Islanders: educator Edith Williams, J. Antonio Jarvis (a founder of the *Daily News*), and educator and author Rothschild Francis. The latter gave many speeches from this location. ⊠ *Main St. across from U.S. Post Office.*

㉕ Edward Wilmoth Blyden Marine Terminal. Locally called "Tortola Wharf," you can catch the *Native Son* and other ferries to the BVI from here. The restaurant upstairs is a good place to watch the Charlotte Amalie harbor traffic and sip an iced tea. Next door is the ramp for the *Seaborne* seaplane, which offers commuter service and flight-seeing tours to St. Croix and the BVI. ⊠ *Waterfront Hwy.*

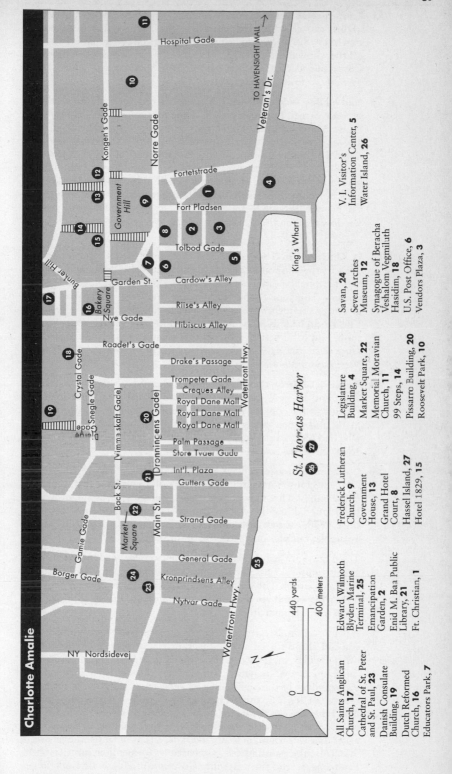

Charlotte Amalie

All Saints Anglican
Church, **17**
Cathedral of St. Peter
and St. Paul, **23**
Danish Consulate
Building, **19**
Dutch Reformed
Church, **16**
Educators Park, **7**

Edward Wilmoth
Blyden Marine
Terminal, **25**
Emancipation
Garden, **2**
Enid M. Baa Public
Library, **21**
Ft. Christian, **1**

Frederick Lutheran
Church, **9**
Government
House, **13**
Grand Hotel
Court, **8**
Hassel Island, **27**
Hotel 1829, **15**

Legislature
Building, **4**
Market Square, **22**
Memorial Moravian
Church, **11**
99 Steps, **14**
Pissarro Building, **20**
Roosevelt Park, **10**

Savan, **24**
Seven Arches
Museum, **12**
Synagogue of Beracha
Veshalom Vegmiluth
Hasidim, **18**
U.S. Post Office, **6**
Vendors Plaza, **3**

V. I. Visitor's
Information Center, **5**
Water Island, **26**

② Emancipation Garden. Built to honor the freeing of slaves in 1848, the garden was refurbished to mark the 150th anniversary of emancipation in 1998. The gazebo here is used for official ceremonies. Two monuments show the island's Danish-American tie—a bust of Danish King Christian and a scaled-down model of the U.S. Liberty Bell. ⊠ *Between Tolbod Gade and Ft. Christian.*

㉑ Enid M. Baa Public Library. Like so many structures on the north side of Main Street, this large pink building is a typical 18th-century town house. Merchants built their houses (stores downstairs, living quarters above) across from the brick warehouses on the south side of the street. The library was once the home of merchant and landowner Baron von Bretton. It's the first recorded fireproof building, meaning that it was built of ballast brick instead of wood. Its interior of high ceilings and cool stone floors is the perfect refuge from the afternoon sun. You can browse through historic papers or just sit in the breeze by an open window reading the paper. ⊠ *Main St.,* ☎ *340/774–0630.* ⊙ *Weekdays 9–5, Sat. 9–3.*

⟲ ① Ft. Christian. St. Thomas's oldest standing structure, this monument anchors the shopping district. It was built in 1672–80, and now has U.S. national landmark status. The clock tower was added in the 19th century. This remarkable redoubt has, over time, been used as a jail, governor's residence, town hall, courthouse, and church. It now houses **The Virgin Islands Museum** (☞ Nightlife and the Arts, *above*) , a gift shop, and local artists' exhibits that change monthly. ⊠ *Waterfront Hwy. just east of shopping district,* ☎ *340/776–4566.* ☜ *Free.* ⊙ *Weekdays 8:30–4:30.*

⑨ Frederick Lutheran Church. This historic church has a massive mahogany altar, and its pews—each with its own door—were once rented to families of the congregation. Lutheranism is the state religion of Denmark, and, when the territory was without a minister, the governor—who had his own elevated pew—filled in. ⊠ *Norre Gade,* ☎ *340/776–1315.* ⊙ *Mon.–Sat. 9–4.*

⑬ Government House. Built as an elegant residence in 1867, today Government House serves as the governor's office with the first floor open to the public. The staircases are of native mahogany, as are the plaques hand-lettered in gold with the names of the governors appointed and, since 1970, elected. Brochures detailing the history of the building are available, but you may have to ask for them.

The three murals at the back of the lobby were painted by Pepino Mangravatti in the 1930s as part of the U.S. government's Works Projects Administration. The murals depict Columbus's landing on St. Croix during his second voyage in 1493; the transfer of the islands from Denmark to the United States in 1917; and a sugar plantation on St. John.

A deputy administrator can take you on a tour of the second floor. You can call ahead for an appointment, or you can take a chance that an official will be in. It's worth the extra effort, if for no other reason than the terrace view. Imagine colonial affairs of state being conducted in the grandeur of the high-ceiling, chandeliered ballroom. In the reception room are four small paintings by Camille Pissarro, but unfortunately they are hard to appreciate because they're enclosed in frosted-glass cases. More interesting, and visible, is the large painting by an unknown artist that was found in Denmark: it depicts a romanticized version of St. Croix; the painting was purchased by former governor Ralph M. Paiewonsky, who then gave it to Government House. ⊠ *Government Hill,* ☎ *340/774–0001.* ☜ *Free.* ⊙ *Weekdays 8–5.*

8 **Grand Hotel Court.** This imposing building stands at the head of Main Street. Once the island's premier hotel, it has been converted into offices and shops. ⊠ *Tolbod Gade at Norre Gade.*

27 **Hassel Island.** East of ☞ Water Island in Charlotte Amalie harbor, Hassel Island is part of the Virgin Islands National Park, due in part to the fact that it has the ruins of a British military garrison (built during a brief British occupation of the USVI during the 1800s) and the remains of a marine railway (where ships were hoisted into drydock for repairs). Also on Hassel Island is the shell of the hotel that writer Herman Wouk's fictitious character Norman Paperman tried to turn into his own paradise in the book *Don't Stop the Carnival.* There's a small ferry that runs from the Crown Bay Marina to the island; departure times are posted at Tickles Dockside Pub, and the fare is $3.

15 **Hotel 1829.** As its name implies, it was built in 1829, albeit as a residence of a prominent merchant named Lavalette rather than as a hotel. The building's bright coral-color exterior walls are accented with fancy black wrought iron, and the interior is paneled in a dark wood, which makes it feel delightfully cool. From the dining terrace, where gourmet food is served, there's an exquisite view of the harbor framed by tangerine-color bougainvillea. ⊠ *Government Hill,* ☎ *340/776–1829.*

4 **Legislature Building.** Its pastoral-looking lime-green exterior conceals the vociferous political wrangling of the Virgin Islands Senate going on inside. Built originally by the Danish as a police barracks, the building was later used to billet U.S. Marines, and much later it housed a public school. You're welcome to sit in on sessions in the upstairs chambers. ⊠ *Waterfront Hwy. across from Ft. Christian,* ☎ *340/774–0880.* ⊗ *Daily 8–5.*

22 **Market Square.** Formally called Rothschild Francis Square, this is a good place to find tropical produce. A cadre of old-timers sells mangoes and papayas, strange-looking root vegetables, and herbs; sidewalk vendors offer a variety of African fabrics and artifacts and tie-dyed cotton clothes at good prices. ⊠ *North side of Main St. at Strand Gade.*

11 **Memorial Moravian Church.** Built in 1884, it was named to commemorate the 150th anniversary of the Moravian Church in the VI. ⊠ *17 Norre Gade,* ☎ *340/776–0066.* ⊗ *Weekdays 8–5.*

14 **99 Steps.** This staircase "street," built by the Danes in the 1700s, leads to the residential area above Charlotte Amalie and Blackbeard's Castle. The castle's tower, built in 1679, was used by the notorious pirate Edward Teach. Today, this lookout serves at the backdrop for a trendy restaurant. If you count the stairs as you go up, you'll discover, as have thousands before you, that there are more than 99. ⊠ *Look for steps heading north from Government Hill.*

20 **Pissarro Building.** Home to several shops and an art gallery, this was the birthplace and childhood home of Camille Pissarro, who later moved to France and became an acclaimed Impressionist painter. In the art gallery, you'll find three original pages from Pissarro's sketchbook and two pastels by Pissarro's grandson, Claude.

10 **Roosevelt Park.** A good spot to people-watch, you'll see members of the local legal community head to the nearby court buildings while you rest on a bench. The small monument on the park's south side is dedicated to USVI war veterans. Kids enjoy the wood-and-tire playground. ⊠ *Norre Gade.*

24 **Savan.** A neighborhood of small streets and small houses, it was first laid out in the 1700s as the residential area for a growing community of middle-class black artisans, clerks, and shopkeepers. You'll find a row of Rastafarian shops along the first block and restaurants that sell pâté—a delicious turnover-type pastry stuffed with meat or vegetables. ✉ *Turn north off lower Main St. onto General Gade.*

⑫ Seven Arches Museum. This restored 18th-century home is a striking example of classic Danish West Indian architecture. There seem to be arches everywhere—seven to be exact—all supporting a "welcoming arms" staircase that leads to the second floor and the flower-framed front doorway. The Danish kitchen is a highlight: it's housed in a separate building just off the main house, as were all cooking facilities in the early days (in case of fire). Inside the house, you'll find mahogany furnishings and gas lamps. Tall, cool glasses of *bush*—the local lingo for herb-tea—are served in a charming courtyard. ✉ *Government Hill, 3 buildings east of Government House,* ☎ *340/774–9295.* 🎫 *$5 (suggested donation).* ⊙ *Tues.–Sun. 10–3 or by appointment.*

⑱ Synagogue of Beracha Veshalom Vegmiluth Hasidim. The synagogue's Hebrew name translates to the Congregation of Blessing, Peace, and Loving Deeds. The small building's white pillars contrast with rough stone walls, as does the rich mahogany of the pews and altar. The sand on the floor symbolizes the exodus from Egypt. Since the synagogue first opened its doors in 1833, it has held a weekly Sabbath service, making it the oldest synagogue building in continuous use under the American flag and the second oldest (after the one on Curaçao) in the Western Hemisphere. Next door, the **Weibel Museum** (☞ Nightlife and the Arts, *above*) showcases Jewish history on St. Thomas. ✉ *15 Crystal Gade,* ☎ *340/774–4312.* ⊙ *Weekdays 9–4.*

⑥ U.S. Post Office. While you buy your postcard stamps, contemplate the murals of waterfront scenes by *Saturday Evening Post* artist Stephen Dohanos. His art was commissioned as part of the WPA in the 1930s. ✉ *Tolbod Gade and Main St.*

③ Vendors Plaza. Here merchants sell everything from T-shirts to African attire to leather goods. Look for local art among the ever-changing selections at this busy market. ✉ *West of Ft. Christian at the waterfront.* ⊙ *Weekdays 8–6, weekends 9–1.*

⑤ V.I. Visitor's Information Center. This hospitality lounge comes complete with bathrooms and a place to stash your luggage if you want to shop on your way to the airport. ✉ *Tolbod Gade across from Emancipation Garden,* ☎ *340/774–8784.* ⊙ *Weekdays 8–5, Sat. 9–noon.*

㉖ Water Island. This island, about ¼ mi (½ km) out in Charlotte Amalie harbor, was once a peninsula of St. Thomas, but a channel was cut through so U.S. submarines could get to their base in a bay just to the west, known as Sub Base. On December 12, 1996, the U.S. Department of the Interior transferred 50 acres of the island, which included beaches and roads, to the territorial government, making it the fourth largest of the USVI. A ferry goes between Crown Bay Marina and the island several times daily, at a cost of $3.

Around the Island

To explore outside of Charlotte Amalie, you'll need to rent a car or hire a taxi. Your rental car should come with a good map; if not, pick up the "St. Thomas–St. John Road Map" at a tourist information center. The roads are marked with route numbers, but they're confusing and seem to switch numbers suddenly. If you stop to ask for directions, it's best to have your map in hand because the locals probably know the road you're looking for by another name. Allow yourself a full day to explore St. Thomas by car, especially if you want to stop for picture taking or to enjoy a light bite or refreshing swim. Most of the gas stations are on the more populated eastern end of the island, so fill up before heading to the north side. And remember to drive on the left.

Although the eastern end has many major resorts and spectacular beaches, don't be surprised if a cow or a herd of goats crosses your path as you drive through the relatively flat, dry terrain. The north side of the island is more lush and hush—fewer houses and less traffic. Here you'll find roller-coaster routes (made all the more scary because the roads have no shoulders) and be rewarded with incredible vistas. Plan to spend a day on a driving tour, leaving time in the afternoon for a swim at the beach. Pick up some sandwiches from delis in the Red Hook area for a picnic lunch or enjoy a slice of pizza at Magens Bay. A day in the country will reveal the tropical pleasures that have enticed more than one visitor to become a resident.

Numbers in the margin correspond to points of interest on the St. Thomas map.

SIGHTS TO SEE

㉙ Compass Point Marina. It's fun to park your car and walk around this marina. The boaters—many of whom have sailed here from points around the globe—are easy to engage in conversation. ✉ *Turn south off Red Hook Rd. at well-marked entrance road just east of Independent Boat Yard.*

㉜ Coral World Marine Park. Reopened in August 1998 after extensive renovation, Coral World is home to an off-shore underwater observatory that houses the Predator Tank, one of the world's largest coral reef tanks, and an aquarium with more than 20 portholes providing close-up views of Caribbean sealife. There are also several outdoor pools where you can touch starfish, pet a baby shark, feed stingrays, and view endangered sea turtles. In addition you'll find a mangrove lagoon and a natural trail full of lush tropical flora. Daily feedings and talks take place at most every exhibit. ✉ *Coki Point, turn north off Rte. 38 at sign,* ☎ *340/775–1555.* 🎟 *$18.* �l *Daily 9–5:30.*

㉟ Drake's Seat. Sir Francis Drake was supposed to have kept watch over his fleet and looked for enemy ships of the Spanish fleet from this vantage point. The panoramic vista is especially breathtaking (and romantic) at dusk, and if you arrive late in the day you'll miss the hordes of day-trippers on taxi tours who stop at Drake's Seat to take a picture and buy a T-shirt from one of the many vendors. ✉ *Rte. 40.*

㊱ Estate St. Peter Greathouse & Botanical Gardens. This unusual spot is perched on a mountainside 1,000 ft above sea level, with views of more than 20 other islands and islets. You can wander through a gallery displaying local art, sip a complimentary rum or Virgin Punch while looking out at the view, or follow a nature trail that leads through nearly 200 varieties of tropical trees and plants, including an orchid jungle. ✉ *Rte. 40, St. Peter Mountain Rd.,* ☎ *340/774–4999.* 🎟 *$8.* �l *Mon.–Sat. 9–4:30.*

㊲ Frenchtown. Popular with tourists for its several bars and restaurants, Frenchtown also serves as home to the descendants of immigrants from St. Barthélemy (St. Barts). You can watch them pull up their brightly painted boats and display their equally colorful catch of the day along the waterfront. If you have the opportunity to chat with them, you'll hear speech patterns slightly different from those of other St. Thomians. Get a feel for the residential district of Frenchtown by walking west to some of the town's winding streets, where the tiny wooden houses have been passed down from generation to generation. ⊠ *Turn south off Waterfront Hwy. at the U.S. Post Office.*

🖐 ㉞ **Mountain Top.** Stop here for a banana daiquiri and spectacular views from the observation deck more than 1,500 ft above sea level. There are also shops that sell everything from Caribbean art to nautical antiques, ship models, and T-shirts. Kids will like talking to the tropical parrots—and hearing them answer back. ⊠ *Head north off Rte. 33; look for signs.*

🖐 ㉘ **Paradise Point Tramway.** Fly skyward in a gondola straight up the hill to Paradise Point, a scenic overlook with breathtaking views of Charlotte Amalie and the harbor. There are several shops, a bar, and a restaurant. A ¼-mi (½-km) hiking trail leads to spectacular sights of St. Croix to the south. Wear sturdy shoes, since the trail is steep and rocky. ⊠ *Rte. 30 at Havensight,* ☎ *340/774–9809.* 🎫 *$10.* ⊙ *Daily 7:30–4:30.*

㉛ **Red Hook.** In this nautical mecca of St. Thomas, you'll find fishing and sailing charter boats, dive shops, and power-boat rental agencies at the American Yacht Harbor marina. There are also several bars and restaurants, including Tickles Dockside Pub, Duffy's Love Shack, and the seafood-oriented Cafe Wahoo (☞ Dining, *above*). Two grocery stores (including the Marina Market) and two delis offer picnic fixings ranging from sliced meats and cheeses to rotisserie-cooked chickens, gourmet salads, and fresh baked breads.

㉝ **Tillett Gardens.** Clustered in a booming local shopping area, you'll find a colony where local artisans craft stained glass, pottery, gold jewelry, and ceramics. Tillett's paintings and silk-screened fabrics are also on display and for sale. The gardens encircle a shaded courtyard with fountains and Polli's Mexican restaurant (☞ Dining, *above*). ⊠ *Rte. 38 across from Tutu Park Shopping Center,* ☎ *340/775–1929.* 🎫 *Free.*

㉚ **Virgin Islands National Park Headquarters.** This park facility consists of a dock, a small grassy area with picnic tables, and a visitor center where maps and brochures are available. Iguanas are common here. If you see one, hold out a hibiscus flower, which is this prehistoric-looking creature's favorite food. ⊠ *Turn east off Rte. 32 at sign,* ☎ *340/ 775–6238.* ⊙ *Weekdays 8–5.*

ST. CROIX

Updated by
Lynda Lohr

St. Croix, the largest of the three USVI at 84 square mi (218 square km), lies 40 mi (65 km) to the south of St. Thomas. But unlike the bustling island-city of St. Thomas, its harbor teeming with cruise ships and its shopping district crowded with bargain hunters, St. Croix has a slower pace and a more diverse economy, mixing tourism with light and heavy industry on rolling land that was once covered with waving carpets of sugarcane.

St. Croix's population has grown dramatically over the last 30 years, and its diversity reflects the island's varied history. The cultivation of sugarcane was more important here than on St. Thomas or St. John and continued as an economic force into the 1960s. After the end of slavery in 1848, the need for workers brought waves of immigrants from other Caribbean islands, particularly nearby Puerto Rico. St. Croix was divided into plantation estates, and the ruins of great houses and more than 100 sugar mills that dot the island's landscape are evidence of an era when St. Croix rivaled Barbados as the greatest producer of sugar in the West Indies.

Tourism began and boomed in the 1960s, bringing visitors and migrants from the mainland United States (referred to by locals as Continentals). In the late 1960s and early 1970s industrial development brought St. Croix yet another wave of immigrants. This time they came mostly from Trinidad and St. Lucia, to seek work at the Hess oil refinery or at the south-shore aluminum-processing plants.

St. Croix is a study of contrasting beauty. The island isn't as hilly as St. Thomas or St. John. A lush rain forest envelops the northwest, the eastern end is dry, and palm-lined beaches with startlingly clear aquamarine water ring the island. The capital, Christiansted, is a restored Danish port on a coral-bound bay on the northeastern shore. The tin-roof, 18th-century buildings in both Christiansted and Frederiksted, on the island's western end, are either pale yellow, pink, or ocher, resplendent with bright blazes of bougainvillea and hibiscus. The prosperous Danes built well (and more than once as both towns were devastated by fire in the 19th century), using imported bricks or blocks cut from coral, fashioning covered sidewalks (galleries) and stately colonnades, and leaving an enduring cosmopolitan air as their legacy.

Lodging

From plush resorts to simple beachfront digs, St. Croix's variety of accommodations is bound to suit every type of traveler. If you sleep in either Christiansted or Frederiksted, you'll be close to shopping, a variety of restaurants, and nightlife. Any of the island's other hotels will put you just steps from the beach. St. Croix has several small-but-special properties that offer personalized service. If you enjoy all the comforts of home while you travel, you may prefer to stay in a condominium or villa. Room rates on St. Croix are competitive with those on other islands, and if you travel off-season, you'll find substantially reduced prices. Many properties offer honeymoon and dive packages that are also big money savers. Whether you stay in a hotel, a condominium, or a villa, you'll find up-to-date amenities, including cable TV.

A room in Christiansted or its environs puts you close to shopping and restaurants. Although a stay right in this historic town may mean putting up with a little urban noise, you probably won't have trouble sleeping. Christiansted rolls up the sidewalks fairly early. Frederiksted is perfect for folks who want peace and quiet. A small, charming town—hardly more than a village—with a lovely waterfront, it has beaches within walking distance of its shops and restaurants. Solitude is guaranteed in the West End. Old ruins dot the landscape where the green mountains meet the dark blue and turquoise sea. It's the perfect region for independent folks who like to explore. For price categories, *see* the chart *under* Lodging *in* St. Thomas, *above*.

Hotels

CHRISTIANSTED

$$-$$$ 🏨 **Hilty House.** For an alternative to beach and in-town lodgings, try this tranquil hilltop bed-and-breakfast. Built on the ruins of an 18th-century rum factory, it has the feel of a Florentine villa. You can escape to a patio and while away an afternoon in sun or shade, or mingle with others in the immense great room, where a prix-fixe dinner is served on Monday to guests and locals (reservations essential). Unless you want to spend your entire vacation reading or sunning at the large tiled pool, however, you'll need a rental car to venture forth from here. ⊠ *Queste Verde Rd. (Box 26077), Gallows Bay 00824,* ☎ FAX *340/773–2594. 4 rooms, 3 cottages. Dining room, pool. No credit cards. CP.*

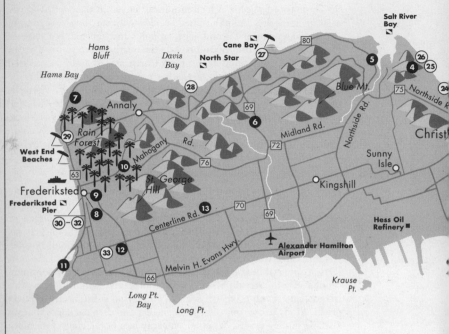

TO
ST. THOMAS

Salt River
Bay

Hams
Bluff

Davis
Bay

Cane Bay **27**

North Star

Hams Bay

Blue Mt.

5

26 **25**

4

7

Annaly

28

69

Northside Rd.

75 Northside R

24

Christ

29

Rain
Forest

Mahogany Rd.

6

Midland Rd.

72

West End
Beaches

10

76

Sunny
Isle

63

St. George
Hill

Kingshill

Frederiksted

9

Centerline Rd.

70

69

Frederiksted
Pier

8

13

Hess Oil
Refinery

30 **32**

33 **12**

Melvin H. Evans Hwy.

Alexander Hamilton
Airport

11

66

Long Pt.
Bay

Long Pt.

Krause
Pt.

KEY

Beaches

1 Exploring Sights

Cruise Ship Terminal

1 Hotels and Restaurants

Dive Sites

Rain Forest

Lodging
Breakfast Club, **4**
Buccaneer, **16**
Chenay Bay Beach
Resort, **18**
Club St. Croix, **22**
Colony Cove, **24**
Cormorant Beach
Club and Villas, **25**
The Frederiksted, **30**
Hibiscus Beach
Hotel, **26**

Hilty House, **13**
Hotel Caravelle, **11**
King's Alley
Hotel, **12**
Schooner Bay, **15**
Sprat Hall, **29**
Sugar Beach, **23**
Sunterra Carambola
Beach Resort, **28**
Tamarind
Reef Hotel, **17**

Villa Madeleine, **20**
Waves at Cane
Bay, **27**

Dining
Antoine's, **5**
Blue Moon, **31**
Bombay Club, **1**
The Galleon, **19**
Great House at Villa
Madeleine, **20**
Harvey's, **6**
Indies, **7**
Kendricks, **14**
Paradise Cafe, **2**

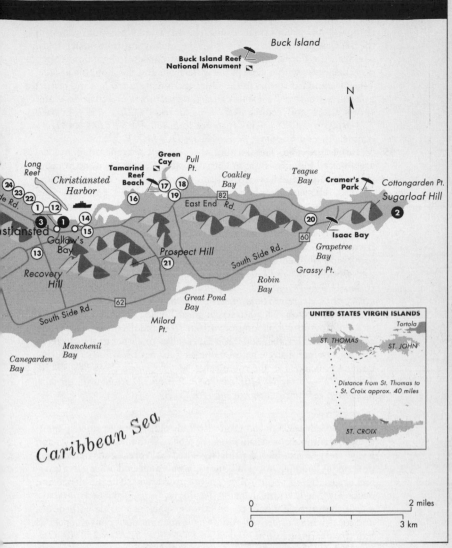

Buck Island

Buck Island Reef
National Monument

N

Long
Reef

Christiansted
Harbor

Tamarind
Reef
Beach

Green
Cay

Pull
Pt.

Coakley
Bay

Teague
Bay

Cramer's
Park

Cottongarden Pt.

Sugarloaf Hill

24
23
22

e Rd.

1
12

3

1

14

15

13

stiansted

Gallow's
Bay

16

17
18

19

East End Rd.

20

60

Isaac Bay

2

Recovery
Hill

Prospect Hill

21

South Side Rd.

Grapetree
Bay

Grassy Pt.

62

South Side Rd.

Great Pond
Bay

Milord
Pt.

Robin
Bay

UNITED STATES VIRGIN ISLANDS

Tortola

ST. THOMAS

ST. JOHN

Distance from St. Thomas to
St. Croix approx. 40 miles

ST. CROIX

Manchenil
Bay

Canegarden
Bay

Caribbean Sea

0   2 miles
0   3 km

$$–$$$ ☎ **King's Alley Hotel.** In the center of Christiansted's hustle and bus-
★   tle, this small hotel (part of the King's Alley shopping and restaurant
         complex) mixes convenience with charm. The 14 premium rooms in
         the section across the courtyard have mahogany four-poster beds,
         Mexican tile floors, and Indonesian print fabrics. French doors open
         onto balconies with a view of the waterfront and the shopping arcade.
         The 21 standard rooms in the older section are a tad less interesting
         but still attractive. The staff can arrange all sorts of activities: water
         sports, tours, golf, tennis. ⊠ *57 King St. (Box 4120), 00822, ☎ 340/
         773–0103 or 800/843–3574 (direct to hotel),* FAX *340/773–4431. 35
         rooms. Air-conditioning, pool. AE, D, DC, MC, V. EP.*

$$ ☎ **Hotel Caravelle.** The fetching, three-story Caravelle offers moder-
         ately priced lodgings right in Christiansted. Rooms are done in taste-
         ful dusky blues and have floral-print bedspreads and curtains, vaulted
         ceilings, refrigerators, phones, and TV with free HBO. Baths are clean
         and fresh, though the unique tile in the showers is a holdover from when
         the hotel was built in 1968. Most rooms have some sort of ocean view;
         the best overlook the harbor. Owners Sid and Amy Kalmans are
         friendly and helpful. The Wahoo Willie, a casual terrace eatery, serves
         local and Continental cuisine. ⊠ *44A Queen Cross St., 00820, ☎ 340/
         773–0687 or 800/524–0410 (direct to hotel),* FAX *340/778–7004. 43
         rooms, 1 2-bedroom suite. Restaurant, bar, air-conditioning, refriger-
         ators, pool, exercise room, meeting room. AE, D, DC, MC, V. EP.*

$ ☎ **Breakfast Club.** This attractive guest house is within walking dis-
         tance of downtown. Rooms of various sizes and decors are clean, and
         each has a full kitchen and bath. Guests like to gather at the cluttered
         bar, and owner Toby Chapin includes gourmet breakfasts (featuring
         banana pancakes) in the room rates. ⊠ *18 Queen Cross St., 00820,
         ☎ 340/773–7383,* FAX *340/773–8642. 9 rooms. 1 room with air-con-
         ditioning, rest with fans, hot tub. AE, V. BP.*

EAST END

$$$$ ☎ **The Buccaneer.** On the grounds of an old, 300-acre sugar planta-
         tion, this complex has it all: sandy beaches, swimming pools, golf, and
         a vast array of activities. A palm tree–lined main drive leads to the large,
         pink, main building atop a hill; shops, restaurants, and other guest quar-
         ters are scattered about rolling, manicured lawns. The ambience and
         decor are Mediterranean, with tile floors, four-poster beds, massive
         wardrobes of pale wood, pastel fabrics, spacious marble bathrooms,
         and local works of art. All rooms have such modern conveniences as
         hair dryers, refrigerators, and cable TV. ⊠ *Rte. 82 (Box 25200), Gal-
         lows Bay 00824, ☎ 340/773–2100 or 800/255–3881 (direct to hotel),*
         FAX *340/778–8215. 150 rooms. 4 restaurants, air-conditioning, in-
         room safes, refrigerators, 2 pools, spa, 8 tennis courts, jogging, beach,
         shops. AE, D, DC, MC, V. CP.*

$$$$ ☎ **Villa Madeleine.** A West Indian plantation great house is the cen-
★   terpiece of this exquisite hotel. Richly upholstered furniture, Asian rugs,
         teal walls, and whimsically painted driftwood set the mood in the bil-
         liards room, the library, and the sitting room. The great house sits on
         a hill, and there are villas on both sides of it. Each has a full kitchen
         and a private pool. The decor is modern tropical: rattan furniture with
         plush cushions, rocking chairs, and in many villas, bamboo four-poster
         beds. Special touches include pink-marble showers and hand-painted
         floral wall borders. Enjoy fine dining on the terrace at the ☞ **Great
         House at Villa Madeleine** or steak at the Turf Club. ⊠ *Off Rte. 82 at
         Teague Bay (Box 26160), Gallows Bay 00824, ☎ 340/778–8782 or
         800/496–7379 (direct to hotel),* FAX *340/773–2150. 43 villas. 2 restau-
         rants, bar, air-conditioning, kitchenettes, tennis court, billiards, li-
         brary, concierge. AE, D, MC, V. EP.*

$$$–$$$$ 🏨 **Chenay Bay Beach Resort.** The beachfront location and complimentary tennis and water-sports equipment (including kayaks) make this resort a real find. Rooms are basic with ceramic-tile floors, bright-peach or yellow walls, rattan furnishings, kitchenettes, and front porches. Gravel paths connect the terraced gray-and-white wood cottages with the shore, where you'll find a large L-shape pool, a protected beach, a picnic area, and a casual restaurant. The all-you-can-eat pasta night is a bargain. The hotel offers an inexpensive day camp for children 4–12. ⊠ *Rte. 82 (Box 24600), Christiansted 00824,* 🕾 *340/773–2918 or 800/548–4457 (direct to hotel),* FAX *340/773–6665. 50 rooms. Restaurant, bar, picnic area, air-conditioning, kitchenettes, pool, 2 tennis courts, volleyball, beach, snorkeling, kayaking, baby-sitting, children's programs. AE, MC, V. EP.*

$$$ 🏨 **Tamarind Reef Hotel.** At this casual, motel-like, seaside spot, you can sunbathe at the large pool and sandy beach or snorkel in the reef, which comes right to the shore (serious swimming here is difficult). The spacious, modern rooms have rattan furniture, tropical-print drapes and bedspreads, and either a terrace or a deck with views of the water and St. Croix's sister islands to the north. Many rooms have basic kitchenettes—handy for preparing light meals—and three rooms have facilities for guests with disabilities. There's a snack bar just off the beach and a restaurant at the adjacent Green Cay Marina. ⊠ *Off Rte. 82, 5001 Tamarind Reef, 00820,* 🕾 *340/773–4455 or 800/619–0014 (direct to hotel),* FAX *340/773–3989. 46 rooms. Snack bar, air-conditioning, kitchenettes, pool. AE, MC, V. EP.*

FREDERIKSTED

$–$$ 🏨 **The Frederiksted.** Don't be put off by the unprepossessing exterior. This modern four-story inn is your best bet for lodging in Frederiksted. In the inviting, tile courtyard, the glass tables and yellow chairs of the bar and restaurant crowd around a small freshwater swimming pool. Yellow-striped awnings and tropical greenery add still more cheer to the atmosphere. Guest rooms have light-color rattan furniture, print bedspreads, mini-refrigerators, and microwaves. Bathrooms are on the small side but are bright and clean. The nicest quarters have an ocean view and a bathroom with a tub instead of just a shower. ⊠ *442 Strand St., 00840,* 🕾 *340/772–0500 or 800/595–9519 (direct to hotel),* FAX *340/772–0500, ext. 151. 40 rooms. Restaurant, bar, air-conditioning, refrigerators, pool. AE, D, DC, MC, V. EP.*

NORTH SHORE

$$$$ 🏨 **Sunterra Carambola Beach Resort.** The 26 quaint, two-story red-roof ★ villas (including one that's wheelchair-accessible) are connected by lovely, lush arcades. The rooms are identical except for the view— ocean or garden. The decor is English country with a touch of Caribbean: terra-cotta floors, ceramic lamps, mahogany ceilings and furnishings, and rocking chairs and sofas upholstered in soothing floral fabrics. Each room has a patio and a huge bath (shower only). The two-bedroom suite, with its 3-ft-thick plantation walls and large patio, is the perfect Caribbean family dwelling—it has its own exquisite ecru beach and lots of secluded nooks. The on-site ☞ **Picnics at the Carambola Beach Club** open-air restaurant has a sophisticated, contemporary menu. ⊠ *Rte. 80 (Box 3031), Kingshill 00851,* 🕾 *340/778–3800 or 888/316–9648,* FAX *340/778–1682. 150 rooms, 1 2-bedroom cottage. 2 restaurants, deli, air-conditioning, pool, golf course, 4 tennis courts, exercise room, beach, dive shop, snorkeling, library. AE, D, DC, MC, V. EP.*

$$$–$$$$ 🏨 **Cormorant Beach Club and Villas.** At these connected, Moorish-style villas you can slip into a hammock strung between two breeze-bent palms and relax to the thrum of waves. The open-air public spaces are filled with tropical plants and comfy wicker furniture in peach and mint green. Beachfront rooms have dark-wicker furniture, pale-peach

walls, white-tile floors, and floral-print spreads and curtains; all rooms have a patio or balcony and a phone, cable TV, and safes. Bathrooms stand out for their coral-rock shower walls, marble-top double sinks, and brass fixtures. The hotel offers partial and all-inclusive meal plans that include all drinks. The guest are sophisticated travelers, many of whom are gay men and lesbian women. ⊠ *Off Rte. 752, 4126 La Grande Princesse, Christiansted 00820,* ☏ *340/778–8920 or 800/548–4460 (direct to hotel),* 𝖥𝖠𝖷 *340/778–9218. 34 rooms, 4 suites, 14 2- and 3-bedroom villas. Restaurant, bar, air-conditioning, in-room safes, pool, 2 tennis courts, beach, snorkeling. AE, D, DC, MC, V. All-inclusive, EP, MAP.*

$$$ 🏨 **Hibiscus Beach Hotel.** Guest rooms here are in five two-story, pink buildings—each named for a tropical flower. Most rooms have views of the ocean, but those in the Hibiscus building are closest to the water. All rooms have such welcome amenities as roomy balconies, cable TV, safes, and minibars, and all are tastefully decorated with white-tile floors, white walls, pink-stripe curtains, floral spreads, and fresh-cut hibiscus blossoms. Bathrooms are clean but nondescript—both the shower stalls and the vanity mirrors are on the small side. ⊠ *Off Rte. 752, 4131 Estate La Grande Princesse, Christiansted 00820-4441,* ☏ *340/773–4042 or 800/442–0121 (direct to hotel),* 𝖥𝖠𝖷 *340/773–7668. 37 rooms. Restaurant, air-conditioning, in-room safes, minibars, pool, beach, snorkeling. AE, D, MC, V. EP.*

$$–$$$ 🏨 **Waves at Cane Bay.** Lapping waves lull you to sleep at this isolated inn. Although the beach here is rocky, Cane Bay Beach is next door, and the world-famous Cane Bay Reef is just 100 yards offshore (divers take note). You can also sunbathe on a small patch of sand beside the very unusual pool: it's carved from the coral along the shore, and waves crash dramatically over its side, creating a foamy whirlpool on blustery days. Two peach and mint-green buildings house enormous, balconied guest rooms (all have kitchens or kitchenettes, but not all have air-conditioning) that are done in cream and soft pastel prints. ⊠ *Rte. 80 (Box 1749), Kingshill 00851,* ☏ *340/778–1805 or 800/545–0603 (direct to hotel),* 𝖥𝖠𝖷 *340/778–4945. 12 rooms, 1 suite. Restaurant, bar, in-room safes, kitchenettes, pool, snorkeling. AE, MC, V. EP.*

WEST END

$$–$$$ 🏨 **Sprat Hall.** This 20-acre seaside property appeals to guests who enjoy the vagaries of a visit to someone's home. Joyce Hurd presides over the slightly ramshackle antiques-filled plantation where she was born. Some of the guest rooms in the cluttered great house have four-poster beds and planter's chairs. More-modern rooms and cottages are spread out all over the estate. A glorious strand of beach lies a good hike down a gentle hill. Joyce prepares dinner for guests and nonguests, but you have to make your menu selection when she delivers your complimentary Continental breakfast. To explore the island from here, you need to rent a car. Those who prefer the reins to the wheel can take advantage of the Hurd family's horseback-riding facilities. ⊠ *Rte. 63 (Box 695), Frederiksted 00841,* ☏ *340/772–0305 or 800/843–3584 (direct to hotel). 9 rooms, 8 suites, 1 1-bedroom cottage, 2 2-bedroom cottages. Restaurant, horseback riding, beach. No credit cards. CP.*

Cottages and Condominiums

$$$–$$$$ 🏨 **Club St. Croix.** Popular with honeymooners, this complex's studio, one-, and two-bedroom apartments are spacious and bright. Indian-print throw rugs and cushions complement the bamboo furniture and rough, white-tile floors; glass-top tables and mirrored closet doors are lovely modern touches. Penthouses have loft bedrooms atop spiral staircases; studios have Murphy beds in their sitting rooms. All units have full kitchens and sundecks with waterfront views of Christiansted and Buck Island. On the beach you'll find a poolside restaurant, a bar, and a dock. ⊠ *Rte. 752, 3230 Estate Golden Rock, Christiansted 00820,* ☎ *340/773–4800 or 800/524–2025,* FAX *340/778–4009. 54 suites. Restaurant, bar, air-conditioning, kitchenettes, pool, 3 tennis courts, beach, dock. AE, D, MC, V. EP.*

$$$–$$$$ ⊞ **Colony Cove.** Next door to ☞ **Sugar Beach,** this condo-style resort has sunny, tropical apartments done up with pastel prints, white tile, and rattan furnishings. Each unit has two bedrooms, two baths, a balcony, a washer and dryer, and a kitchen so complete that it even has a lasagna pan. You'll find a large pool, a water-sports center, and tennis courts on the grounds, and you can walk along the beach to the restaurant next door. ⊠ *Rte. 752, 3221 Golden Rock, Christiansted 00820,* ☎ *340/773–1965 or 800/828–0746 (direct to hotel),* FAX *340/773–5397. 60 apartments. Snack bar, air-conditioning, kitchenettes, pool, 2 tennis courts, beach, snorkeling. AE, MC, V. EP.*

$$$ ⊞ **Schooner Bay.** This red-roof condo village climbs a hill above Gallows Bay and just outside Christiansted. Each modern two- or three-bedroom apartment has a balcony, ceiling fans, air-conditioning, a washer and dryer, and a full kitchen with a dishwasher and a microwave. Rattan furnishings are set on beige-tile floors; floral-print fabrics add splashes of color. Three-bedroom units have spiral staircases. Sun worshipers might be disappointed that the nearest beach is east, at the Buccaneer, but those with a yen to explore Christiansted will find the location ideal—within walking distance of downtown, yet away from its bustle. ⊠ *5002 Gallows Bay, Christiansted 00820,* ☎ *340/773–7670 or 800/524–2025,* FAX *340/778–4760. 40 apartments. Air-conditioning, fans, kitchenettes, 2 pools, tennis court. AE, D, MC, V. EP.*

$$–$$$$ ⊞ **Sugar Beach.** A stay here puts you on the beach at the north side of the island and just five minutes from Christiansted. The apartments, which range from studios to units with four bedrooms, are immaculate and breezy. Each has a full kitchen and a large patio or balcony with an ocean view; larger units have washers and dryers. Though the exteriors of these condos are ordinary beige stucco, the interiors are lovely (white with tropical furnishings). The pool is amid the ruins of a 250-year-old sugar mill. ⊠ *Rte. 752, 3245 Estate Golden Rock, Christiansted 00820,* ☎ *340/773–5345 or 800/524–2049 (direct to hotel),* FAX *340/773–1359. 46 apartments. Air-conditioning, kitchenettes, pool, 2 tennis courts, beach, meeting room. AE, D, MC, V. EP.*

Private Homes and Villas

Renting a private house gives you the convenience of home as well as top-notch amenities. Many houses have pools, hot tubs, and deluxe furnishings. Most companies meet you at the airport, arrange for a rental car, and provide useful information to make your vacation more interesting. Call **The Collection** (☎ 609/751–2413), **Island Villas** (☎ 340/773–8821), **Rent A Villa** (☎ 800/533–6863), **Richards & Ayer** (☎ 340/772–0420), or **Teague Bay Properties** (☎ 340/773–4850).

Dining

Seven flags have flown over St. Croix, and each has left its legacy in the island's cuisine. You can feast on Italian, French, Danish, and American dishes; there are even Chinese and Mexican restaurants in Christiansted. Fresh local seafood is plentiful and always good; wahoo, mahimahi, and conch are popular. Island chefs often add Caribbean twists to familiar dishes. For a true island experience, stop at a local restaurant for goat stew, curry chicken, or fried pork chops. Regardless of where you eat, your meal will be an informal affair. But be forewarned, prices are a lot higher than you'd pay on the mainland. For price categories, *see* the chart *under* Dining *in* St. Thomas, *above.*

Christiansted

CARIBBEAN/CREOLE

$$$–$$$$ ✕ **Indies.** A historic courtyard full of tables covered with handmade
★ floral-print cloths is the setting for a wonderful dining experience. Owner-
chef Catherine Plav-Drigger prepares island-inspired dishes, and the
menu changes each day to take advantage of St. Croix's freshest boun-
ties. Indulge in the crab cakes or the spicy Caribbean spring rolls to
start, then the spice-rubbed chicken (every bite reveals a new, subtle
flavor) or dolphinfish baked in coconut milk, ginger, tomato, and
spicy peppers. Enjoy live jazz Saturday evening. ⊠ *55–56 Company
St.,* ☎ *340/692–9440. AE, D, MC, V. No lunch weekends.*

$–$$$$ ✕ **Harvey's.** The plain, even dowdy, dining room has just 12 tables,
and plastic floral tablecloths constitute the sole attempt at decor. But
who cares? The food is some of the island's most delicious. Daily spe-
cials, such as mouthwatering goat stew and tender whelks in butter,
served with heaping helpings of rice, fungi, and vegetables, are listed
on the blackboard. Genial owner Sarah Harvey takes great pride in
her kitchen, bustling out from behind the stove to chat and urge you
to eat up. ⊠ *11B Company St.,* ☎ *340/773–3433. No credit cards.
Closed Sun. No dinner Mon.–Wed.*

CONTEMPORARY

$$$$ ✕ **Kendricks.** The chef at this open-air restaurant—a longtime favorite
★ with locals—conjures up creative, tasty cuisine. Try the lobster spring
rolls with warm ginger and soy butter to start, or the warm *chipotle*
pepper with garlic and onion soup. Move on to the house specialty:
pecan-crusted roast pork loin with ginger mayonnaise. ⊠ *21–32 Com-
pany St.,* ☎ *340/773–9199. AE, MC, V.*

CONTINENTAL

$$$–$$$$ ✕ **Top Hat.** Owned by a delightful Danish couple, this restaurant has
★ been serving international cuisine (with Danish specialties, of course)
since 1970. Dishes include roast duck stuffed with apples and prunes,
frikadeller (savory meatballs in a tangy cocktail sauce), fried Camem-
bert with lingonberries, and smoked eel. The signature dessert is a rum-
ice-cream-filled chocolate windmill with blades that turn. ⊠ *52
Company St.,* ☎ *340/773–2346. AE, D, MC, V. Closed May–Aug.*

$$–$$$ ✕ **Antoine's.** Listen to the waves lap at the beach while you dine in
this open-air restaurant tucked into Mill Harbour Condominiums.
Chef Antoine Doos, a Swiss native, whips up international, Austrian,
and German dishes. If you like sauerbraten, knockwurst, or bratwurst,
this is the place. Seafood lovers will enjoy the selection: snapper, tuna,
dolphinfish, and shrimp. ⊠ *3220 Golden Rock,* ☎ *340/773–0263. AE,
MC, V.*

$$–$$$ ✕ **Tivoli Gardens.** Fresh breezes and bowers of hanging plants virtu-
★ ally transform this restaurant in the heart of Christiansted into a gar-
den. The Continental menu features steak, lobster, and more lobster.
To make it easy to eat, the chef takes all the succulent meat from a whole
lobster, puts it into half the lobster's shell, and drips butter over the
top. For dessert, try the bittersweet chocolate velvet—a chocoholic's
dream that's closer to candy than cake. ⊠ *39 Strand St.,* ☎ *340/773–
6782. MC, V. No lunch weekends.*

ECLECTIC

$$–$$$ ✕ **Bombay Club.** This dimly lit spot—made cheerier with bright local
artwork—is in a historic pub. The bar, with its cool, exposed stone walls,
is a favorite expat hangout. The typical pub grub includes fine salads,
nachos, scrumptious buffalo wings, pastas, and simple chicken and steak
dishes. Don't pass up the heavenly stuffed crabs with roast garlic herb

sauce. ⊠ *5A King St.,* ☎ *340/773–1838. MC, V. No lunch weekends.*

$$–$$$ ✕ **Paradise Cafe.** The exposed brick walls of this tiny, lively spot are splashed with colorful island prints. Stop in for lunch or a light supper: sandwiches and burgers are the big draw, though the daily seafood special, often wahoo or mahimahi, is also popular. ⊠ *Company and Queen Cross Sts.,* ☎ *340/773–2985. No credit cards.*

ITALIAN

$$–$$$$ ✕ **Tutto Bene.** Its yellow walls, brightly striped cushions, and painted trompe l'oeil tables make Tutto Bene look more like a sophisticated Mexican cantina than an Italian cucina. One bite of the food, however, will clear up any confusion. Written on hanging mirrors is the daily menu, which includes such fare as veal chop with sun-dried tomatoes and *zuppa di mare* (clams, shrimp, and mussels poached in white wine and served over cappellini). Desserts are prepared by one of the island's finest pastry chefs. ⊠ *2 Company St.,* ☎ *340/773–5229. AE, D, MC, V.*

$–$$ ✕ **Pizza Mare–Cafe Sol.** This trendy spot does dual duty. It serves up
★ terrific pizza, panini sandwiches stuffed with bacon and eggs, and other Italian fare on one side of the walk-up counter. On the other, you'll find 40 varieties of pastries (try the chocolate suicide cake) and exotic coffees. Although you'll have to stand in line to order your lunch, dinner brings wait service and music. ⊠ *1111 Strand St.,* ☎ *340/773–0553;* ⊠ *Sunny Isle Shopping Center, Rte. 70,* ☎ *340/778–5556. AE, D, MC, V. No dinner Sun.–Wed.*

East End
CONTEMPORARY

$$$–$$$$ ✕ **Great House at Villa Madeleine.** The elegant restaurant at the ☞ Villa Madeleine resort serves such diverse cuisine as penne pasta sautéed with grilled chicken breast and served with roasted pepper *coulis* (a puree of peppers and spices) or broiled wahoo with a topping of sweet pepper relish, there are also a number of fine beef dishes. The wine list is extensive. ⊠ *19A Teague Bay (take Rte. 82 out of Christiansted, turn right at Reef Condominiums),* ☎ *340/778–7377. AE, D, MC, V.*

ECLECTIC

$$$–$$$$ ✕ **The Galleon.** Popular with both locals and visitors, this dockside restaurant has something for everyone. Start with the Caesar salad or gravlax (fresh salmon with dill and pepper). Pasta lovers should sample the eggplant ravioli: the homemade pasta is filled not only with grilled eggplant but also with Parmesan, ricotta, and mozzarella cheeses. The osso buco and rack of lamb are legendary. ⊠ *Teague Bay (take Rte. 82 out of Christiansted, turn left at sign for Green Cay Marina),* ☎ *340/773–9949. AE, V. No lunch.*

$$–$$$ ✕ **South Shore Cafe.** This casual bistro sits near the Great Salt Pond on the island's south shore. Popular with locals for its good food and cozy ambience, the restaurant features dishes drawn from a variety of cuisines. Meat lovers and vegetarians can find common ground with a menu that runs from handmade pasta to prime rib. The selection isn't extensive, but the chef puts together a blackboard full of specials every day. ⊠ *Junction of Rtes. 62 and 624,* ☎ *340/773–9311. V. Closed Mon.–Tues. No lunch.*

Frederiksted
CARIBBEAN/CREOLE

$–$$$ ✕ **Villa Morales.** Locals come to this family-run spot for the food and the dancing (in the cavernous back room). The kitchen turns out such well-prepared Cruzan and Spanish dishes as goat stew and baked chicken, all served with heaping helpings of fungi, rice, and vegetables. ⊠ *Plot 82C (off Rte. 70), Estate Whim,* ☎ *340/772–0556. Reservations essential. D, MC, V. Closed Sun.–Mon. No dinner Tues. or Wed.*

CONTEMPORARY

$$$–$$$$ ✕ **Picnics at the Carambola Beach Club.** Don't be fooled by the name. While this open-air restaurant is right at the beach, you're more likely to find salmon fillet stuffed with lobster or shrimp mousse in a puff pastry on the menu than more casual fare. The chefs weave the best of the West Indies into their delightful dishes. The Sunday brunch is popular with both locals and visitors, especially those from the affiliated ☞ **Sunterra Carambola Beach Resort.** ⊠ *Rte. 80 (adjacent to Carambola Beach Resort),* ☎ *340/778–1212. AE, MC. Closed Mon. and July–Oct. No lunch.*

ECLECTIC

$$$–$$$$ ✕ **Le St. Tropez.** A ceramic-tile bar and soft lighting add to the Mediterranean atmosphere at this pleasant bistro, tucked into a courtyard off Frederiksted's main thoroughfare. Seated either inside or on the adjoining patio, you can enjoy such items as grilled meats in delicate French sauces. The menu changes daily, often taking advantage of fresh local seafood. The fresh basil, tomato, and mozzarella salad is heavenly. ⊠ *67 King St.,* ☎ *340/772–3000. AE, MC, V. Closed Sun.*

$$–$$$$ ✕ **Blue Moon.** This terrific little bistro, popular for its live jazz on Friday night, has a changing menu that draws on Asian, Cajun, and local flavors. Try the seafood chowder or *luna* pie (veggies and cheese baked in phyllo dough) as an appetizer; the roasted vegetables and shrimp over linguine as an entrée; and the almond joy sundae for dessert. ⊠ *17 Strand St.,* ☎ *340/772–2222. AE, D, MC, V. Closed Mon.*

Beaches

Buck Island. A visit to this island, part of the U.S. National Park system, is a must on any trip to St. Croix. The beach is beautiful, but its finest treasures are those you can see when you plop off the boat and adjust your mask, snorkel, and flippers. To get here, you'll have to charter a boat (☞ Sailing *in* Outdoor Activities and Sports, *below*).

Cane Bay. The waters aren't always gentle at this breezy north shore beach, but there are never many people around and the scuba diving and snorkeling are wondrous (☞ Scuba Diving and Snorkeling *in* Outdoor Activities and Sports, below). You'll see elkhorn and brain corals, and less than 200 yards out is the drop-off called Cane Bay Wall.

Cramer's Park. This USVI territorial beach on the northeast coast (Route 82) is very popular with locals. It's a good spot for beach picnics and camping. Because of its isolation, though, it's not a good place to linger if you're traveling solo.

Isaac Bay. This East End beach is almost impossible to reach without a four-wheel-drive vehicle, but it's worth the effort. You'll find secluded sands for sunbathing, calm waters for swimming, and a barrier reef for snorkeling. You can also get here via footpaths from Jacks Bay.

Tamarind Reef Beach. Small but attractive Tamarind Reef Beach is east of Christiansted. Both Green Cay and Buck Island seem smack in front of you—an arresting view. The snorkeling is good.

West End Beaches. There are several unnamed beaches along the coast road north of Frederiksted. Just pull over at whatever piece of powdery sand catches your fancy. The beach at the Rainbow Beach Club has a bar, casual restaurant, water sports, and volleyball.

Outdoor Activities and Sports

BICYCLING

Pedal through paradise. A bike tour to some of the island's top sights adds a new dimension to your vacation and helps you stay in shape. **St. Croix Bike and Tours** (⊠ Pier 69 Courtyard, Frederiksted, ☎ 340/772–2343 or 340/773–5004) offers two tours (both cost $35). One heads through historic Frederiksted before cycling on a fairly flat road to Hamm's Bluff. The second, for more hearty folks, takes you up and through the rain forest.

FISHING

In the past quarter-century, some 20 world records—many for blue marlin—have been set in these waters. Sailfish, skipjack, bonito, tuna (allison, blackfin, and yellowfin), and wahoo are abundant.

Ruffian Enterprises (⊠ St. Croix Marina, Gallows Bay, ☎ 340/773–6011) will take you out on a 38-ft powerboat, the *Fantasy*.

GOLF

St. Croix's courses welcome you with spectacular vistas and well-kept greens. Check with your hotel or the tourist board (☞ Visitor Information *in* U.S. Virgin Islands A to Z, *below*) to determine when major celebrity tournaments will be held. There's often an opportunity to play with the pros. **The Buccaneer**'s (⊠ Off Rte. 82 at Teague Bay, ☎ 340/773–2100) 18-hole course is conveniently close to (east of) Christiansted. **The Reef Golf Course** (☎ 340/773–8844), in the northeastern part of the island, has 9 holes. The spectacular course at **Sunterra Carambola Beach Resort** (⊠ Rte. 80, ☎ 340/778–5638), in the northwest valley, was designed by Robert Trent Jones.

HIKING

Although you can set off by yourself on a hike through a rain forest or along a shore, a guide will point out what's important and tell you why. The nonprofit **St. Croix Environmental Association** (⊠ Arawak Bldg., Suite 3, Gallows Bay, 00820, ☎ 340/773–1989) offers hikes through several of the island's ecological treasures, including Estate Mt. Washington, Estate Caledonia in the rain forest, and Salt River. The hikes take nearly two hours and cost $20 per person.

HORSEBACK RIDING

Well-kept roads and expert guides make horseback riding on St. Croix pleasurable. At Sprat Hall, near Frederiksted, Jill Hurd runs **Paul and Jill's Equestrian Stables** (⊠ Rte. 58, ☎ 340/772–2880 or 340/772–2627) and will take you clip-clopping through the rain forest (explaining the flora, fauna, and ruins on the way), along the coast, or on moonlit rides. Costs range from $50 to $75 for two-hour rides.

SAILING

Day sail to Buck Island aboard one of the island's charter boats. Most leave from the Christiansted waterfront or from Green Cay Marina. They stop for a snorkel at the eastern end of the island before dropping anchor off a gorgeous sandy beach for a swim, a hike, and lunch.

Big Beard's Adventure Tours (☎ 340/773–4482) takes you on a catamaran, the *Renegade*, from the Christiansted Waterfront to Buck Island for snorkeling before dropping anchor at a private beach for a barbecue lunch. **Buck Island Charters**' (☎ 340/773–3161) trimaran *Teroro II* leaves Green Cay Marina for full- or half-day sails. Bring your own lunch. **Mile Mark Charters** (☎ 340/773–2628 or 800/523–3483) departs from the Christiansted waterfront for half- and full-day sails on a variety of boats.

SCUBA DIVING AND SNORKELING

St. Croix has several excellent dive sites. At **Buck Island,** a short boat ride from Christiansted or Green Cay Marina, the reef is so spectacular that it's the site of a national monument. You can dive right off the beach at **Cane Bay,** which has a spectacular drop-off. **Frederiksted Pier** is home to a colony of seahorses, creatures seldom seen in the waters off the Virgin Islands. At **Green Cay,** just outside Green Cay Marina in the East End, you'll see colorful fish swimming around the reefs and rocks. Two exceptional **North Shore sites** are North Star and Salt River, which you can reach only by boat. You can float downward through a canyon filled with colorful fish and coral.

The island's dive shops take you out for one- or two-tank dives. Plan to pay about $50 for a one-tank dive and $70 for a two-tank dive, including equipment and an underwater tour. **Anchor Dive Center** (⊠ Salt River Marina, Rte. 801, ☎ 340/778–1522 or 800/532–3483) explores the wall at Salt River Canyon from its base at Salt River Marina. It provides PADI certification. **Dive Experience** (⊠ Strand St., Christiansted, ☎ 340/773–3307 or 800-235-9047) is a five-star PADI training facility providing a range of activities from introductory dives to certification. It takes divers to the north shore walls and reefs. **Dive St. Croix** (☎ 340/773–3434 or 800/523–3483) takes divers to 35 different sites from its base on the Christiansted Wharf. It's the only operation that runs dives to Buck Island. **Scuba West** (☎ 340/772–3701 or 800/352–0107) operates out of Frederiksted. Although it runs trips to reefs and wrecks, its specialty is the seahorses that live around the Frederiksted Pier. **V.I. Divers Ltd.** (☎ 340/773–6045 or 800/544–5911) is near the water in the Pan Am Pavilion. It's a PADI five-star training facility and takes divers to their choice of 28 sites.

TENNIS

The public courts in Frederiksted and out east at Cramer Park are in questionable shape. It's better to pay a fee and play at one of the island's many hotel courts. There are eight courts (two lighted), plus a pro and a full tennis pro shop at the **Buccaneer Hotel** (⊠ Rte. 82, ☎ 340/773–2100); two courts (no lights) at the **Chenay Bay Beach Resort** (⊠ Rte. 82, ☎ 340/773–2918); three lighted courts at **Club St. Croix** (⊠ Rte. 752, ☎ 340/773–4800); and four courts (two lighted) at the **Sunterra Carambola Beach Resort** (⊠ Rte. 80, ☎ 340/778–3800).

WINDSURFING

St. Croix's trade winds make windsurfing a breeze. Most hotels rent Windsurfers and other water-sports equipment to nonguests. **Tradewindsurfing Inc.** (⊠ Hotel on the Cay, ☎ 340/773–7060) offers Windsurfer rentals, sales, and rides; parasailing; and a wide range of water-sports equipment, such as Jet Skis and kayaks.

Shopping

Areas and Malls

Although St. Croix doesn't offer as many shopping opportunities as St. Thomas, the island does have an array of small stores with unique merchandise. In Christiansted, the best shopping areas are the **Pan Am Pavilion** and **Caravelle Arcade** off Strand Street, **Kings Alley Walk,** and along **King** and **Company streets.** These streets give way to arcades filled with boutiques. **Gallows Bay** has a blossoming shopping area in a quiet neighborhood. Stores are often closed on Sunday.

The best shopping in Frederiksted is along **Strand Street** and in the side streets and alleyways that connect it with **King Street.** Most stores close Sunday except when a cruise ship is in port.

Specialty Items

ART

The Gallery at the Pentheny. Even if you don't want to send home any of the pricey art works sold at this interesting cooperative gallery, it's worth a browse. Housed in the lobby of an old hotel, the thick, whitewashed stone walls are the perfect backdrops for works by a changing group of St. Croix artists. Look for Sylvia Maratoba's pieces; she creates exquisite baskets and wire sculptures out of discards she finds around the island. ⊠ 1138 King St., Christiansted, ☎ FAX 340/773-2781.

BOOKS

The Bookie. This shop carries paperback novels, stationery, newspapers, and cards. Stop in for the latest gossip and to find out about upcoming events. ⊠ 1111 Strand St., Christiansted, ☎ 340/773-2592.
Trader Bob's Dockside Book Store. For Caribbean books or the latest good read, try this bookstore across from the post office in the Gallows Bay shopping area. ⊠ 5030 Anchor Way, ☎ 340/773-6001.

CHINA AND CRYSTAL

Little Switzerland. The St. Croix branch of this VI institution sells a variety of Rosenthal flatware, Lladro figurines, Waterford and Baccarat crystal, Lalique figurines, and Wedgwood china. ⊠ 1 Strand St., Christiansted, ☎ 340/773-1976.

CLOTHES

Caribbean Clothing Company. This fashionable store features contemporary sportswear for men and women by top American designers. ⊠ 41 Queen Cross St., Christiansted, ☎ 340/773-5012.
From the Gecko. Come here for the hippest clothes on St. Croix, from superb batik sarongs to hand-painted silk scarves. ⊠ 1233 Queen Cross St., Christiansted, ☎ 340/778-9433.
Urban Threadz. Urban island wear by No Fear and many other lines for men and women are available here. Check the **Urban Kidz** store three doors down for Guess, Calvin Klein, Boss, Nautica, and Fila children's clothes. ⊠ 52C Company St., Christiansted, ☎ 340/773-2883.
The White House. This contemporary store sells clothes in all-white and natural colors. Look for exquisite lingerie, elegant evening wear, and unusual casual outfits. ⊠ 8B Kings Alley Walk, Christiansted, ☎ 340/773-9222.

FOODSTUFFS

If you've rented a condominium or a villa, you'll appreciate the fact that St. Croix offers excellent shopping at its stateside-style supermarkets. Fresh vegetables, fruits, and meats arrive frequently. Try the open-air stands strung out along Route 70 for island produce. Supermarkets include **Pueblo** (⊠ Orange Grove Shopping Center, Rte. 75, ☎ 340/773-0118; ⊠ Sunny Isle Shopping Center, Rte. 70, ☎ 340/778-5005; ⊠ Villa La Reine Shopping Center, Rte. 75, ☎ 340/778-1272), **Plaza Extra** (⊠ United Shopping Plaza, Rte. 70, ☎ 340/778-6240), **Schooner Bay Market** (⊠ Rte. 82, ☎ 340/773-3232), and **Sunshine Supermarket** (⊠ Sunshine Mall, Rte. 70, ☎ 340/692-2720). **Cost-U-Less** (⊠ Rte. 70, ☎ 340/692-2220) is a warehouse-style store (no membership fee) across from the Sunshine Mall.

GIFTS

Island Webe. The coffees, jams, and spices—produced locally or elsewhere in the Caribbean—here will tempt your taste buds. Small *mocko jumbie* dolls depict an African tradition transported to the islands during slave days (they represent the souls of the ancestors of African slaves). The fabric dolls wearing Caribbean costumes will delight kids of all ages. Turn the double dolls upside down to see a white face on one side and a black one on the other. ⊠ *210 Strand St., Frederiksted,* ☎ *340/772–2555.*

The Royal Poinciana. You'll find island seasonings and hot sauces, West Indian crafts, bath gels, and herbal teas at this attractive shop. ⊠ *1111 Strand St., Christiansted,* ☎ *340/773–9892.*

Trade Winds Shop. This shop seems to carry whatever has recently blown in from the four corners of the earth. Look for the exquisite model wooden sailboats (perfect for your coffee table); dishes the color of the sea and shaped like fish; attractive stationery with seashore motifs; and fashionable tropical clothing. ⊠ *Kings Alley Walk, Christiansted,* ☎ *340/713–9200.*

Gone Tropical. Whether you're looking for inexpensive souvenirs of your trip or a special, singular gift, you'll probably find it at this shop. On her travels about the world, owner Margo Meacham keeps her eye out for items with which to stock her shop—from tablecloths and napkins in bright Caribbean colors to carefully crafted metal birds. ⊠ *5 Company St., Christiansted,* ☎ *340/773–4696.*

HANDICRAFTS

Folk Art Traders. Owners Patty and Charles Eitzen travel to Guyana as well as Haiti, Jamaica, and elsewhere in the Caribbean to find treasures for their shop. The baskets, ceramic masks, pottery, jewelry, and sculpture they find are unique examples of folk-art traditions. ⊠ *1B Queen Cross St., at Strand St., Christiansted,* ☎ *340/773–1900.*

JEWELRY

Colombian Emeralds. Specializing—of course—in emeralds, this store also carries diamonds, rubies, sapphires, and gold. A branch store, **Jewelers' Warehouse** (⊠ 1 Queen Cross St., Christiansted, ☎ 340/773–5590), is across the street. The chain, the Caribbean's largest jeweler, offers certified appraisal and international guarantees. ⊠ *43 Queen Cross St., Christiansted,* ☎ *340/773–1928 or 340/773–9189.*

Crucian Gold. This store, in a small courtyard of a West Indian–style cottage, carries the unique gold creations of St. Croix native Brian Bishop. His trademark piece is the Turk's Head ring (a knot of interwoven gold strands). ⊠ *59 King's Wharf, Christiansted,* ☎ *340/773–5241.*

Karavan West Indies. The owner here designs her own jewelry and also sells an assortment of tchotchkes, including handmade Christmas ornaments and magical beads, from amber to amethyst. ⊠ *5030 Anchor Way, Gallows Bay,* ☎ *340/773–9999.*

Sonya's. Sonya Hough opened this store in 1964 to showcase her jewelry creations; now she runs it with her daughter, Diana. Sonya invented the hook bracelet, popular among locals. Hurricane Georges's visit to the island in 1998 inspired a "hurricane" bracelet. Its unique clasp features a gold and silver strand shaped like the storm's swirling winds as they hit St. Croix, St. John, and St. Thomas. ⊠ *1 Company St., Christiansted,* ☎ *340/778–8605.*

LEATHER GOODS

Kicks. This upscale shop carries a good, if small, selection of shoes and leather goods. ⊠ *57 Company St., Christiansted,* ☎ *340/773–7801.*

LIQUOR

Cruzan Rum Distillery. A tour of the company's rebuilt factory culminates in a tasting of its products, all sold here at bargain prices. ⊠ *West Airport Rd.,* ☎ *340/692–2280.*

Kmart. The two branches of this discount department store—a large one in the Sunshine Mall and a smaller one mid-island at Sunny Isle Shopping Center—carry a huge line of discount, duty-free liquor. ⊠

Sunshine Mall, Rte. 70, Frederiksted, ☎ *340/692–5848;* ✉ *Sunny Isle Shopping Center, Rte. 70,* ☎ *340/719–9191.*

PERFUMES

Violette Boutique. Perfumes, cosmetics, and skin-care products are the draws here. ✉ *Caravelle Arcade, 38 Strand St., Christiansted,* ☎ *340/ 773–2148.*

Nightlife and the Arts

The island's nightlife is ever-changing, and its arts scene is eclectic— ranging from Christmastime performances of the *Nutcracker* to whatever local group got organized enough to put on a show. Folk-art traditions, such as the island's quadrille dancers, are making a comeback. To find out what's happening, pick up the local newspapers— *V.I. Daily News* and *St. Croix Avis*—which are available at newsstands.

Nightlife

Christiansted has a lively and eminently casual club scene near the waterfront. On Thursday night during the winter season, the **Cormorant** (✉ 4126 La Grande Princesse, ☎ 340/778–8920) dishes up a West Indian buffet with a musical accompaniment. **Hotel on the Cay** (✉ Protestant Cay, ☎ 340/773–2035) has a West Indian buffet on Tuesday night in the winter season that features a broken-bottle dancer (a dancer who braves a carpet of broken bottles) and mocko jumbie characters. Easy jazz flows from the courtyard bar at **Indies** (✉ 55– 56 Company St., ☎ 340/692–9440) Saturday evening. The **2 Plus 2 Disco** (✉ 17 La Grande Princesse, ☎ 340/773–3710) spins a great mix of calypso, soul, disco, and reggae; there's live music on weekends.

Although less hopping than Christiansted, Frederiksted has a couple of restaurants and clubs with a variety of weekend entertainment. **Blue Moon** (✉ 17 Strand St., ☎ 340/772–2222), a waterfront restaurant, is the place to be for live jazz on Friday 9 PM–1 AM. **Pier 69** (✉ 69 King St., ☎ 340/772–0069) has blues, jazz, and reggae every Friday and Saturday at 9:30 PM.

The Arts

The **Island Center for the Performing Arts** (✉ Rte. 79, ☎ 340/778– 5272) hosts St. Croix's major concerts, plays, and performances by visiting entertainers.

Exploring St. Croix

Though there are things to see and do in St. Croix's two towns, Christiansted and Frederiksted (both named after Danish kings), there are lots of interesting spots in between them and to the east of Christiansted. Just be sure you have a map in hand (pick one up at rental-car agencies, or stop by the tourist office for an excellent free one). Many secondary roads remain unmarked; if you get confused, ask for help.

Numbers in the margin correspond to points of interest on the St. Croix map.

Christiansted and the East

Christiansted is a historic, Danish-style town that always served as St. Croix's commercial center. Your best bet is to spend the morning, when it's still cool, exploring the historic sites. This two-hour endeavor won't tax your walking shoes and will leave you with energy to poke around the town's eclectic shops. Break for lunch at an open-air restaurant before spending as much time as you like shopping.

An easy drive (roads are flat and well marked) to St. Croix's eastern end takes you through some choice real estate. Ruins of old sugar estates dot the landscape. You can make the entire loop on the road that circles the island in about an hour, a good way to end the day. If you want to spend a full day exploring, you'll find some nice beaches and easy walks, with places to stop for lunch.

SIGHTS TO SEE

❶ **Christiansted.** Trade here in the 1700s and 1800s was in sugar, rum, and molasses. Today the town is home to law offices, tourist shops, and restaurants, but many of the buildings, built from the harbor up into the gentle hillsides, date from the 18th century. You can't get lost. All streets lead gently downhill to the water. Still, if you want some friendly advice, stop by the **Visitor's Center** (✉ 53A Company St., ☎ 340/773–0495) weekdays between 8 and 5 for maps and brochures.

Large, yellow **Ft. Christiansvaern** dominates the waterfront. Because it's so easy to spot, it makes a good place to start a walking tour. In 1749 the Danish built the fort to protect the harbor, but the structure was repeatedly damaged by hurricane-force winds and was partially rebuilt in 1771. It's now a national historic site and the best preserved of the five remaining Danish-built forts in the VI. ✉ *Hospital St.,* ☎ *340/773–1460.* ▣ *$2 (includes admission to Steeple Building,* ☞ *below).* ☉ *Weekdays 8–5, weekends and holidays 9–5.*

When you're tired of sightseeing, stop at **D. Hamilton Jackson Park**— on the street side of Ft. Christiansaern—for a rest. It's named for a famed labor leader, judge, and journalist who started the first newspaper not under the thumb of the Danish crown. ✉ *Between Ft. Christiansvaern and the Danish Customs House.*

Built in 1830 on foundations that date from 1734, the **Danish Customs House**—near Ft. Christiansvaern—originally served as a both a customs house and a post office (second floor). In 1926 it became the Christiansted Library, and it has been a National Park Service office since 1972. ✉ *King St.* ☉ *Weekdays 8–5.*

Constructed in 1856, the **Scale House** was once the spot where goods passing through the port were weighed and inspected. It now serves at the Christiansted Historic Site's visitors center and is just across the street from the Danish Customs House. ✉ *King St.,* ☎ *340/773–1460.* ☉ *Mon.–Fri. 8–5, weekends and holidays 9–5.*

Built by the Danes in 1753, the **Steeple Building** was the first Danish Lutheran church on St. Croix. It's now a national park museum and contains exhibits that document the island's Indian habitation. It's worth the block-long walk from Ft. Christiansvaern to see the building's collection of archaeological artifacts; displays on plantation life; and exhibits on the architectural development of Christiansted, the early history of the church, and Alexander Hamilton, the first secretary of the U.S. Treasury, who grew up in St. Croix. ✉ *Church St.,* ☎ *340/ 773–1460.* ▣ *$2 (includes admission to Ft. Christiansvaern;* ☞ *above).* ☉ *Open when staffing permits; check at Ft. Christiansvaern.*

The **Post Office Building,** built in 1749, was once the Danish West India & Guinea Company warehouse. It's across the street from the Steeple Building. ✉ *Church St.*

One of the town's most elegant structures, **Government House** was built as a home for a Danish merchant in 1747. Today it houses USVI government offices. If the building is open, slip into the peaceful inner courtyard to admire the still pools and gardens. A sweeping staircase leads you to a second-story ballroom, still the site of official government functions. ⊠ *King St.,* ☏ *340/773–1404. Closed for renovations at press time.*

Around the corner and down a block from Government House, the tanks at the **St. Croix Aquarium** contain an ever-changing variety of local sea creatures. Children are invited to explore the discovery room, with its microscopes, interactive displays, and educational videos. They'll especially enjoy the petting tank, where they can feel starfish relax to their touch. ⊠ *Caravelle Arcade,* ☏ *340/773–8995.* ⊐ *$4.50.* ⊙ *Tues.–Sat. 11–4.*

Built in 1735 as a slave market, today **the market,** which is housed in a wood-and-galvanized-aluminum structure, is where farmers and others sell their goods every Wednesday and Saturday from 8 to 5. The market is a three-block walk from the aquarium and is a great place to end a walking tour. ⊠ *Company St.*

The **Buck Island Reef National Monument,** off the northeast coast, has pristine beaches that are just right for sunbathing, but there's enough shade for those who don't want to fry. The spectacular snorkeling trail set in the reef allows close-up study of coral formations and tropical fish. After your arrival by charter boat, crew members give special attention to novice snorkelers and children. There's an easy hiking trail to the island's highest point, where you'll be rewarded for your efforts by spectacular views of the reef and St. John. Charter-boat trips leave daily from the Christiansted waterfront or from Green Cay Marina, about 2 mi (3 km) east of Christiansted. Check with your hotel for recommendations. ⊠ *North Shore,* ☏ *340/773–1460 (park headquarters).*

2 Point Udall. This rocky promontory, the easternmost point in the United States, is about a half-hour's drive from Christiansted. A paved road takes you to an overlook with glorious views. More adventurous folks can hike down to the pristine beach below. On the way back, look for The Castle, an enormous mansion that can only be described as a cross between a Moorish mosque and the Taj Mahal. It was built by an extravagant recluse known only as the Contessa. ⊠ *Rte. 82.*

Between Christiansted and Frederiksted

A drive through the countryside between Christiansted and Frederiksted will take you past ruins of old plantations, many bearing whimsical names—Morningstar, Solitude, Upper Love—bestowed by early owners. The traffic moves quickly—by island standards—on the main roads, but you can pause and poke around if you head down some side lanes. It's easy to find your way west, but driving from north to south requires good navigation. Don't leave your hotel without a map. Allow an entire day for this trip so you'll have enough time for a swim at a north shore beach. Although you'll find lots of casual eateries on the main roads, pick up a picnic lunch if you plan to head off the beaten path.

SIGHTS TO SEE

4 Judith's Fancy. In this upscale neighborhood you'll find the ruins of an old great house and tower of the same name, both remnants of a circa-1750 Danish sugar plantation. The "Judith" comes from the first name of a woman buried on the property. From the guard house at the neighborhood entrance, follow Hamilton Drive past some of St. Croix's loveliest homes. At the end of Hamilton Drive, the road overlooks Salt River Bay, where Christopher Columbus anchored in 1493. A skirmish between members of Columbus's crew and a group of Carib Indians resulted in the first bloody encounter between Europeans and West Indians. The peninsula on the east side of the bay is named for the event: Cabo de las Flechas (Cape of the Arrows). On the way back, make a detour left off Hamilton Drive onto Caribe Road, for a close look at the ruins. ⊠ *Turn north onto Rte. 751 off Rte. 75.*

❸ **Little Princess Estate.** If the old plantation ruins decaying here and there around St. Croix intrigue you, a visit to this nature conservancy project will give you even more of a glimpse into the past. The staff has carved walking paths out of the bush that surrounds what's left of a 19th-century plantation. It's easy to stroll among well-labeled fruit trees and see the ruins of the windmill, the sugar and rum factory, and the laborers' village. This is the perfect place to reflect on St. Croix's agrarian past fueled with labor from African slaves. The property also has a community garden. ⊠ *Just off Rte. 75 (turn north at the Five Corners traffic light),* ☎ *340/773–5575.* ⊠ *Free.* ☉ *Daily 9–5.*

❻ **Mt. Eagle.** This is St. Croix's highest peak (1,165 ft). Leaving Cane Bay and passing North Star Beach, follow the coastal road that dips briefly into a forest, then turn left on Rte. 69. Just after you make the turn, the pavement is marked with the words THE BEAST and a set of giant paw prints. The hill you're about to climb is the location of the famous Beast of the America's Paradise Triathlon, an annual event during which participants must bike this intimidating slope. ⊠ *Rte. 69.*

❺ **Salt River Bay National Historical Park and Ecological Preserve.** This joint national and local park was dedicated in November 1993. In addition to sights with cultural significance, it encompasses a bio-diverse coastal estuary with the largest remaining mangrove forest in the USVI, a submarine canyon, and several endangered species, including the hawksbill turtle and the roseate tern. Plans are afoot to create a museum, interpretive walking trails, and a replica of a Carib village. A ceremonial ball court was discovered at the spot where the taxis park. Take a short hike up the dirt road to the ruins of an old earthen fort and great views of Salt River Bay and the surrounding countryside. ⊠ *Rte. 75 to Rte. 80.*

Frederiksted and Environs

St. Croix's second-largest town, Frederiksted, was founded in 1751. A stroll around its historic sights will take you no more than an hour. Allow a little more time if you want to browse in the few small shops. Although Frederiksted is the hub, the area just outside town has old plantations. Some have been preserved as homes or historic structures that are open to the public.

SIGHTS TO SEE

❼ **Estate Mount Washington Plantation.** Several years ago, while surveying the property, the owners discovered the ruins of a sugar plantation beneath the rain-forest brush. The grounds have since been cleared and opened to the public. You can take a self-guided walking tour of the mill, the rum factory, and other ruins, and there's an antiques shop in what were once the stables. ⊠ *Rte. 63 (watch for antiques shop sign),* ☎ *340/772–1026.* ☉ *Ruins open daily; antiques shop open by appointment only.*

☜ ⑫ **Estate Whim Plantation Museum.** The lovingly restored estate, with a windmill, cook house, and other buildings, will give you a sense of what life was like on St. Croix's sugar plantations in the 1800s. The oval-shape great house has high ceilings and antique furniture, decor, and utensils. Notice its fresh, airy atmosphere—the waterless stone moat around the great house was used not for defense but for gathering cooling air. The apothecary exhibit is the largest in all the West Indies. If you have kids, the grounds are the perfect place for them to stretch their legs, perhaps while you browse in the museum gift shop. ⊠ *Rte. 70, Frederiksted,* ☎ *340/772–0598.* 🖼 *$6.* ☉ *Mon.–Sat. 10–4.*

8 Frederiksted. The town is noted less for its Danish than for its Victorian architecture, which dates from after the slave uprising and the great fire of 1878. One long cruise-ship pier juts into the sparkling sea. The pier is the perfect place to start a tour of this quaint city. The **Visitor's Center** (⊠ Waterfront, ☎ 340/772–0357), right on the pier, was built in the late 1700s; the two-story gallery was added in the 1800s. The building once served as the customs house; today you can stop in weekdays from 8 to 5 and pick up brochures or view the exhibits on St. Croix.

On July 3, 1848, 8,000 slaves marched on the redbrick **Ft. Frederik** to demand their freedom. Danish Governor Peter von Scholten, fearing they would burn the town to the ground, stood up in his carriage parked in front of the fort and granted them their freedom. The fort, completed in 1760, houses a number of interesting historical exhibits as well as an art gallery and a display of police memorabilia. It's within earshot of the Visitor's Center. ⊠ *Waterfront,* ☎ *340/772–2021.* 🖼 *Free.* ☉ *Weekdays 8:30–4:30.*

St. Patrick's Roman Catholic church, complete with three turrets, was built in 1843 of coral. Wander inside and you'll find woodwork handcrafted by Frederiksted artisans. The churchyard, four blocks inland from Ft. Frederik, is filled with 18th-century gravestones. ⊠ *Prince St.*

Two blocks south of St. Patrick's, **St. Paul's Anglican Church** (circa 1812) is a mix of Georgian and Gothic Revival architecture. The bell tower of exposed sandstone was added later. The simple interior has gleaming woodwork and a tray ceiling (it looks like an upside-down tray) popular in Caribbean architecture. It has survived several hurricanes. ⊠ *Prince St.*

Built in 1839, **Apothecary Hall** is a good example of 19th-century architecture; its facade has both Gothic and Greek Revival elements. This historic building is about a minute away from St. Paul's; head toward the sea on King Cross Street, and you can't miss it. ⊠ *King Cross St.*

Stop at the **market** for fresh fruits and vegetables (be sure to wash or peel this produce before eating it) sold each morning, just as they have been for more than 200 years. ⊠ *Queen St.*

9 Karl and Marie Lawaetz Museum. For a trip back in time, tour this circa-1750 farm. Owned by the prominent Lawaetz family since 1899, just after Karl arrived from Denmark, the lovely two-story house is nestled in a valley at La Grange. A Lawaetz family member shows you the four-poster mahogany bed Karl and Marie shared, the china Marie painted, the family portraits, and the fruit trees that fed the family for several generations. Initially a sugar plantation, it was subsequently used to raise cattle and produce. ⊠ *Estate Little La Grange, Rte. 76, Mahogany Rd.,* ☎ *340/772–1539.* 🖼 *$5.* ☉ *Tues.–Sat. 10–4.*

10 St. Croix Leap. This workshop sits in the heart of the rain forest, about a 15-minute drive from Frederiksted. It sells a wide range of articles, including mirrors, tables, bread boards, and mahogany jewelry boxes crafted by local artisans. ⊠ *Rte. 76,* ☎ *340/772–0421.*

13 St. George Village Botanical Gardens. At this 17-acre estate you'll find lush, fragrant flora amid the ruins of a 19th-century sugarcane plantation village. There are miniature versions of each ecosystem on St. Croix, from a semiarid cactus grove to a verdant rain forest. ⊠ *Turn*

north off Rte. 70 at sign, Kingshill, ☎ *340/692–2874.* ✉ *$5.* ☉ *Mon.–
Sat. 9–4. Closed holidays.*

⓫ **West End Salt Pond.** A bird-watcher's delight, this salt pond attracts a
vast variety of winged creatures, including flamingos. ⊠ *Veteran's
Shore Dr.*

ST. JOHN

Updated by
Lynda Lohr

Beautiful and largely undisturbed St. John is 3 mi (5 km) east of St.
Thomas across the Pillsbury Sound (a 20-minute ferry ride from Red
Hook). In 1956 Laurence Rockefeller, who founded the Caneel Bay
Resort, donated ⅔ of St. John's 20 square mi (53 square km) to the
United States as a national park. Because of this, the island comes close
to realizing that travel-brochure dream of "an unspoiled tropical paradise." It's covered with tropical vegetation, including a bay-tree forest that once supplied St. Thomas with the raw material for its fragrant
bay rum. Along St. John's north shore, clean, gleaming, white-sand
beaches fringe bay after bay, each full of iridescent water that's perfect for swimming, fishing, snorkeling, diving, and underwater photography.

In 1675 Jorgen Iverson claimed the unsettled island for Denmark. The
British residents of nearby Tortola, however, considered St. John theirs,
and when a small party of Danes from St. Thomas moved onto the
uninhabited island, the British "invited" them to leave (which they did).
Despite this, in 1717 a group of Danish planters founded the first per-
manent settlement at Coral Bay. The question of who owned St. John
wasn't settled until 1762, when Britain decided that maintaining good
relations with Denmark was more important than keeping St. John.

By 1728 St. John had 87 plantations and a population of 123 whites
and 677 blacks. By 1733, there were more than 1,000 slaves working
more than 100 plantations. In that year, the island was hit by a drought,
hurricanes, and a plague of insects that destroyed the summer crops.
Everyone felt the threat of famine, particularly the slaves, whose living and working conditions were already harsh. Sensing the growing
desperation, the landowners enacted even more severe measures in a
misguided attempt to keep control. On November 23 the slaves revolted.
With great military prowess, they captured the fort at Coral Bay, took
control of the island, and held on to it for six months. During this time
nearly a quarter of the island's population—black and white—was killed.
The rebellion was eventually put down by 100 Danish militia and 220
Creole troops that were brought in from Martinique. Slavery continued until 1848, when slaves in St. Croix marched on Frederiksted to
demand their freedom from the Danish government. After emancipation, St. John fell into decline, with its inhabitants eking out a living
on small farms. Life continued in much the same way until the national
park was established in 1956 and tourism became an industry.

Today St. John may well be the most racially integrated of the three
USVI. Its 5,000 residents, black and white, have a strong sense of community that seems rooted in a desire to protect the island's natural beauty.
Cruz Bay, the administrative capital, is home to the Virgin Islands National Park Visitor's Center and a few small shopping centers. It's
more a small West Indian village (calm except when cruise ships arrive) than a major urban hub, and its residents want to keep it that
way. When the government tried to install the island's first traffic light
here, the citizens successfully opposed it, claiming it would change the
character of the island and do little to help traffic. The consensus that

the island's natural resources are sacrosanct may be curbing excesses on private land as well. Except for Cruz Bay, most of St. John—even areas outside the national park—still has a natural, undeveloped feel to it. Here you can truly escape the pressures of 20th-century life for a day, a week—perhaps, forever.

Lodging

St. John doesn't have many beachfront hotels, but that's a small price to pay for all the pristine sand. However, the island's two world-class hotels—Caneel Bay Resort and the Westin Resort, St. John—*are* on the beach. Sandy, white beaches string out along the north coast, which is popular with sunbathers and snorkelers and is the home of Caneel Bay Resort and Cinnamon and Maho Bay campgrounds. Most villas are in the residential south shore area, a 15-minute drive from the North Shore beaches. If you head east you'll come to the laid-back community of Coral Bay, where you'll find a few villas and cottages. A stay outside of Coral Bay will be peaceful and quiet.

If you're looking for West Indian–village charm, there are a few inns in Cruz Bay. Just know that when bands play at any of the town's bars (some of which stay open till the wee hours), the noise can be a problem. Your choice of accommodations also includes condominiums and cottages near town; two campgrounds, both at the edges of beautiful beaches (bring bug repellent); eco-resorts; and luxurious villas, often with a pool or a hot tub (sometimes both), and a stunning view.

If your lodging comes with a fully equipped kitchen, you'll be happy to know that St. John's handful of grocery stores sell everything from the basics to sun-dried tomatoes and green chilies—though the prices will take your breath away. If you're on a budget, consider bringing some staples (pasta, canned goods, paper products) from home. Throughout the island, rates (which some may consider expensive) at many hotels include most water sports and endless privacy. For price categories, *see* the chart *under* Lodging *in* St. Thomas, *above.*

Hotels and Inns

$$$$ ☷ **Caneel Bay Resort.** Set on 170 lush peninsular acres—originally part
★ of the Danish West India Company's Durloo plantation—Caneel Bay Resort mixes a good bit of peace and quiet into its luxurious air. You won't find crowds or glitz; your room won't have air-conditioning, a TV, or even a phone (though management will loan you a cellular). Instead, you'll discover spacious, restful rooms that are open to the breezes and are tastefully decorated with tropical furnishings; seven beaches, each more gorgeous than the last; and an attentive staff that will fill your every need. ⊠ *Rte. 20 (Box 720), Cruz Bay 00830,* ☎ *340/776–6111 or 800/928–8889. 166 rooms. 3 restaurants, 11 tennis courts, beaches, dive shop, dock, snorkeling, windsurfing, boating, children's program, meeting rooms. AE, MC, V. EP, FAP, MAP.*

$$$$ ☷ **Gallows Point Suite Resort.** These soft-gray buildings with peaked roofs and shuttered windows are clustered on a peninsula south of the Cruz Bay ferry dock. The garden apartments have kitchens and sky-lighted, plant-filled showers that are big enough to frolic in. The upper-level apartments have loft bedrooms and better views. There's air-conditioning only in the first-floor units; the harborside villas get better trade winds, but they're also noisier. The entranceway is bridged by ☞ **Ellington's** restaurant, which serves delicious contemporary cuisine. ⊠ *Gallows Point (Box 58), Cruz Bay 00831,* ☎ *340/776–6434 or 800/323–7229 (direct to hotel),* ☒ *340/776–6520. 60 rooms. Restaurant, pool, beach, snorkeling. AE, DC, MC, V. EP.*

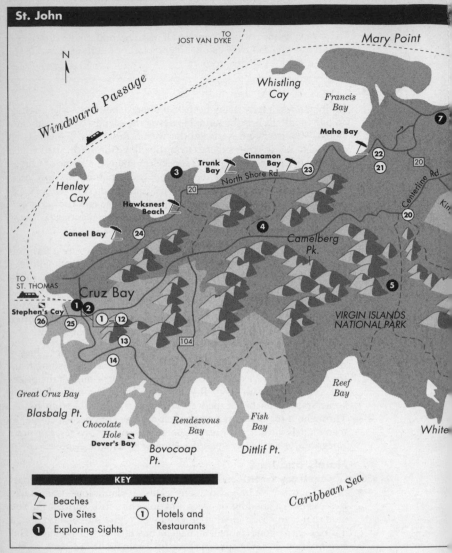

KEY

Beaches
Dive Sites
Exploring Sights
Ferry
Hotels and Restaurants

Lodging
Caneel Bay Resort, **24**
Cinnamon Bay Campground, **23**
Coconut Coast Villas, **26**
Estate Concordia, **15**
Estate Zootenvaal, **19**
Gallows Point Suite Resort, **2**
Harmony, **21**
Inn at Tamarind Court, **12**
Maho Bay Camps, **22**
Park Isle Villas, **25**
Serendip, **13**
Westin Resort, St. John, **14**

Dining
Asolare, **3**
Cafe Roma, **1**
Le Chateau Bordeaux, **20**
Ellington's, **2**
Fish Trap, **4**
Global Village Cuisine at Lattitude 18, **7**
Lime Inn, **5**
Luscious Licks, **6**
Paradiso, **8**
Pusser's, **9**
Serafina Seaside Bistro, **17**
Shipwreck Landing, **16**
Skinny Legs Bar and Restaurant, **18**
Sun Dog Cafe, **11**
La Tapa, **10**

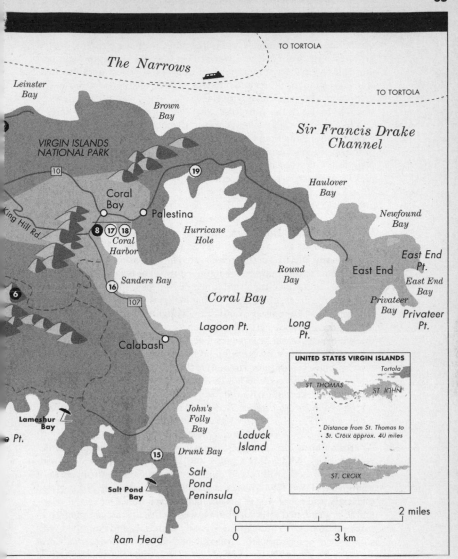

TO TORTOLA

TO TORTOLA

The Narrows

Leinster Bay

Brown Bay

Sir Francis Drake Channel

VIRGIN ISLANDS NATIONAL PARK

10

(19)

Coral Bay

Palestina

Haulover Bay

Newfound Bay

King Hill Rd.

(8) (17) (18)

Coral Harbor

Hurricane Hole

East End Pt.

East End

East End Bay

6

(16)

Sanders Bay

107

Round Bay

Coral Bay

Privateer Bay

Privateer Pt.

Calabash

Lagoon Pt.

Long Pt.

Lameshur Bay

Pt.

John's Folly Bay

Loduck Island

(15)

Drunk Bay

Salt Pond Bay

Salt Pond Peninsula

Ram Head

UNITED STATES VIRGIN ISLANDS

Tortola

ST. THOMAS   ST. JOHN

Distance from St. Thomas to St. Croix approx. 40 miles

ST. CROIX

0 _____ 2 miles

0 _____ 3 km

$$$$ ⊡ **Westin Resort, St. John.** Spread out over 47 acres adjacent to Great Cruz Bay, the Westin has lushly planted gardens, a pool, a beach (the swimming is good), and enough amenities to make stepping off the grounds unnecessary. If you want to get out and about, though, taxi jaunts into Cruz Bay are a breeze. Rooms have yellow and blue bedspreads, rattan furniture, and phones and computer ports for those who just *have* to keep in touch with the world. Many rooms have views of boats bobbing in the turquoise sea. You can keep very busy here, if you like; perhaps play some tennis in the morning, go windsurfing in the afternoon, and then get a massage before heading to dinner in one of the on-site restaurants. Younger guests will appreciate the children's program. Guests at the Westin Vacation Club, a condominium complex located across the street, enjoy all the hotel amenities. ⊠ *Rte. 104 (Box 8310), Cruz Bay 00831,* ☎ *340/693–8000 or 800/937–8461,* ℻ *340/693–8888. 285 rooms. 3 restaurants, air-conditioning, in-room modem lines, minibars, pool, massage, 6 tennis courts, exercise room, beach, dive shop, snorkeling, windsurfing, boating, fishing, shops, children's program, meeting room. AE, D, DC, MC, V. EP.*

$$$ ⊡ **Harmony.** Nestled in the tree-covered hills adjacent to the ☞ **Maho Bay Camps** is this Stanley Selengut eco-tourism resort. The spacious two-story units have the usual amenities—decks, sliding glass doors, living-dining areas, great views. What makes this place unusual are the materials that were used to build it. Though you can't tell when you look at them, the carpets are made of recycled milk cartons, the pristine white walls of old newspapers. Energy for the low-wattage appliances is generated entirely by the wind and the sun, and each unit has a laptop computer programmed to monitor energy consumption. Tile floors, undyed cotton linens, and South American handicrafts create a decor that seems in keeping with the ideals. There's a water-sports outfitter on the beach. ⊠ *Maho Bay (Box 310), Cruz Bay 00830,* ☎ *340/776– 6240, 212/472–9453, or 800/392–9004;* ℻ *212/861–6210. 12 units. Restaurant, beach, snorkeling, windsurfing. MC, D, V. EP.*

$$–$$$ ⊡ **Estate Concordia.** The latest brainchild of Stanley Selengut, the developer of ☞ **Maho Bay Camps** and ☞ **Harmony,** these "environmentally correct" studios and duplexes are on 51 oceanfront acres of remote Salt Pond Bay. The spacious units are constructed of recycled materials, and energy for all the appliances (even the ice makers) is wind- and solar-generated. Next door are five eco-tents, upscale camping structures made of environmentally friendly materials and equipped with solar power and composting toilets. ⊠ *20–27 Estate Concordia, Coral Bay 00830,* ☎ *340/693–5855, 212/472–9453, or 800/392–9004;* ℻ *212/861–6210. 14 units. Kitchenettes, pool, beach. MC, D, V. EP.*

$–$$ ⊡ **Inn at Tamarind Court.** Within walking distance of Cruz Bay's shops and restaurants, this inn offers not only a convenient location but also affordable accommodations with a touch of charm. Though the rooms are plain, the courtyard is attractive: mature trees, plants, and umbrellas provide plenty of shade in which to enjoy your barbecue ribs in its open-air restaurant. Locals gather in the small bar, which seems particularly hoppin' on Friday night. ⊠ *Rte. 104 (Box 350), Cruz Bay 00831,* ☎ *340/776–6378 or 800/221–1637,* ℻ *340/776–6722. 20 units. Restaurant, air-conditioning. MC, V. CP.*

Campgrounds

$$ ⚠ **Maho Bay Camps.** Eight miles (13 km) from Cruz Bay, this eco-camp is a lush hillside community of rustic structures. The 16x16-ft tents (wooden platforms protected from the elements by canvas and screening) are linked by wooden stairs, ramps, and walkways—some of them elevated—so that you can trek around camp and down to the beach with-

out disturbing the terrain. The tents sleep as many as four people and have beds, tables and chairs, electric lamps, propane stoves, coolers, and kitchenware and cutlery. Though all the units are surrounded by tropical greenery, some have spectacular views of the Caribbean. The camp has the chummy feel of a retreat, making it very popular; book well in advance. ⊠ *Maho Bay (Box 310), Cruz Bay 00830,* ☎ *340/776–6240, 212/472–9453, or 800/392–9004;* FAX *212/861–6210. 113 tent cottages. Restaurant, beach, snorkeling, windsurfing. MC, D, V. EP.*

$–$$ 🔥 **Cinnamon Bay Campground.** Camping here puts you in the national park, surrounded by jungle and at the edge of Cinnamon Bay Beach. The unlockable, concrete "cottages" have electric lights, and the tents have propane lanterns; both come with propane camping stoves, coolers, cooking gear, and linens. Bring your own tent and supplies for the bare sites (a steal at $18 a night), which, like the cottages and tents, have a grill and a picnic table. The showers (on the cool side) and flush toilets, as well as a restaurant and a small store, are a trek down the hill. Hiking, snorkeling, swimming, and evening environmental or history programs are free and at your doorstep. Spaces for the winter months fill up far in advance (by as much as a year), so call for reservations. ⊠ *Rte. 20 (Box 720), Cruz Bay 00830-0720,* ☎ *340/776–6330 or 800/539– 9998,* FAX *340/776–6458. 44 tents, 38 cottages, 26 bare sites. Restaurant, hiking, beach, snorkeling, windsurfing. AE, MC, V. EP, FAP, MAP.*

Condominiums and Cottages

Most of the island's condos are just minutes from the hustle and bustle of Cruz Bay, but you'll find cottages in more far-flung locations.

$$$$ 🏠 **Estate Zootenvaal.** Set at the far reaches of the island, this small complex provides modest cottages right at the water or across the street. It's a quiet spot perfect for people who like to sit in the hammock and read. ⊠ *Hurricane Hole, Coral Bay 00830,* ☎ *340/776–6321. 3 units. Fans, kitchenettes, beach. No credit cards. EP.*

$$$–$$$$ 🏠 **Coconut Coast Villas.** Within walking distance of Cruz Bay's shops and restaurants, this small condominium complex sits so close to the water you'll fall asleep to the sound of waves. ⊠ *Turner Bay (Box 618), Cruz Bay 00831,* ☎ *340/693–9100 or 800/858–7989,* FAX *340/779– 4157. 9 units. Air-conditioning, kitchenettes, beach. MC, V. EP.*

$$$–$$$$ 🏠 **Park Isle Villas.** This company manages Battery Hill and Villa Caribe condominiums, small complexes close to Cruz Bay. Both are modern properties with great views. Some units have air-conditioning, others have ceiling fans. ⊠ *Genip St. (Box 1263), Cruz Bay 00831,* ☎ FAX *340/693–8261 or* ☎ *800/416–1205. 12 units. Air-conditioning, fans, kitchenettes. No credit cards. EP.*

$–$$$ 🏠 **Serendip.** This complex offers modest units on lush grounds with lovely views. You definitely need a rental car if you stay here, though; it's about 1 mi (1½ km) up a killer hill out of Cruz Bay. If air-conditioning is important to you, be sure to mention it when booking as some units only have ceiling fans. ⊠ *Enighed (Box 273), Cruz Bay 00831,* ☎ FAX *340/776–6646 or* ☎ *888/800–6445. 10 units. Air-conditioning, fans, kitchenettes. MC, V. EP.*

Villas

Tucked here and there between Cruz Bay and Coral Bay are about 350 villas (prices range from $ to $$$$). With pools and/or hot tubs, full kitchens, and living areas, they provide a home away from home. They're perfect for couples and extended groups of families or friends. You'll need a car since most are up in the hills (very few are at the beach). Villa managers usually pick you up at the dock, arrange for your rental car, and answer questions you have upon arrival as well as during your stay.

To rent a luxury villa contact one of the following rental agents: **Caribbean Villas and Resorts** (✉ Box 458, 00831, ☎ 340/776–6152 or 800/338–0987, FAX 340/779–4044), which handles condo rentals for Cruz Views, Cruz Bay Villas, and Pastory Estates; **Catered To, Inc.** (✉ Box 704, 00830, ☎ 340/776–6641, FAX 340/693–8191); **Destination St. John** (✉ Box 8306, 00831, ☎ FAX 340/779–4647 or ☎ 800/562–1901), which handles Lavender Hill condos; **Private Homes for Private Vacations** (✉ Mamey Peak, 00830, ☎ FAX 340/776–6876); **Star Villa** (✉ Box 599, 00830, ☎ 340/776–6704, FAX 340/776–6183); **Vacation Homes** (✉ Box 272, 00831, ☎ 340/776–6094, FAX 340/693–8455); **Vacation Vistas** (✉ Box 476, 00831, ☎ 340/776–6462); or **Windspree** (✉ 6-2-1A Estate Carolina, 00830, ☎ 340/693–5423, FAX 340/693–5623).

Dining

The cuisine on St. John seems to get better every year, with culinary school–trained chefs vying to see who can come up with the most imaginative dishes. There are restaurants to suit every taste and budget—from the elegant establishments at Caneel Bay Resort (where men may be required to wear a jacket at dinner) to the casual in-town eateries of Cruz Bay. For quick lunches, try the West Indian food stands in Cruz Bay Park and across from the post office. The cooks prepare fried chicken legs, *pates* (meat- and fish-filled pastries), and callaloo.

Bordeaux Mountain

CONTEMPORARY

$$$–$$$$ ✕ **Le Chateau Bordeaux.** Whether you eat on the terrace or in the air-
★   conditioned dining room, the view is terrific. This rustic restaurant is practically a tree house, albeit one that's made very elegant and romantic by wrought-iron chandeliers, lace tablecloths, and antiques. The innovative preparations appeal equally to eye and palate. You might start with the chicken crawfish gumbo. Segue into rosemary-perfumed rack of lamb with a honey-Dijon-nut crust in a shallot-and-port-wine sauce or salmon poached with white wine and capers and served on a bed of pasta. Don't miss the mussels, which are done to perfection. The comprehensive, moderately priced wine list is predictably strong on Bordeaux reds. ✉ *Rte. 10,* ☎ *340/776–6611. AE, MC, V.*

Coral Bay and Environs

AMERICAN

$ ✕ **Skinny Legs Bar and Restaurant.** Sailors who live aboard boats an-
★ chored just off shore and an eclectic coterie of residents gather for lunch and dinner at this funky spot. If owners Doug Sica and Mo Chabuz are around, take a gander at their gams; you'll see where the restaurant got its name. It's a great place for burgers, fish sandwiches, and watching whatever sports event is on cable TV. ✉ *Rte. 107 (near the Coral Bay dinghy dock),* ☎ *340/779–4982. No credit cards.*

CONTEMPORARY

$$$–$$$$ ✕ **Serafina Seaside Bistro.** This cozy restaurant on the water's edge has a menu that's interesting, indeed. Many dishes are unique twists on old favorites such as New York strip steak—here it's marinated in Guinness stout and coated with pink, green, black, and white peppercorns. Look for fresh fish in parchment paper, chicken quesadilla, and salad made with local produce. ✉ *Rte. 107,* ☎ *340/693–5630. AE, MC, V.*

ECLECTIC

$–$$$ ✕ **Shipwreck Landing.** Start with one of the house drinks, perhaps a fresh-squeezed concoction of lime, coconut, and rum, then move on to hearty taco salads, fried shrimp, teriyaki chicken, and conch fritters. The birds keep up a lively chatter in the bougainvillea that surrounds you at this open-air restaurant, and there's live music on Sunday night in season. ⊠ *Rte. 107,* ☎ *340/693–5640. MC, V.*

Cruz Bay

ASIAN

$$$–$$$$ ✕ **Asolare.** Contemporary Asian cuisine dominates the menu at this elegant open-air eatery in an old St. John house. Come early and relax over drinks while you enjoy the sunset over the harbor. Start with an appetizer, say, crab summer roll (a variation on the spring roll theme) with tamarind peanut sauce. Entrées include such delights as salmon rolled in Szechuan spices with a wasabi and passion-fruit cream sauce. If you still have room for dessert, try the chocolate pyramid, a luscious cake with homemade ice cream melting in the middle. ⊠ *Caneel Hill,* ☎ *340/779–4747. AE, MC, V. No lunch.*

CONTEMPORARY

$$$–$$$$ ✕ **Ellington's.** This peaceful, appealing spot extends out onto the second-story veranda of the ☞ **Gallows Point Suite Resort**'s central building. The outside tables are particularly quiet and romantic. The menu has chicken, fish, and steak dishes. You might start with the jumbo shrimp cooked in sweet coconut and served with mango sauce or the seafood chowder. Entrées include sea scallops with garlic and olive oil, three cheeses and paprika, swordfish scampi, filet mignon, and fresh lobster. For dessert, the banana–chocolate chip cake or the white-chocolate brownie are good bets. ⊠ *Gallows Point (5-min walk from Cruz Bay),* ☎ *340/693–8490. AE, MC, V. No lunch.*

$$–$$$$ ✕ **Lime Inn.** This open-air restaurant attracts mainland transplants who call St. John home as well as visitors who come for the congenial atmosphere and good food. There are shrimp and steak dishes and such specials as sautéed chicken with artichoke hearts in lemon sauce. On Wednesday night there's an all-you-can-eat shrimp feast, and prime rib is the specialty every Saturday night. ⊠ *Downtown, east of Chase Manhattan Bank,* ☎ *340/776–6425. AE, MC, V. Closed Sun.*

ECLECTIC

$$$–$$$$ ✕ **Paradiso.** This popular spot is on the upper level of the island's largest
★ shopping complex. The menu is a mix of everything from grilled beef fillet with red onion vinaigrette to almond-and-bran-encrusted grouper. You can dine indoors, in the comfort of air-conditioning, or outdoors on a small terrace that overlooks the street. ⊠ *Mongoose Junction shopping center,* ☎ *340/693–8899. AE, MC, V.*

$$–$$$$ ✕ **Fish Trap.** The rooms and terraces here all open to the breezes and buzz with a mix of locals and visitors. Chef Aaron Willis conjures up such tasty appetizers as conch fritters and Fish Trap chowder (a creamy soup of snapper, white wine, paprika, and secret spices). The menu also includes an interesting pasta of the day, steak and chicken dishes, and hamburgers. ⊠ *Downtown, next to Our Lady of Mount Carmel Church,* ☎ *340/693–9994. AE, D, MC, V. Closed Mon. No lunch.*

$$–$$$$ ✕ **Global Village Cuisine at Latitude 18.** Open to the breezes, this restaurant attracts an eclectic local crowd that tends to drop by for lunch at the bar. They aren't the only ones: tiny yellow birds peck at the wine glasses of sugar that are used as feeders. For lunch, there are hamburgers, sandwiches, and salads; for dinner, grilled local tuna, wahoo, or other fresh fish; sirloin steak; and daily pasta specials. ⊠ *Mongoose Junction shopping center,* ☎ *340/693–8677. AE, MC, V.*

$$–$$$$ ✕ **Pusser's.** Its dark paneling and brass rails make you feel as if you just stepped into an old British pub. But this feeling will only be fleeting: tropical temperatures, lazily rotating ceiling fans, and menu items with a Caribbean twist are reminders that this is Cruz Bay, not Cambridge. Step outside the bar to the covered deck, have a seat, take in

the view, and order up some terrific conch chowder or fish and chips. The rum Painkillers pack a punch. ⊠ *Wharfside Village,* ☎ *340/693–8489. AE, MC, V.*

$$–$$$$ ✕ **La Tapa.** Locals congregate here to feast on tapas and sip sangria. Although streetside tables let you watch the world go by, they're a little noisy; head inside for a quiet, cozy, bistro-like atmosphere. Owner Alex Ewald dishes up a changing menu of delicious soups, tapas as lighter fare or dinner, and yummy desserts. The buffalo mozzarella served with tomatoes and basil is made in her own tiny kitchen. ⊠ *Across from Scotia Bank on unnamed street that heads inland from ferry dock,* ☎ *340/693–7755. AE, MC, V. No lunch Sat. Closed Sun.*

$–$$ ✕ **Sun Dog Cafe.** You'll find an unusual assortment of dishes at this charming restaurant tucked into a courtyard in the upper reaches of the Mongoose Junction shopping center. Kudos to the white artichoke pizza with roasted garlic, artichoke hearts, mozzarella cheese, and capers. The Jamaican jerk chicken sub or the three-cheese quesadilla are also good choices. ⊠ *Mongoose Junction shopping center,* ☎ *340/693–8340. No credit cards.*

ITALIAN

$$–$$$ ✕ **Cafe Roma.** This casual, second-floor restaurant in the heart of Cruz Bay is *the* place for traditional Italian cuisine: lasagna, spaghetti and meatballs, chicken Parmesan. There are also a variety of excellent pizzas. Polenta cake with raspberry sauce is a dessert specialty. ⊠ *Downtown on Vesta Gade,* ☎ *340/776–6524. MC, V. No lunch.*

VEGETARIAN

$–$$ ✕ **Luscious Licks.** This funky hole-in-the-wall serves up mostly health food—all-natural fruit smoothies, veggie pita sandwiches, and homemade muffins. Try the barbecue tofu in sweet-and-sour sauce, the spinach and olive fettuccine, or the local's platter (a bit of this and that—really whatever owner Bonny Corbeil feels like whipping up on any given day). You can also get Ben & Jerry's ice cream and specialty coffees here. ⊠ *Across from V.I. National Park Visitor's Center,* ☎ *340/693–8400. No credit cards. Closed Sun. No dinner.*

Beaches

St. John is blessed with so many beaches, and all of them fall into the good, great, and don't-tell-anyone-else-about-this-place categories. The beaches along the north shore are all within the national park. Some are more developed than others—and all are crowded on weekends, holidays, and in high season—but by and large they're still pristine. Beaches along the south and eastern shores are still quiet and isolated.

Caneel Bay. Caneel Bay is actually a catch-all name for seven white-sand north-shore beaches, six of which can be reached only by water if you aren't a guest at the Caneel Bay Resort. (Access to beaches is a civil right in the USVI, but access to land that leads to the beaches is not.) The seventh, **Caneel Beach,** is open to the public and is easy to reach from the main entrance of the resort; just ask for directions at the gatehouse. Nonguests can also dine at the hotel's two restaurants and browse in its gift shop.

Cinnamon Bay. This long, sandy beach faces beautiful cays and abuts the national park campground. The facilities are open to the public and include cool showers, toilets, a commissary, and a restaurant. You can rent water-sports equipment here—a good thing, because there's excellent snorkeling off the point to the right; look for the big angelfish and large schools of purple triggerfish. Afternoons on Cinnamon Bay can be windy, so arrive early to beat the gusts. The Cinnamon Bay hiking trail begins across the road from the beach parking lot; the ruins of a sugar mill mark the trailhead. There are actually two paths here: a level nature trail (signs along it identify the flora) that loops through the woods and passes an old Danish cemetery, and a steep trail that starts where the road bends past the ruins and heads straight up to Centerline Road.

Hawksnest Beach. Sea-grape trees line this narrow beach, and there are rest rooms, cooking grills, and a covered shed for picnicking. It's the closest beach to town, so it's often crowded.

Lameshur Bay. This nifty beach is toward the end of a very long dirt road on the southeast coast. It offers solitude, good snorkeling, and a chance to spy on some pelicans. The ruins of the old plantation are a five-minute walk down the road past the beach.

Maho Bay. This popular beach is below the Maho Bay Camps—a wonderful hillside enclave of tents. The campground offers informal talks and slide and film presentations on nature, environmentally friendly living, and whatever else crosses the manager's mind. In spring, jazz and jungle harmonize during a music series in the outdoor pavilion.

Salt Pond Bay. If you're adventurous, this somewhat rocky beach on the scenic southeastern coast—next to Coral Bay and rugged Drunk Bay—is worth exploring. It's a short hike down a hill from the parking lot, and the only facilities are an outhouse and a few picnic tables scattered about. There are interesting tidal pools, and the snorkeling is good. Take special care to leave nothing valuable in your car; reports of thefts are common.

Trunk Bay. St. John's most-photographed beach is also the preferred spot for beginning snorkelers because of its underwater trail. (Cruise-ship passengers interested in snorkeling for a day come here, so if you're looking for seclusion, check cruise-ship schedules in *St. Thomas This Week* before heading here.) Crowded or not, this stunning beach is sure to please. There are changing rooms, a snack bar, picnic tables, a gift shop, phones, lockers, and snorkeling-equipment rentals.

Outdoor Activities and Sports

BOATING AND SAILING

For a speedy trip to offshore cays and remote beaches, a power boat is a necessity. More leisurely day sails to islands not far offshore or longer sails to points east are also possibilities. If you're boatless, book with one of the island's agents. Most day sails include lunch, beverages, and at least one stop to snorkel.

Connections (⊠ Cruz Bay, a block up from the ferry dock and cater-corner from Chase Manhattan Bank, ☎ 340/776–6922) pairs you up with the sailboat that suits you. Have simple tastes? The smiling staff can help. If luxury is more your style, they can book that, too. **Ocean Runner** (☎ 340/693–8809), on the waterfront in Cruz Bay, rents one-and two-engine boats for fast trips around the island's seas. **Proper Yachts** (☎ 340/776–6256) books day sails and longer charters on its fleet of luxury yachts that depart from Caneel Bay Resort.

FISHING

Well-kept charter boats head out to the north and south drops or troll along the inshore reefs. The captains usually provide bait, drinks, and lunch, but you'll need your hat and sunscreen. **American Yacht Harbor** (☎ 340/775–6454) offers sportfishing trips, and though they're in Red Hook on St. Thomas, they'll come and pick you up on St. John. The **Charterboat Center** (☎ 340/775–7990), in Red Hook on St. Thomas, also arranges fishing trips for folks in St. John. **Gone Ketchin'** (☎ 340/693–8657) in St. John arranges trips with old salt Wally

Leopold. **St. John World Class Anglers** (☎ 340/779–4281) offers light-tackle shore and offshore half- and full-day trips.

Although it's fun to go hiking with a Virgin Islands National Park guide, don't be afraid to strike out on your own. To find a hike that suits your ability, stop by the park's visitors center in Cruz Bay and pick up the free trail guide; it details points of interest, dangers, trail lengths, and estimated hiking times. Although the park staff recommends pants to protect against thorns and insects, most people hike in shorts because pants are too hot. Wear sturdy shoes or hiking boots even if you're hiking to the beach. Don't forget to bring water and insect repellant.

The **Virgin Islands National Park** (☎ 340/776–6201) maintains more than 20 trails on the north and south shores and offers guided hikes along popular routes. A full-day trip to Reef Bay is a must; it's an easy hike through lush and dry forest, past the ruins of an old plantation, and to a sugar factory adjacent to the beach. Take the public Vitran bus to the trailhead where you'll meet a ranger who will serve as your guide. The park provides a boat ride back to Cruz Bay for $14.50 to save you the walk back up the mountain. The schedule changes from season to season; call for times and reservations, which are essential.

Clip-clop along the island's byways for a slower-pace tour of St. John. **Carolina Corral** (☎ 340/693–5778) offers horseback, donkey-back, and donkey-cart rides as well as riding lessons. Rates start at $45 for a 1½-hour ride.

While just about every beach has nice snorkeling—Trunk Bay, Cinnamon Bay and Waterlemon Cay at Leinster Bay get the most kudos—you'll need a boat to head out to the more remote snorkeling locations and the best scuba spots. Sign on with any of the island's water-sports operators. Their boats will take you to hot spots between St. John and St. Thomas, including the tunnels at **Thatch Cay,** the ledges at **Congo Cay,** and the wreck of the **General Rogers.** (☞ Scuba Diving and Snorkeling *in* St. Thomas, *above.*) Dive off St. John at **Stephens Cay,** a short boat ride out of Cruz Bay, where fish swim around the reefs as you float downward. At **Devers Bay,** on St. John's south shore, fish dart about in colorful schools.

Count on paying $55 for a one-tank dive and $75 for a two-tank dive. Rates include equipment and a tour. **Cruz Bay Watersports** (☎ 340/776–6234) has three locations. You'll find them in Cruz Bay, at the Westin Resort, and in the Palm Plaza Shopping Center. Owners Marcus and Patty Johnston offer regular reef, wreck, and night dives and USVI and BVI snorkel tours. **Low Key Watersports** (☎ 340/693–8999), at Wharfside Village, offers PADI certification and resort courses, one- and two-tank dives, and specialty courses. **St. John Watersports** (☎ 340/776–6256) is a five-star PADI dive center in the Mongoose Junction shopping center.

Poke around crystal bays and explore undersea life from a sea kayak. **Arawak Expeditions'** (☎ 340/693–8312 or 800/238–8687) professional guides use traditional kayaks to ply coastal waters. Prices start at $40 for a half-day trip.

With hot weather the norm, tennis players take to the courts in the morning or late afternoon. The **Westin Resort, St. John** (⌂ Rte. 104, ☎ 340/

693–8000) has six lighted courts. Nonguests are welcome to play here for a fee of $15 an hour. The **public courts,** near the fire station in Cruz Bay, are lighted until 10 PM and are available on a first-come, first-served basis.

WINDSURFING

Steady breezes and expert instruction make learning to windsurf a snap. Try **Cinnamon Bay Campground** (✉ Rte. 20, ☏ 340/776–6330), where rentals are available for $12–$15 per hour. Lessons are available right at the waterfront; just look for the Windsurfers stacked up on the beach. The cost for a 1-hour lesson is about $40.

Shopping

Areas and Malls

You'll find luxury items and handicrafts on St. John. Most shops carry a little of this and a bit of that, so it pays to poke around. The Cruz Bay shopping district runs from **Wharfside Village,** just around the corner from the ferry dock, through the streets of town to North Shore Road and **Mongoose Junction,** an inviting shopping center with stonework walls. (Its name is a holdover from a time when those furry island creatures gathered at a garbage bin that was here.) Steps connect the two sections of the center, which has unique, upscale shops. Out on Route 104, stop in at **Palm Plaza** to explore its handful of gift and crafts shops. At the island's other end, you'll find a few stores—selling clothes, jewelry, and artwork—here and there from the village of **Coral Bay** to the small complex at **Shipwreck Landing.**

Specialty Items

ART

Coconut Coast Studios. This waterside shop, a five-minute walk from Cruz Bay, showcases the work of Elaine Estern. She specializes in undersea scenes. ✉ *Frank Bay,* ☏ *340/776–6944.*

Bajo el Sol. A cooperative gallery, Bajo el Sol features Aimee Trayser's expressionistic Caribbean scenes, Les Anderson's island scenes in oil, Kat Sowa's watercolors, and works by a handful of other artists. ✉ *Mongoose Junction,* ☏ *340/693–7070.*

BOOKS

MAPes MONDe. Here you'll find a huge selection of books on the Caribbean, including the exquisite-looking publications that are the hallmark of Virgin Islands publisher MAPes MONDe. You'll also find many reproductions of old maps as well as contemporary prints and greeting cards. ✉ *Mongoose Junction,* ☏ *340/779–4545.*

National Park Headquarters. The headquarters sells several good histories of St. John, including *St. John Back Time,* by Ruth Hull Low and Rafael Lito Valls, and for linguists, Valls's *What a Pistarckle!*—an explanation of the colloquialisms that make up the local version of English (*pistarckle* is a Dutch Creole word that means "noise" or "din," which pretty much sums up the language here). ✉ *At the Creek,* ☏ *340/776–6201.*

St. John Books. This is the place to come for current newspapers and magazines and a variety of books, including those by local authors. ✉ *Wharfside Village,* ☏ *340/779–4260.*

CLOTHES

Big Planet Adventure Outfitters. You knew when you arrived that some place on St. John would sell Birkenstock sandals. Well, this outdoor-clothing store is where you'll find them along with colorful and durable cotton clothing and accessories by Patagonia, the North Face, Sierra Designs, and others. The adjacent **Little Planet** sells children's clothes, often made from such unlikely materials as recycled plastic bottles. ⊠ *Mongoose Junction,* ☎ *340/776–6638.*

Bougainvillea Boutique. If you want to look like you stepped out of the pages of the resort-wear spread in an upscale travel magazine, try this store. Owner Susan Stair carries *very* chic men's and women's resort wear, straw hats, leather handbags, and fine gift items. ⊠ *Mongoose Junction,* ☎ *340/693–7190.*

The Clothing Studio. Several talented artists hand-paint original designs on clothing for all members of the family. You'll find T-shirts, beach cover-ups, pants, shorts, and even bathing suits with beautiful hand-painted creations. ⊠ *Mongoose Junction,* ☎ *340/776–6585.*

Pusser's Company Store. Pusser's stores originated in the BVI, and this branch carries all the items these stores are famous for: nautical memorabilia, casual sportswear, books, and, of course, famous Pusser's Rum. ⊠ *Wharfside Village, Cruz Bay,* ☎ *340/693–8489.*

St. John Editions. Shop here for nifty cotton shifts that go from beach to dinner with a change of shoes and accessories. Owner Ann Soper also carries nifty straw hats and inexpensive jewelry. ⊠ *North Shore Rd., Cruz Bay,* ☎ *340/693–8444.*

FOODSTUFFS

If you're renting a villa, condo, or cottage and doing your own cooking, there are several good places to shop for food; just be aware that prices are much higher than those at home. **Starfish Market** (☎ 340/779–4949) is in the Boulon Center, **Marina Market** (☎ 340/779–4401) is on Route 104, and **Tropicale** (☎ 340/693–7474) is also on Route 104 in Palm Plaza.

GIFTS

Bamboula. Owner Jo Sterling travels the Caribbean and the world to find unusual housewares, rugs, bedspreads, accessories, shoes, and men's and women's clothes for this multicultural boutique. ⊠ *Mongoose Junction,* ☎ *340/693–8699.*

The Canvas Factory. If you're a true shopper who needs an extra bag to carry all your treasures home, this store offers every kind of tote and carrier imaginable—from simple bags to suitcases with numerous zippered compartments—all made of canvas, naturally. It also sells great canvas hats. ⊠ *Mongoose Junction,* ☎ *340/776–6196.*

Donald Schnell Pottery. In addition to pottery, this place sells unique hand-blown glass, wind chimes, kaleidoscopes, fanciful water fountains, and more. Your purchases can be shipped worldwide. ⊠ *Mongoose Junction,* ☎ *340/776–6420.*

Fabric Mill. Shop here for handmade dolls, place mats, napkins, and batik wraps. Or take home a bolt of tropical brights from the upholstery-fabric selection. ⊠ *Mongoose Junction,* ☎ *340/776–6194.*

Isola. An eclectic array of handicrafts and clothing from around the world fills this store. You'll also find pottery and jewelry by local artists, CDs of Caribbean music, and whatever else owner Lorena Sitka has picked up in her travels. ⊠ *Wharfside Village,* ☎ *340/779–4212.*

Pink Papaya. This store is the home of longtime Virgin Islands resident M. L. Etre's well-known artwork plus a huge collection of one-of-a-kind gift items, including bright tablecloths, unusual trays, dinnerware, and unique tropical jewelry. ⊠ *Lemon Tree Mall, Cruz Bay,* ☎ *340/693–8535.*

JEWELRY

Blue Carib Gems. Here you'll find custom-made jewelry, loose gemstones, and old coins as well as a small art gallery. ⊠ *Wharfside Village,* ☎ *340/693–8299.*

Caravan Gallery. Owner Radha Speer creates much of the unusual jewelry you'll find here. And the more you look, the more you see—folk art, tribal art, and masks for sale cover the walls and tables, making this a great place to browse. ⊠ *Mongoose Junction,* ☎ *340/779–4566.*
Colombian Emeralds (⊠ Mongoose Junction, ☎ 340/776–6007) has high-quality emeralds, and also sells rubies, diamonds, and other jewels set in attractive gold and silver settings. This is also the only place on St. John that sells the latest perfumes. You can find still more jewels at Columbian Emeralds' sister store, **Jeweler's Warehouse** (⊠ Wharfside Village, ☎ 340/693–7490).
Free Bird Creations. Head here for the unique handcrafted jewelry—earrings, bracelets, pendants, chains—as well as the good selection of waterproof watches great for your excursions to the beach. ⊠ *Wharfside Village,* ☎ *340/693–8625.*
R&I Patton Goldsmiths. Rudy and Irene Patton design most of the unique silver and gold jewelry in this shop. The rest comes from various jeweler friends of theirs. Sea fans (those large, lacy plants that sway with the ocean's currents) in filigreed silver, lapis set in long drops of gold, starfish and hibiscus pendants in silver or gold, and gold sand dollar–shape charms and earrings are tempting choices. ⊠ *Mongoose Junction,* ☎ *340/776–6548.*

Nightlife

St. John isn't the place to go for glitter and all-night partying. Still, after-hours Cruz Bay can be a lively little village in which to dine, drink, dance, chat, or flirt. Notices posted on the bulletin board outside the **Connections** telephone center—up the street from the ferry dock in Cruz Bay—or listings in the island's two small newspapers (the *St. John Times* and *Tradewinds*) will keep you apprised of special events, comedy nights, movies, and the like.

After a sunset drink at **Ellington's** (⊠ Gallows Point Suite Resort, ☎ 340/693–8490), up the hill from Cruz Bay, you can stroll here and there in town (much is clustered around the small waterfront park). Many of the young people from the U.S. mainland who live and work on St. John will be out sipping and socializing, too.

You'll find friendly hubbub at the rough-and-ready **Backyard** (⊠ Cruz Bay, ☎ 340/693–8886), which is *the* place for sports-watching as well as grooving to Bonnie Raitt, et al. Outside of town, **Caneel Bay Resort** (⊠ Rte. 20, ☎ 340/776–6111) usually has entertainment (generally, of the quiet calypso variety) several nights a week in season. There's calypso and reggae on Wednesday and Friday at **Fred's** (⊠ Cruz Bay, ☎ 340/776–6363). The **Inn at Tamarind Court** (⊠ Rte. 104, ☎ 340/776–6378) serves up country rock on Friday and reggae on Saturday. At Coral Bay, on the far side of the island, check out the action at **Skinny Legs Bar and Restaurant** (⊠ Rte. 107, ☎ 340/779–4982). Young folks like to gather at **Woody's** (⊠ Cruz Bay, ☎ 340/779–4625). Its sidewalk tables provide a close-up view of Cruz Bay's action.

Exploring St. John

St. John is an easy place to explore. One road runs along the north shore, another across the center of the mountains. There are a few roads that branch off here and there, but it's hard to get lost. Pick up a map at the visitor center before you start out, and you'll have no problems. Few residents remember the route numbers, so have your map in hand if you stop to ask for directions. Bring along a swimsuit for stops at some of the most beautiful beaches in the world. You can spend all day or just a couple of hours exploring, but be advised that the roads are narrow and wind up and down steep hills, so don't expect to get anywhere in a hurry. There are lunch spots at Cinnamon Bay and in Coral Bay, or you can do what the locals do—picnic. The grocery stores in Cruz Bay sell Styrofoam coolers just for this purpose.

If you plan to do a lot of touring, renting a car will be cheaper and will give you much more freedom than relying on taxis, which are re-luctant to go anywhere until they have a full load of passengers. Al-though you may be tempted by an open-air Suzuki or Jeep, a conventional car can get you just about everywhere on the paved roads, and you'll be able to lock up your valuables. You may be able to share a van or open-air vehicle (called a safari bus) with other passengers on a tour of scenic mountain trails, secret coves, and eerie bush-covered ruins.

Numbers in the margin correspond to points of interest on the St. John map.

SIGHTS TO SEE

❼ Annaberg Plantation. In the 18th century, sugar plantations dotted the steep hills of the USVI. Slaves and free Danes and Dutchmen toiled to harvest the cane that was used to create sugar, molasses, and rum for export. Built in the 1780s, the partially restored plantation at Leinster Bay was once an important sugar mill. Though there are no official visiting hours, the National Park Service has regular tours, and some well-informed taxi drivers will show you around. Occasionally you'll find a living-history demonstration—someone making johnnycake or weaving baskets. For information on tours and cultural demonstrations, contact the St. John National Park Service Visitor's Center. ⊠ *Leinster Bay Rd.,* ☎ *340/776–6201.* ☜ *$4.*

❻ Bordeaux Mountain. St. John's highest peak rises to 1,277 ft. Center-line Road passes near enough to the top to offer breathtaking views. Drive nearly to the end of the dirt road for spectacular views at Pic-ture Point and for the trailhead of the hike downhill to Lameshur. Get a trail map from the park service before you start. ⊠ *Rte. 70.*

❹ Catherineberg Ruins. At this fine example of an 18th-century sugar and rum factory there's a storage vault beneath the windmill. Across the road, look for the round mill, which was later used to hold water. In the 1733 slave revolt, Catherineberg served as headquarters for Amina warriors, a tribe of Africans captured into slavery. ⊠ *Rte. 70.*

❽ Coral Bay. This laid-back community at the island's dry, eastern end is named for its shape rather than for its underwater life—the word *coral* comes from *krawl,* Danish for "corral." It's a small, quiet, neigh-borhoody settlement; a place to get away from it all. You'll need a Jeep if you plan to stay at this end of the island, as some of the rental houses are up unpaved roads that wind around the mountain. If you come just for lunch, a regular car will be fine.

❶ Cruz Bay. St. John's main town may be compact (it consists only of several blocks), but it's definitely a hub: the ferries from St. Thomas and the BVI pull in here, and it's where you can get a taxis or rent a car to travel around the island. There are plenty of shops in which to browse, a number of watering holes where you can stop for a breather, many restaurants, and a grassy square with benches where you can sit back and take everything in. Look for the current edition of the handy, amusing "St. John Map" featuring Max the Mongoose.

To pick up a handy guide to St. John's hiking trails, see various large maps of the island, and find out about current park service programs, including guided walks and cultural demonstrations, stop by the **V.I. National Park Visitor's Center.** ⊠ *In an area known as the Creek, near Cruz Bay bulkhead and baseball field, Cruz Bay, 00831,* ☎ *340/776–6201.* ⊞ *Free.* ⊙ *Daily 8–4:30.*

② **Elaine Ione Sprauve Library and Museum.** On the hill just above Cruz Bay is the **Enighed Estate Great House,** built in 1757. *Enighed* is the Danish word for "concord" (unity or peace). The great house and its outbuildings (a sugar-production factory and horse-driven mill) were destroyed by fire and hurricanes, and the house sat in ruins until 1982. Today it houses a library and museum, and contains a dusty collection of Indian pottery and colonial artifacts. ⊠ *Rte. 104 (make a right past Texaco station),* ☎ *340/776–6359.* ⊞ *Free.* ⊙ *Weekdays 9–5.*

③ **Peace Hill.** It's worth stopping at this spot just past the Hawksnest Bay overlook for great views of St. John, St. Thomas, and the BVI. The flat promontory features an old sugar mill. ⊠ *Off North Shore Rd.*

⑤ **Reef Bay Trail.** Although this is one of the most interesting hikes on St. John, unless you are a rugged individualist who wants a physical challenge (and that describes a lot of people who stay on St. John), you'll probably get the most out of the trip if you join a hike led by a park service ranger, who can identify the trees and plants on the hike down, fill you in on the history of the Reef Bay Plantation, and tell you about the petroglyphs on the rocks at the bottom of the trail. If you're without a car, take the public Vitran bus from the Cruz Bay ferry dock. If you're on a park service hike, take the bus to the trailhead, where you'll meet a ranger for the hike downhill. A boat will take you to Cruz Bay ($14.50), saving you the uphill return climb.

The **Reef Bay Plantation,** according to architectural historian Frederik C. Gjessing, is the most architecturally ambitious structure of its kind on St. John. Though gutted, the great house is largely intact, and its classical beauty is still visible. It sits on a side trail to the north off the trail to Lameshur Bay, and the sugar works are near the beach. Reef Bay was the last working plantation on St. John when it stopped production in 1920. ⊠ *Rte. 10 between Cruz Bay and Coral Bay; parking area is on the left, trail is to the right.*

U.S. VIRGIN ISLANDS A TO Z

Arriving and Departing
BY AIRPLANE

One advantage to visiting the USVI is the abundance of nonstop and connecting flights that can have you at the beach in three to four hours from most eastern United States departures. You may fly direct to **St. Thomas's Cyril E. King Airport** (☎ 340/774–5100) on **American** (☎ 340/774–6464 or 340/778–1140) from Miami and New York, **Delta** (☎ 340/777–4177) from Atlanta, and **US Airways** (☎ 340/774–7885) from Philadelphia. Another option is to pick up a local flight from San Juan on **American Eagle** (☎ 340/776–2560 or 340/778–2000).

From the Airport: Most hotels on **St. Thomas** don't have airport shuttles, but taxi vans at the airport are plentiful. From the airport, fees (set by the VI Taxi Commission) for two or more people sharing a cab are: $12 to the Ritz-Carlton, $9 to Renaissance Grand Beach Resort, $7.50 to Marriott Frenchman's Reef, and $5 to Bluebeard Castle. Expect to be charged 50¢ per bag and to pay a higher fee if you're riding alone. During rush hour the trip to East End resorts can take up to 40 minutes, but ½ hour is typical. Driving time from the airport to

Charlotte Amalie is 15 minutes. Getting from the airport to **St. Croix** hotels by taxi costs about $10–$13.

Visitors to **St. John** fly into St. Thomas and take a taxi to either Charlotte Amalie or Red Hook, where they catch a ferry to Cruz Bay, St. John. The ferry from Charlotte Amalie makes the 45-minute trip several times a day and costs $7 a person. From Red Hook, the ferry leaves on the hour; the 20-minute trip costs $3 a person.

BY BOAT

Virtually every type of ship and major cruise line calls at St. Thomas; only a few call at St. Croix. Many of the ships that call at St. Thomas also call in St. John or offer an excursion to that island.

From the Docks: On **St. Thomas** taxi vans line up along Havensight and Crown Bay docks when a cruise ship pulls in. If you booked a shore tour, the operator will lead you to a designated vehicle. Otherwise, there are plenty of air-conditioned vans and open-air safari buses to take you to Charlotte Amalie or the beach. The cab fare from Havensight to Charlotte Amalie is $2.50 per person; you can, however, walk to town in about 30 minutes (1½ mi/2½ km) along the beautiful waterfront. From Crown Bay to town the taxi fare is $3 per person whether you travel solo or you share; it's a 1-mi (1½-km) walk, but the route passes along a busy highway. Transportation from Havensight to Magens Bay for swimming is $6.50 per person ($4 if you share).

In **St. Croix,** taxis greet arriving cruise ships at the Frederiksted pier. All the shops are just a short walk away, and you can swim off the beach in Frederiksted. Most ship passengers visit Christiansted on a tour. A taxi will cost $20 for one to two people. Some cruise ships stop at **St. John** to let passengers disembark for a day. The main town of Cruz Bay is near the ship terminal. If you want to swim, the famous Trunk Bay is a $7.50 taxi ride (for two) from town.

Electricity

The USVI use the same current as the U.S. mainland—110 volts. Since power fluctuations occasionally occur, bring a heavy-duty surge protector (available at hardware stores) if you plan to use your computer.

Emergencies

GENERAL

Ambulance, Fire, and Police: ☎ 911. **Air Ambulance: Air Ambulance Network** (☎ 800/327–1966) serves the USVI area from Florida. **Bohlke International Airways** (☎ 340/778–9177) serves both St. Thomas and St. Croix, though it's based on St. Croix. **Medical Air Services** (☎ 340/777–8580 or 800/643–9023) has its Caribbean headquarters in St. Thomas. If you're on St. John, you'll have to go by ambulance boat to St. Thomas and by ambulance to St. Thomas airport.

Coast Guard: For emergencies, call the **Marine Safety Detachment** (☎ 340/776–3497 for St. Thomas and St. John or 340/772–5557 for St. Croix) from 7 to 3:30 weekdays. If there's no answer at either number, call the **Rescue Coordination Center** (☎ 787/729–6800, ext. 140) in San Juan, Puerto Rico; it's open 24 hours a day. **Scuba-Diving Accidents:** The only **hyperbaric chamber** (☎ 340/776–2686) in the territory is at St. Thomas's Roy L. Schneider Hospital & Community Health Center (☞ *below*).

HOSPITALS

St. Thomas: The emergency room of the **Roy L. Schneider Hospital & Community Health Center** (✉ Sugar Estate, 1 mi/1½ km east of Charlotte Amalie, ☎ 340/776–8311) is open 24 hours a day.

St. Croix: Outside Christiansted there's the **Gov. Juan F. Luis Hospital and Health Center** (⌖ 6 Diamond Ruby, north of Sunny Isle Shopping Center on Rte. 79, ☎ 340/778–6311). You can also try the **Frederiksted Health Center** (⌖ 516 Strand St., ☎ 340/772–1992).

St. John: For medical emergencies, visit the **Myrah Keating Smith Community Health Center** (⌖ Rte. 10, about 7 min east of Cruz Bay, ☎ 340/693–8900).

PHARMACIES

St. Thomas: Havensight Pharmacy (☎ 340/776–1235), in the Havensight Mall, is open daily 9–9. **Kmart** (☎ 340/777–3854) operates a pharmacy inside the Tutu Park Mall; it's open 8 AM–9 PM. **Sunrise Pharmacy** (☎ 340/775–6600), in Red Hook, is open daily 9–7.

St. Croix: Although most drugstores are open daily 8–8, off-season hours may vary; call ahead to confirm times. **Kmart** (☎ 340/692–2622) operates a pharmacy at its Sunshine Mall store. **People's Drug Store, Inc.** has two branches: on the Christiansted Wharf (☎ 340/778–7355) and at the Sunny Isle Shopping Center (☎ 340/778–5537), just a few miles west of Christiansted on Route 70. In Frederiksted, try **D&D Apothecary Hall** (⌖ 501 Queen St., ☎ 340/772–1890).

St. John: The **St. John Drug Center** (☎ 340/776–6353) is in the Boulon shopping center, up Centerline Road in Cruz Bay. It's open Monday–Saturday 9–5.

Festivals and Seasonal Events

ST. THOMAS

January–April sees **Classics In The Garden** (☎ 340/775–1405), a chamber music series at Tillett Gardens, where young musicians from all over the world perform. Tillett Gardens also hosts annual **Arts Alive** (☎ 340/775–1405) festivals in November, March, and August. In April, St. Thomas Yacht Club hosts the **Rolex Cup Regatta** (☎ 340/775–6320), which is part of the three race Caribbean Ocean Racing Triangle (CORT) that pulls in yachties and their pals from all over. **Carnival** (☎ 340/776–3112) is a weeklong, major-league blowout of parades, parties, and island-wide events. The dates change from year to year, following the Easter calendar. Marlin mania begins in May and so do the **sportfishing tournaments.** There are also several locally sponsored fishing events throughout summer and fall.

The St. Thomas Gamefishing Club hosts its **July Open Tournament** (☎ 340/775–9144) over the Fourth of July weekend. There are categories for serious marlin anglers, just-for-fun fishermen, and even kids who want to try their luck from docks and rocks. The mid-July celebration of **Bastille Day**—which commemorates the French Revolution—is marked by a minicarnival in Frenchtown. August's **Texas Society Chili Cook-Off** (☎ 340/776–3595) is a party on Sapphire Beach—you'll find country music performances, dancing, games, and, of course, chili tasting. During full moon in August, anglers compete for big-money prizes in the **USVI Open/Atlantic Blue Marlin Tournament** (☎ 340/775–9500). In November the **St. Thomas–St. John Agricultural Fair** (☎ 340/693–1080) showcases fresh produce, home-grown herbs, and local dishes, such as callaloo, salt fish and dumplings, and fresh fish simmered with green banana, pumpkin, and potato-like tannia.

ST. CROIX

The island celebrates Carnival with its **Crucian Christmas Festival,** which starts in late December. After weeks of beauty pageants, food fairs, and concerts, the festival wraps up with a parade in early January. During the **St. Croix Blues and Heritage Festival** (☎ 800/260–

2603), in late January, blues artists from the national and local scene play at various locations. In February and March, the **St. Croix Landmarks Society House Tours** (☎ 340/772–0598) visit some of the island's most exclusive or historic homes, and give you a chance to peek inside places you can usually view only from the road.

Serious swimmers should join island residents in early November for the **Coral Reef Swim** (☎ 340/773–2100). Participants swim about 5 mi (8 km) from Buck Island to Christiansted. The event also includes an awards dinner. **The Mumm's Cup Regatta** (☎ 340/773–9531) sets sail on Veteran's Day weekend at the St. Croix Yacht Club. Sailors converge on Teague Bay for three days of sailing and parties.

ST. JOHN

The island dishes up its own version of Carnival with the **July 4th Festival.** Weeks of festivities—including beauty pageants and a food fair—culminate in a parade through the streets of Cruz Bay on July 4.

On the two days after Thanksgiving, an eclectic group of sailors takes to the waters of Coral Bay for the annual **Coral Bay Thanksgiving Regatta.** Some boats are "live-aboards," whose owners only pull up anchor for this one event; other boats belong to Sunday sailors; and a very few are owned by hot-shot racers. If you'd like to crew, stop by Skinny Legs Bar and Restaurant (☞ Dining *in* St. John, *above*).

Getting Around

AIRPLANES

American Eagle (☞ Arriving and Departing, *above*) offers frequent flights daily from St. Thomas to St. Croix's Henry E. Rohlsen Airport (☎ 340/778–0589). **Seaborne Seaplane** (☎ 340/777–4491) also flies between St. Thomas and St. Croix several times daily as well as to Beef Island Airport on Tortola, British Virgin Islands. **LIAT** (☎ 340/774–2313) has service from St. Thomas and St. Croix to Caribbean islands to the south.

BUSES

St. Thomas: The island's 20 deluxe, mainland-size buses make public transportation a very comfortable—though slow—way to get from east and west to Charlotte Amalie and back (service to the north is limited). Buses run about every 30 minutes from stops that are clearly marked with VITRAN signs. Fares are $1 between outlying areas and town and 75¢ in town.

St. Croix: Privately owned **taxi vans** crisscross St. Croix regularly, providing reliable service between Frederiksted and Christiansted along Route 70. This inexpensive ($1.50 one-way) mode of transportation is favored by locals, and though the many stops on the 20-mi (32-km) drive between the two main towns make the ride slow, it's never dull. The public **Vitran** buses aren't the quickest way to get around the island, but they're comfortable and affordable. The fare is $1 between Christiansted to Frederiksted or to places in between.

St. John: Modern **Vitran** buses run from the Cruz Bay ferry dock through Coral Bay to the far eastern end of the island at Salt Pond, making numerous stops in between. The fare is $1 to any point.

CAR RENTALS

Any U.S. driver's license is good for 90 days on the USVI, as are valid driver's licenses from other countries; the minimum age for drivers is 18, although many agencies won't rent to anyone under the age of 25.

Driving is on the left side of the road (although your steering wheel will be on the left side of the car). The law requires *everyone* in a car to wear seat belts; many of the roads are narrow, and the islands are dotted with hills, so there's ample reason to put safety first. Even at a sedate speed of 20 mph, driving can be an adventure—for example, you may find yourself in a stick-shift Jeep slogging behind a slow tourist-packed safari bus at a steep hairpin turn. Give a little beep at blind turns. Note that the general speed limit on these islands is only 25 mph–35 mph, which will seem fast enough for you on most roads. If you don't think you'll need to lock up your valuables, a Jeep or open-air Suzuki with four-wheel-drive will make it easier to navigate pot-holed dirt side roads and to get up slick hills when it rains. All main roads are paved. Gas is pricey: about $1.50 per gallon on St. Thomas, $1.10 on St. Croix, and $1.70 on St. John.

St. Thomas. Traffic can get pretty bad, especially in Charlotte Amalie at rush hour (7 AM–9 AM and 4:30 PM–6 PM). Cars often line up bumper to bumper along the waterfront. If you need to get from an East End resort to the airport during these times, find the alternate route (starting from the East End, Route 38 to 42 to 40 to 33) that goes up the mountain and then drops you back onto Veteran's Highway. If you plan to explore by car, be sure to pick up the "2000 Road Map St. Thomas–St. John" that includes the route numbers *and* the names of the roads that are used by locals. It's available anywhere you find maps and guidebooks.

You can rent a car from **ABC Rentals** (☎ 340/776–1222 or 800/524–2080), **Anchorage E-Z Car** (☎ 340/775–6255), **Avis** (☎ 340/774–1468 or 800/331–1084), **Budget** (☎ 340/776–5774 or 800/626–4516), **Cowpet Rent-a-Car** (☎ 340/775–7376), **Dependable Car Rental** (☎ 340/774–2253 or 800/522–3076), **Discount** (☎ 340/776–4858), or **Hertz** (☎ 340/774–1879 or 800/654–3131).

St. Croix. Unlike St. Thomas and St. John, where narrow roads wind through hillsides, St. Croix is relatively flat, and it even has a four-lane highway. The speed limit on the Melvin H. Evans Highway is 55 mph and ranges from 35 mph to 40 mph elsewhere. Roads are often unmarked, so be patient; sometimes, getting lost is half the fun.

Occasionally, all the rental companies run out of cars at once. To avoid disappointment, make your reservations early. Call **Atlas** (☎ 340/773–2886 or 800/426–6009), **Avis** (☎ 340/778–9355 or 800/331–1084), **Budget** (☎ 340/778–9636 or 888/227–3359), **Caribbean Jeep & Car** (☎ 340/773–7227), **Midwest** (☎ 340/772–0438), **Olympic** (☎ 340/773–2208 or 888/878–4227), or **Thrifty** (☎ 340/773–7200 or 800/367–2277).

St. John. Use caution on St. John. The terrain is very hilly, the roads are winding, and the blind curves numerous. You may suddenly come upon a huge safari bus careening around a corner, or a couple of hikers strolling along the side of the road. Major roads are well paved, but once you get off a specific route, dirt roads filled with potholes are common. For such driving, a four-wheel-drive vehicle is your best bet.

At the height of the winter season, it may be tough to find a car; reserve well in advance to ensure you get the vehicle of your choice. Call **Avis** (☎ 340/776–6374 or 800/331–1084), **Best** (☎ 340/693–8177), **Cool Breeze** (☎ 340/776–6588), **Delbert Hill Taxi Rental Service** (☎ 340/776–6637), **Denzil Clyne** (☎ 340/776–6715), **O'Connor Jeep** (☎ 340/776–6343), **St. John Car Rental** (☎ 340/776–6103), or **Spencer's Jeep** (☎ 340/693–8784 or 888/776–6628).

FERRIES

Ferries are a great way to travel around the islands; there's service between St. Thomas and St. John and their neighbors, the BVI. A hydrofoil also runs the 40-mi (65-km) route between St. Thomas and St. Croix. There's something special about spending a day on St. John and then joining your fellow passengers—a mix of tourists, local families, and restaurant staffers en route to work—for a peaceful, sundown ride back to St. Thomas.

Ferries to Cruz Bay, St. John, leave St. Thomas from either the Charlotte Amalie waterfront west of the U.S. Coast Guard dock or from Red Hook. From Charlotte Amalie, ferries depart at 9 and 11 AM and 1, 3, 4, and 5:30 PM. To Charlotte Amalie from Cruz Bay, they leave at 7:15, 9:15, and 11:15 AM and at 1:15, 2:15, and 3:45 PM. The one-way fare for the 45-minute ride is $7 for adults, $3 for children. From Red Hook, the ferries to Cruz Bay leave at 6:30 and 7:30 AM. Starting at 8 AM, they leave hourly until midnight. Returning from Cruz Bay, they leave hourly starting at 6 AM until 11 PM. The 15- to 20-minute ferry ride is $3 one-way for adults, $1 for children under 12.

Reefer (☎ 340/776–8500, ext. 445) is the name of both brightly colored 26-passenger skiffs that run between the Charlotte Amalie waterfront and Marriott Frenchman's Reef hotel daily every hour from 9 to 4, returning from the Reef from 9:30 until 4:30. It's a good way to beat the traffic (and is about the same price as a taxi) to Morning Star Beach, which adjoins the Reef. And you get a great view of the harbor as you bob along in the shadow of the giant cruise ships anchored in the harbor. The captain of the *Reefer* may also be persuaded to drop you at Yacht Haven, but check first. The fare is $4 one-way, and the trip takes about 15 minutes.

The hydrofoil *Katrun II* (☎ 340/776–7417) leaves Friday through Monday from Charlotte Amalie in St. Thomas at 7:15 AM and 3:15 PM and from Gallows Bay outside Christiansted, St. Croix, at 9:15 AM and 5 PM. The 1¼-hour trip costs $45 one-way and $90 round-trip.

There's daily service between either Charlotte Amalie or Red Hook on St. Thomas, and West End or Road Town, Tortola, BVI, by either **Smiths Ferry** (☎ 340/775–7292) or **Native Son, Inc.** (☎ 340/774–8685), and to Virgin Gorda, BVI, by Smiths Ferry. The times and days the ferries run change, so it's best to call for schedules once you're in the islands. The fare is $22 one-way or $40 round-trip, and the trip from Charlotte Amalie takes 45 minutes to an hour to West End, up to 1½ hours to Road Town; from Red Hook, the trip is only half an hour. The twice-weekly, 2¼-hour trip from Charlotte Amalie to Virgin Gorda costs $28 one-way and $40 round-trip. There's also daily service between Cruz Bay, St. John, and West End, Tortola, aboard the *Sundance* (☎ 340/776–6597). The half-hour one-way trip is $21. You'll need to present proof of citizenship upon entering the BVI; a passport is best, but a birth certificate or voter's registration card will suffice.

TAXIS

USVI taxis don't have meters, but you needn't worry about fare-gouging if you check a list of standard rates to popular destinations (required by law to be carried by each driver and often posted in hotel and airport lobbies and printed in free tourist periodicals, such as *St. Thomas This Week* and *St. Croix This Week*), and settle on the fare before you start out. Fares are per person, not per destination, but drivers taking multiple fares (which often happens, especially from the airport) will charge you a lower rate than if you're in the cab alone.

St. Thomas. Taxis of all shapes and sizes are available at various ferry, shopping, resort, and airport areas, and they also respond to phone calls. Try **Islander Taxi** (☎ 340/774–4077), the **VI Taxi Association** (☎ 340/774–4550), or **East End Taxi** (☎ 340/775–6974). There are taxi stands in Charlotte Amalie across from Emancipation Garden (in front of Little Switzerland, behind the post office) and along the waterfront. But you probably won't have to look for a stand, as taxis are plentiful and routinely cruise the streets. Walking down Main Street, you'll be asked "Back to ship?" often enough to make you never want to carry another shopping bag.

St. Croix. Taxis, generally station wagons or minivans, are a phone call away from most hotels and are available in downtown Christiansted, at the Alexander Hamilton Airport, and at the Frederiksted pier during cruise-ship arrivals. Try the **St. Croix Taxi Association** (☎ 340/778–1088) at the airport and **Antilles Taxi Service** (☎ 340/773–5020) or **Cruzan Taxi and Tours** (☎ 340/773–6388) in Christiansted.

St. John. Taxis meet ferries arriving in Cruz Bay. Most drivers use vans or open-air safari buses. You'll find them congregated at the dock and at hotel parking lots. You can also hail them anywhere on the road. You're likely to travel with other tourists en route to their destinations. It's very difficult to get taxis to respond to a phone call. If you need one to pick you up at your rental villa, ask the villa manager for suggestions on who to call or arrange a ride in advance.

Guided Tours

BOAT

St. Thomas's **Kon Tiki** party boat (⊠ Gregorie Channel East dock, ☎ 340/775–5055) is a kick. Put your sophistication aside, climb on this big palm-thatch raft, and dip into bottomless barrels of rum punch along with a couple of hundred of your soon-to-be closest friends. Dance to the steel-drum band, sun on the roof (watch out; you'll fry), and join the limbo dancing on the way home from an afternoon of swimming and beachcombing at Honeymoon Beach on Water Island. This popular three-hour afternoon excursion costs $29 for adults, $15 for children under 13 (although few come to this party).

HELICOPTER AND AIRPLANE

Air Center Helicopters (☎ 340/775–7335), on the Charlotte Amalie waterfront (next to Tortola Wharf) on St. Thomas, has 25-minute island tours priced at $125 (2-person minimum) per trip. You can also arrange longer flights that loop over to the neighboring BVI, as well as photography tours. **Seaborne Seaplane Adventures** (⊠ 5305 Long Bay Rd., ☎ 340/777–1227) offers narrated "flightseeing" tours of the USVI and the BVI from its Havensight base on St. Thomas. The 40-minute "Round-the-Island" tour is $94 per person.

ORIENTATION

V.I. Taxi Association St. Thomas City-Island Tour (☎ 340/774–4550) gives a two-hour $40 tour for two people in an open-air safari bus or enclosed van; aimed at cruise-ship passengers, this tour includes stops at Drake's Seat and Mountain Top. For just a bit more money (about $45–$50 for two) you can hire a taxi and ask the driver to take the opposite route so you'll avoid the crowds. But do see Mountain Top: the view is wonderful.

Tropic Tours (☎ 340/774–1855 or 800/524–4334) offers half-day shopping and sightseeing tours of St. Thomas by bus six days a week ($20 per person). The company also has a full-day ferry tour to St. John that includes snorkeling and lunch. The cost is $60 per person.

Van tours of St. Croix are offered by **St. Croix Safari Tours** (☎ 340/773–6700) and **St. Croix Transit** (☎ 340/772–3333). The tours, which depart from Christiansted and last about three hours, cost from $25 per person. St. John taxi drivers provide tours of the island, making stops at various sites including Trunk Bay and Annaberg Plantation. Prices run around $15 a person.

WALKING

The *St. Thomas–St. John Vacation Handbook,* available free at hotels and tourist centers (☞ Visitor Information, *below*), has an excellent self-guided walking tour of Charlotte Amalie on St. Thomas. The St. Thomas Historical Trust has published a self-guided tour of the historic district; it's available in book and souvenir shops for $1.95.

Possible nature tours include bird-watching, whale-watching, and waiting hidden on a beach while the magnificent hawksbill turtles come ashore to lay their eggs. Contact the **St. Croix Environmental Association** (✉ Arawak Bldg. #3, Gallows Bay, St. Croix 00820, ☎ 340/ 773–1989) or **EAST** (✉ Environmental Association of St. Thomas–St. John, Box 12379, St. Thomas 00801, ☎ 340/776–1976) for more information on hikes and special programs, or check the community calendar in the *Daily News* for up-to-date information. **St. Croix Heritage Tours** (✉ Box 7937, Sunny Isle, 00823, ☎ 340/778–6997) leads walks through the historic towns of Christiansted and Frederiksted, detailing the history of the people and the buildings. Custom tours that cover the island are also available.

Along with providing trail maps and brochures about St. John National Park, the park service also gives a variety of guided tours on- and offshore. Note that some of the tours are offered only at certain times of the year, schedules for them vary, and some of them require reservations. For more information or to arrange a tour, contact the **V.I. National Park Visitor's Center** (✉ At an area known as the Creek; across from the Cruz Bay bulkhead and adjacent to the ballfield, Cruz Bay, ☎ 340/776–6201; ✉ Cinnamon Bay, ☎ 340/776–6330).

Annaberg Ruins Tour. During the $4 tour of this fascinating plantation, park rangers discuss how slaves converted sugarcane to sugar and molasses, and tell you about how the red bricks came from Denmark and the yellow from Holland. They also point out the jail where slaves who were thought to be misbehaving were sent to await their fate.

Bird Walks. Birders are bused during the winter season to Francis Bay for a two-hour trail walk with a park-ranger guide. The $10 fee covers the cost of round-trip bus transportation.

Cinnamon Bay. Two to three evenings a week rangers hold informal talks on park history, marine research, and other topics. Confirm times, because schedules change often.

Reef Bay Hike. Take the Vitran bus (it costs $1 for the ride) from the Cruz Bay ferry dock to the trailhead, where you begin a vigorous hike that visits petroglyph carvings and an old sugar-mill factory. You'll need serious walking shoes and your own food and drink. An optional return trip by boat ($14.50) saves you a hike back up the hill (making this a walk of only average difficulty) and will have you back in Cruz Bay by 3:30 PM.

Snorkel Trips. Easy, 1½-hour, free trips start at the Trunk Bay Beach. Bring your own gear and a T-shirt for protection from the sun.

Water's Edge Walk. This free, one-hour walk along the coral flats and mangrove lagoon starts at the shoreline below the Annaberg Plantation parking lot. You'll need wading shoes.

Language, Culture, and Etiquette

English is the official language, though island residents often speak it with a lilting Creole accent, so you might not recognize certain words at first. If you have trouble understanding someone, ask them to speak slowly. A smile and a "good day" greeting will start any encounter off on the right foot.

Money Matters

The American dollar is used throughout the territory, as well as in the neighboring BVI. All major credit cards and traveler's checks are generally accepted. On St. Thomas, the branch of **First Bank** (☎ 340/776–9494) near Market Square and the waterfront locations of **Banco Popular** (☎ 340/693–2777) and **Chase Manhattan Bank** (☎ 340/775–7777) have automatic teller machines. On St. Croix, contact **Banco Popular** (☎ 340/693–2777) or **Chase Manhattan Bank** (☎ 340/775–7777) for information on branch and ATM locations. On St. John, **Chase Manhattan Bank** (☎ 340/775–7777) has the island's only ATM machine.

SERVICE CHARGES, TAXES, AND TIPPING

Many hotels add a 10% to 15% service charge to cover the room maid and other staff. However, some hotels may use part of that money to fund their operations, passing on only a portion of it to the staff. Check with your maid or bell-boy to determine the hotel's policy. If you discover you need to tip, give bellmen and porters 50¢ to $1 per bag and maids $1 or $2 per day. Special errands or requests of hotel staff always require an additional tip. At restaurants, bartenders and waiters expect a 10% to 15% tip, but always check your tab to see whether or not service is included. Taxi drivers get a 15% tip.

There's no sales tax, but there is an 8% hotel-room tax. Departure taxes ($10 for those leaving by air, $5 for those leaving by sea) are generally written into your ticket. The St. John Accommodations Council members ask that hotel and villa guests voluntarily pay a $1-a-day surcharge to help fund school and community projects and other good works.

Opening and Closing Times

BANKS

Bank hours are generally Monday–Thursday 9–3 and Friday 9–5; a handful have Saturday hours (9–noon). Walk-up windows open at 8:30 on weekdays.

POST OFFICES

Hours may vary slightly from branch to branch and island to island, but they are generally 7:30–8 to 4–5:30 weekdays and 7:30–8 to noon–2:30 Saturday.

SHOPS

In **St. Thomas,** stores on Main Street in Charlotte Amalie are open weekdays and Saturday 9–5. Havensight Mall shops' (next to the cruise-ships dock) hours are the same, though some sometimes stay open until 9 on Friday, depending on how many cruise ships are at the dock. You may also find some shops open on Sunday if a lot of cruise ships are in port. Hotel shops are usually open evenings, as well.

St. Croix shop hours are usually Monday–Saturday 9–5, but you'll find some shops in Christiansted open in the evening. On **St. John,** store hours run from 9 or 10 to 5 or 6. Wharfside Village and Mongoose Junction shops in Cruz Bay are often open into the evening.

HOLIDAYS

Although the government closes down for 28 days a year, most of these holidays have no effect on shopping hours. Unless there's a cruise ship arrival, expect most stores to close for Christmas and a few other holidays in the slower summer months.

In addition to the U.S. federal holidays, the USVI celebrate: Three Kings Day (Jan. 6); Transfer Day (commemorates Denmark's 1917 sale of the territory to the United States, Mar. 31); Holy Thursday and Good Friday (Apr. 20–21); Organic Act Day (the 1936 date when the U.S. Congress granted home rule and suffrage to the islands, June 16); Emancipation Day (when slavery was abolished in the Danish West Indies in 1848, July 3); Supplication Day (3rd Mon. in July, a day for prayer and protection from storms); Columbus Day and USVI–Puerto Rico Friendship Day (Oct. 11); Hurricane Thanksgiving Day (3rd Mon. in Oct., for the end of storm season); and Liberty Day (honoring Judge David Hamilton Jackson who secured freedom of the press and assembly from King Christian X of Denmark, Nov. 1).

Passports

If you're a U.S. or Canadian citizen, you can prove citizenship with a current or expired (but not by more than five years) passport or with a birth certificate (with a raised seal) along with a government-issued photo ID. U.K. citizens need a passport.

Precautions

Vacationers tend to assume that normal preautions aren't necessary in paradise. They are. Though there isn't quite as much crime here as in large U.S. mainland cities, it does exist. To be safe, stick to well-lighted streets at night, and use the same kind of street sense (don't wander the back alleys of Charlotte Amalie after five rum punches, for example) that you would in any unfamiliar territory. If you plan to carry things around, rent a car—not a Jeep—and lock possessions in the trunk. Keep your rental car locked wherever you park. Don't leave cameras, purses, and other valuables lying on the beach while you snorkel for an hour (or even for a minute), whether you're on the deserted beaches of St. John or the more crowded Magens and Coki beaches on St. Thomas. St. Croix has several remote beaches outside of Frederiksted and on the East End; it's best to visit them with a group rather than on your own. You should always wash produce before eating it. Also note that ciguatera, a toxin found in some reef fish (particularly kingfish), can be a problem at local restaurants.

Telephones and Mail

The area code for all of the USVI is 340, and you can dial direct to and from the mainland as well as to and from Australia, Canada, New Zealand, and the United Kingdom. Local calls from a public phone cost 25¢ for each five minutes. If you have a cell phone you can dial 6611 for information on its use locally.

On St. Thomas **Islander Services** (☎ 340/774–8128) at 5302 Store Tvaer Gade, behind the Greenhouse Restaurant in Charlotte Amalie, and **East End Secretarial Services** (☎ 340/775–5262, FAX 340/775–3590), upstairs at the Red Hook Plaza, offer long-distance dialing, copying, and fax services. **AT&T** (☎ 340/777–9201) has a state-of-the-art telecommunications center (it's across from the Havensight Mall) with 15 desk booths, fax and copy services, video phone, and TDD equipment (for people with hearing impairments), across from the Havensight Mall.

On St. John, the place to go for telephone or message needs is **Connections** (✉ Cruz Bay, ☎ 340/776–6922; ✉ Coral Bay, ☎ 340/779–4994).

The main **U.S. Post Office** on St. Thomas is near the hospital, with branches in Charlotte Amalie, Frenchtown, Havensight, and Tutu Mall; there's a post office at Christiansted, Frederiksted, Gallows Bay, and Sunny Isle on St. Croix, and at Cruz Bay on St. John. The postal service offers Express Mail, one-day service to major cities if you mail before noon; outlying areas may take two days. Letters to the United

States are 32¢ and postcards are 20¢. Sending mail home to Canada you'll pay 46¢ for a letter and 40¢ for a postcard. To the United Kingdom and Australia, letters are 60¢, postcards 50¢.

For overnight **Federal Express** (☎ 340/774–3393) service, you must get your package to the office at the Havensight Mall (☎ 340/777–4140) in Charlotte Amalie on St. Thomas before 5 PM or to the St. Croix office in the Villa La Reine Shopping Center (☎ 340/778–8180) before 4 PM. On St. John, **Sprint Courier Service** (☎ 340/693–8130) connects to all major couriers.

Visitor Information

ST. THOMAS

The **U.S.V.I. Division of Tourism** has an office in Charlotte Amalie (✉ Box 6400, Charlotte Amalie 00804, ☎ 340/774–8784 or 800/372–8784). You'll also find a visitor center in downtown Charlotte Amalie (☞ Exploring St. Thomas, *above*) and a cruise-ship welcome center at Havensight Mall. The **National Park Service** has a visitor center across the harbor from the ferry dock at Red Hook.

ST. CROIX

The **U.S.V.I. Division of Tourism** has offices at 53A Company Street in Christiansted (✉ Box 4538, Christiansted 00822, ☎ 340/773–0495) and on the pier in Frederiksted (✉ Strand St., Frederiksted 00840, ☎ 340/772–0357).

ST. JOHN

There's a branch of the **U.S.V.I. Government Tourist Office** (✉ Box 200, Cruz Bay 00830, ☎ 340/776–6450) in the compound between Sparky's and the U.S. Post Office in Cruz Bay. The **National Park Service** (✉ Box 710, 00831, ☎ 340/776–6201) also has a visitor center at the Creek in Cruz Bay.

WORLDWIDE

You can get information from the **U.S.V.I. Government Tourist Office** Web site (www.usvi.net) or from the following locations: ✉ 225 Peachtree St., Suite 760, Atlanta, GA 30303, ☎ 404/688–0906; ✉ 500 N. Michigan Ave., Suite 2030, Chicago, IL 60611, ☎ 312/670–8784; ✉ 3460 Wilshire Blvd., Suite 412, Los Angeles, CA 90010, ☎ 213/739–0138; ✉ 2655 Le Jeune Rd., Suite 907, Coral Gables, FL 33134, ☎ 305/442–7200; ✉ 1270 Ave. of the Americas, Room 2108, New York, NY 10020, ☎ 212/332–2222; ✉ 900 17th Ave. NW, Suite 500, Washington, DC 20006, ☎ 202/293–3707; ✉ 1300 Ashford Ave., Condado, Santurce, U.S.V.I. 00907, ☎ 340/724–3816; ✉ 3300 Bloor St., Suite 3120, Center Tower, Toronto, Ontario, Canada M8X 2X3, ☎ 416/233–1414; and ✉ 2 Cinnamon Row, Plantation Wharf, York Place, London SW11 3TW, ☎ 0171/978–5262.

3 BRITISH VIRGIN ISLANDS

The BVI are a spectacular cluster of mountainous islands, and although they're now regularly visited by cruise ships, they retain their quiet, laid-back, friendly atmosphere.

Updated by
Pamela
Acheson

THE BRITISH VIRGIN ISLANDS (BVI) consist of about 50 islands, islets, and cays. Most are remarkably hilly and all but Anegada are volcanic, having exploded from the depths of the sea some some 25 million years ago. The BVI are serene, seductive, spectacularly beautiful, and still remarkably laid-back. At some points they lie only a mile or so from the U.S. Virgin Islands (USVI), but they remain unique and have maintained their quiet, friendly, and very casual character. Although the past five years have seen a huge increase in the number of automobiles and the construction of a cruise-ship dock and a four-lane highway in Road Town, on Tortola, for the most part, the BVI are still happily free of runaway development.

The pleasures here are understated: sailing around the multitude of tiny, nearby islands; diving to the wreck of the RMS *Rhone,* sunk off Salt Island in 1867; snorkeling in one of hundreds of wonderful spots; walking empty beaches; taking in spectacular views from the islands' peaks; and settling in on a breeze-swept terrace to admire the sunset.

Several factors have enabled the BVI to retain the endearing qualities of yesteryear's Caribbean: no building can rise higher than the surrounding palms—two stories is the limit, and there are no direct flights from the mainland United States, so the tourism tide is held back to some extent. Many visitors travel here by water, either aboard their own ketches and yawls or on one of the convenient ferryboats that cross the turquoise waters between St. Thomas and Tortola. Such a passage is a fine prelude to a stay in these unhurried tropical havens.

Tortola, about 10 square mi (26 square km), is the largest and most populated of the islands; Virgin Gorda, with 8 square mi (21 square km), ranks second. The islands scattered around them include Jost Van Dyke, Great Camanoe, Norman, Peter, Salt, Cooper, Ginger, Dead Chest, and Anegada. Tortola has the most hotels, restaurants, and shops. Virgin Gorda offers a limited number of restaurants and shops, and many of its resorts are self-contained. Jost Van Dyke is a major charter-boat anchorage, and although little bars line the beach at Great Harbour, there are few places to stay. The other islands are either uninhabited or have a single hotel or resort. Many of these, such as Peter Island, offer excellent anchorages, and their bays and harbors are popular with overnighting boaters.

Sailing has always been a popular activity in the BVI. The first arrivals here were a romantic seafaring tribe, the Ciboney Indians. They were followed (circa AD 900) by the Arawak Indians, who sailed from South America, established settlements, and farmed and fished. Still later came the mighty Caribs.

In 1493 Christopher Columbus was the first European visitor. Impressed by the number of islands dotting the horizon, he named them *Las Once Mil Virgines*—The 11,000 Virgins—in honor of the 11,000 virgin-companions of St. Ursula, martyred in the 4th century. In the ensuing years, the Spaniards passed through these waters fruitlessly seeking gold. Then came the pirates, who found the islands' hidden coves and treacherous reefs ideal bases from which to prey on passing galleons crammed with Mexican and Peruvian gold, silver, and spices. Among the most notorious of these fellows were Blackbeard Teach, Bluebeard, Captain Kidd, and Sir Francis Drake, who lent his name to the channel that sweeps through the two main clusters of the BVI. In the 17th century, the colorful cutthroats were replaced by the Dutch who, in turn, were sent packing by the British. It was the British who established a plantation economy, and for the next 150 years developed the sugar industry through the labor of African slaves. When slavery was abolished in 1838,

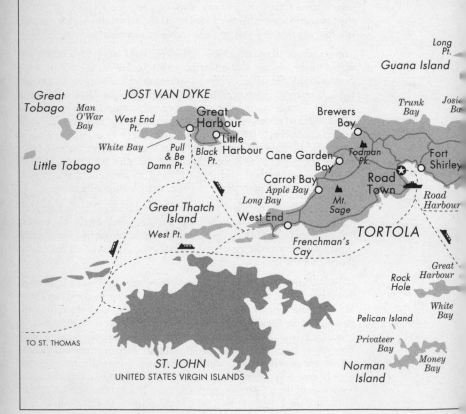

ATLANTIC

Long
Pt.
Guana Island

Great
Tobago

JOST VAN DYKE

Man
O'War
Bay

West End
Pt.

Great
Harbour

Little
Harbour

Brewers
Bay

Trunk
Bay

Josie
Ba

White Bay

Pull
& Be
Damn Pt.

Black
Pt.

Cane Garden
Bay

Todman
Pk.

Fort
Shirley

Little Tobago

Carrot Bay

Apple Bay

Road
Town

Long Bay

Great Thatch
Island

West End

Mt.
Sage

Road
Harbour

West Pt.

Frenchman's
Cay

TORTOLA

Great
Harbour

Rock
Hole

TO ST. THOMAS

Pelican Island

White
Bay

Privateer
Bay

Money
Bay

ST. JOHN
UNITED STATES VIRGIN ISLANDS

Norman
Island

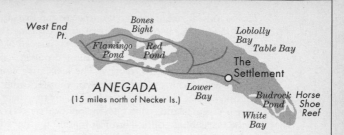

West End
Pt.

Bones
Bight

Flamingo
Pond

Red
Pond

Loblolly
Bay

Table Bay

The
Settlement

ANEGADA
(15 miles north of Necker Is.)

Lower
Bay

Budrock
Pond

Horse
Shoe
Reef

White
Bay

O C E A N

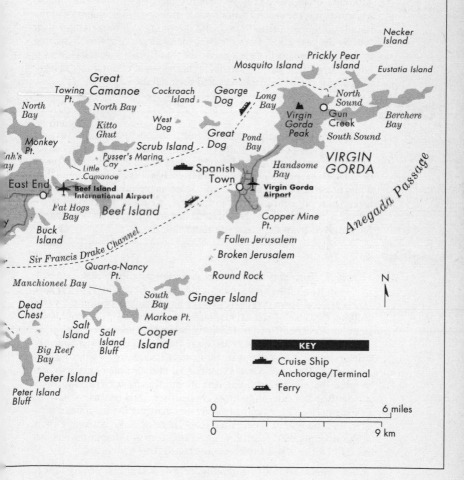

Necker
Island

Prickly Pear
Island

Mosquito Island

Eustatia Island

Great
Camanoe

Towing
Pt.

Cockroach
Island

George
Dog

Long
Bay

North
Sound

North
Bay

North Bay

West
Dog

Kitto
Ghut

Virgin
Gorda
Peak

Gun
Creek

Berchere
Bay

Monkey
Pt.

Scrub Island

Great
Dog

Pond
Bay

South Sound

*VIRGIN
GORDA*

Pusser's Marina

Little
Camanoe

*ah's
ay*

East End

Beef Island
International Airport

Spanish
Town

Handsome
Bay

Virgin Gorda
Airport

Anegada Passage

Fat Hogs
Bay

Beef Island

Copper Mine
Pt.

Buck
Island

Fallen Jerusalem

Sir Francis Drake Channel

Broken Jerusalem

Quart-a-Nancy
Pt.

Round Rock

Manchioneel Bay

South
Bay

Ginger Island

N

Dead
Chest

Markoe Pt.

Salt
Island

Salt
Island
Bluff

Cooper
Island

Big Reef
Bay

Peter Island

Peter Island
Bluff

KEY

Cruise Ship
Anchorage/Terminal

Ferry

0 — 6 miles

0 — 9 km

the plantation economy soon faltered, and the majority of the white population left for Europe.

The islands dozed, a forgotten corner of the British empire, until the early 1960s. In 1966 a new constitution granting the islands greater autonomy was approved. Although the governor is still appointed by the Queen of England, his or her limited powers concentrate on external affairs and local security. The legislative council, with representatives from nine island districts, administers other matters. General elections are held every four years. The arrangement seems to suit the British Virgin Islanders just fine: the political mood is serene, with none of the occasional political turmoil found on other islands. It was also in the 1960s that Laurence Rockefeller and American expatriate Charlie Cary brought tourism to the BVI. In 1965 Rockefeller set about creating the Little Dix resort on Virgin Gorda. Dedicated to preserving the island's natural beauty while providing guests with unpretentious yet elegant surroundings, Little Dix set the standard that still prevails in the BVI. A few years later, Cary and his wife, Ginny, established the Moorings marina complex on Tortola, and sailing in the area burgeoned.

Although offshore banking is currently the BVI's number-one industry, tourism is the second major source of income. The majority of the islands' jobs are tourism-related, and there may well be even more such jobs by the year 2003, when the Beef Island airport expansion is slated to be completed. Still, there's no doubt that British Virgin Islanders—who so love their unspoiled tropical home—will maintain its easygoing charms for both themselves and their guests.

TORTOLA

Unwinding can easily become a full-time occupation on Tortola. Though Tortola offers a wealth of things to see and do, many visitors prefer just to loll about on deserted sands or linger over lunch at one of the island's many delightful restaurants. Beaches are never more than a few minutes away, and the steeply sloping green hills that form Tortola's spine are continuously fanned by gentle trade winds. The neighboring islands glimmer like emeralds in a sea of sapphire. It's a world far removed from the hustle of modern life.

Lodging

Luxury on Tortola is more a state of mind—serenity, seclusion, gentility—than state-of-the-art amenities and facilities. Except for Prospect Reef, hotels in Road Town don't have beaches but do have pools and are within walking distance of restaurants, night spots, and shops. Accommodations outside Road Town are relatively isolated but are on beaches—some of them are exquisite; others are quite small or have been enlarged by bringing in sand. BVI resorts are intimate: none are large—only four have more than 50 rooms. Visitors spend most of their time outside, so bear in mind that the rooms themselves are not the draw. Generally, rooms are on the plain side, and visitors choose their hotel because of location or size or price. Guests are treated as more than just room numbers, however, and many return year after year. This can make booking a room at the more popular resorts difficult, even off-season, despite the fact that nearly half the island's visitors stay aboard their own boats.

A few hotels lack air-conditioning, relying instead on ceiling fans to capture the almost constant trade winds. Nights are cool and breezy, even in midsummer, and never reach the temperatures or humidity levels that are common in much of the United States during the summer.

CATEGORY	COST*
$$$$	over $225
$$$	$150–$225
$$	$75–$150
$	under $75

*All prices are for a standard double room in high season, excluding 7%
hotel tax and 10% (5%–15% on Virgin Gorda) service charge.*

Hotels and Inns

ROAD TOWN

$$$–$$$$ 🏨 **Moorings-Mariner Inn.** This two-story inn is also the headquarters
for the Moorings Charter operation. It's popular with both yachting
folk—who find its facilities convenient and the companionship of fel-
low "boaties" congenial—and landlubbers who want to be within
walking distance of town. The atmosphere is laid-back *and* lively. The
pale-peach decor is picked up in the peach floor tiles, and bright, trop-
ical-print fabrics add splashes of contrasting color. All units are on the
large side and have a small kitchenette and a balcony, and you'll face
the water in all but the eight rooms that overlook the pool or the ten-
nis court. ✉ *Waterfront Dr. (Box 139)*, ☎ *284/494–2332*, FAX *284/494–
2226. 38 rooms, 4 suites. Restaurant, bar, air-conditioning, kitch-
enettes, pool, tennis court, volleyball, dive shop, shop. AE, MC, V. EP.*

$$$–$$$$ 🏨 **Treasure Isle Hotel.** Painted in bright shades of lemon, violet, and
★ mango pink, this hillside resort is very pretty, indeed. Its spacious
guest rooms are simply decorated and are accented by fabrics with Ma-
tisse-like prints. The comfortable lounge of the Spy Glass Bar, which
is open to the breezes and the heady aroma of flowers, is the perfect
place to contemplate the harbor and distant islands. Dinner at the ☞
Lime 'n' Mango restaurant is romantic. Road Town's shops and mari-
nas are nearby, and there's transportation to Cane Garden Bay, Brew-
ers Bay, and Cooper Island on different days each week. ✉ *Waterfront
Dr. (Box 68)*, ☎ *284/494–2501*, FAX *284/494–2507. 34 rooms, 6 suites.
Restaurant, 2 bars, air-conditioning, pool, shop. AE, MC, V. EP.*

$$–$$$$ 🏨 **Prospect Reef Resort.** This sprawling complex of brightly painted
buildings sits on 7 acres laced with rock paths and lagoons. Units vary
from small rooms to larger rooms with kitchenettes to two-story, two-
bedroom apartments with private interior courtyards. All have a balcony or patio. Cool off in the 25-meter swimming pool, the separate
diving pool, or one of the two saltwater swimming areas or test your
driving skills on the rustic pitch-and-putt golf course. The resort has
its own harbor, and sailboats are available for daylong—or longer—
adventures. If all this isn't enough, take a complimentary trip to Cooper
Island, Marina Cay, or Cane Garden Bay. Relax with locals and guests
in the intimate ☞ **Callaloo** restaurant. ✉ *Waterfront Dr. (Box 104)*,
☎ *284/494–3311*, FAX *284/494–5595 or 800/356–8937 (direct to
hotel). 78 rooms, 53 suites. 2 restaurants, 2 bars, air-conditioning, 2
pools, 2 saltwater pools, beauty salon, 6 tennis courts, health club, shops,
convention center, children's program. AE, MC, V. EP.*

$$–$$$ 🏨 **Fort Burt Hotel.** Originally a fort built by the Dutch in the 17th cen-
tury, this hillside landmark is at the edge of town and—like all good
Caribbean forts and hotels—overlooks the harbor. The owners have
expanded the hotel with care, and much of the original stonework exterior remains. New rooms and suites have been added, and older ones
have been completely overhauled. Although room furnishings are still
somewhat modest, you get a private balcony with terrific harbor views.
You could also go all out and book one of the two suites that have private pools. ✉ *Waterfront Dr. (Box 3380)*, ☎ *284/494–2587*, FAX *284/
494–2002. 12 rooms, 5 suites. Restaurant, bar, air-conditioning, pool.
AE, MC, V. EP.*

Tortola

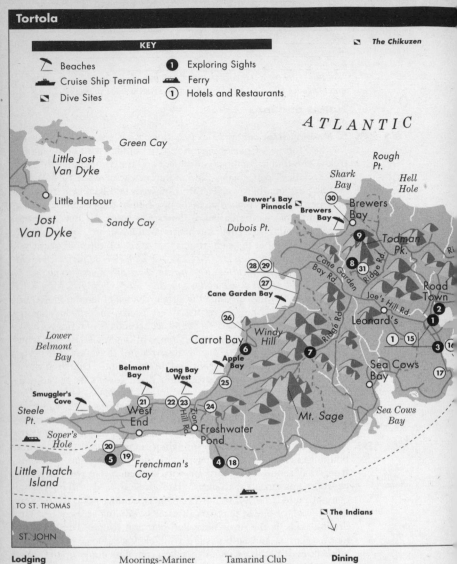

KEY

⚓ The Chikuzen

➤ Beaches
🚢 Cruise Ship Terminal
◥ Dive Sites
❶ Exploring Sights
⛴ Ferry
① Hotels and Restaurants

ATLANTIC

Green Cay

Little Jost
Van Dyke

Little Harbour

Jost
Van Dyke

Sandy Cay

Rough
Pt.

Shark
Bay

Hell
Hole

Brewer's Bay
Pinnacle

Brewers
Bay

③⓪ Brewers
Bay

Dubois Pt.

⑨ Todman
Pk.

Ri

⑧ ③①

Cane Garden
Bay Rd

Ridge Rd

Road
Town

②⑧ ②⑨

Joe's Hill Rd.

②⑦

Cane Garden Bay

Leonard's

①

②⑥

Windy
Hill

① ⑮

③ ⑯

Lower
Belmont
Bay

Carrot Bay

④⑧⑤
Apple
Bay

⑥

⑦

Ridge Rd

Sea Cows
Bay

⑰

Belmont
Bay

Long Bay
West

②⑤

Smuggler's
Cove

②① ②② ②③

②④

Sea Cows
Bay

Steele
Pt.

West
End

Zion Hill Rd

Mt. Sage

Soper's
Hole

Freshwater
Pond

②⓪

⑤ ⑲

Frenchman's
Cay

④⑧

Little Thatch
Island

TO ST. THOMAS

◥ The Indians

ST. JOHN

Lodging

Brewers Bay
Campground, **30**
Fort Burt Hotel, **16**
Frenchman's Cay
Hotel, **19**
Hotel Castle
Maria, **11**
Long Bay Beach
Resort, **21**
Maria's Hotel
by the Sea, **6**

Moorings-Mariner
Inn, **12**
Mount Sage
Villas, **15**
Ole Works Inn, **28**
Prospect Reef
Resort, **17**
Sebastian's on the
Beach, **23**
Sugar Mill Hotel, **25**
Sunset House and
Villas, **22**

Tamarind Club
Hotel and Villas, **32**
Treasure Isle
Hotel, **13**
Village Cay
Resort, **3**
The Villas at Fort
Recovery Estates, **18**

Dining

The Apple, **24**
Brandywine Bay, **35**
C and F
Restaurant, **9**
Callaloo, **17**
Capriccio di Mare, **5**
The Captain's
Table, **14**
Conch Shell Point, **33**
The Fishtrap, **1**

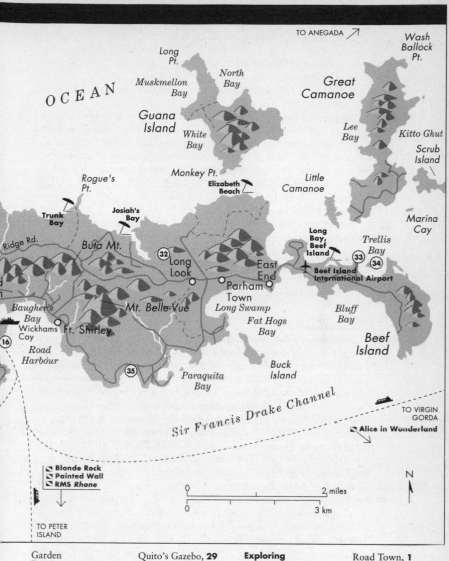

TO ANEGADA ↗

*Wash
Ballock
Pt.*

*Long
Pt.*

*North
Bay*

*Muskmellon
Bay*

O C E A N

*Great
Camanoe*

*Guana
Island*

*Lee
Bay*

Kitto Ghut

*White
Bay*

*Scrub
Island*

Monkey Pt.

**Elizabeth
Beach**

*Little
Camanoe*

*Marina
Cay*

*Rogue's
Pt.*

**Trunk
Bay**

**Josiah's
Bay**

**Long
Bay,
Beef
Island**

*Trellis
Bay*

Ridge Rd.

Bufa Mt.

32

*Long
Look*

*East
End*

33 **34**

**Beef Island
International Airport**

*Parham
Town*

*Baugher's
Bay*

Mt. Belle-Vue

Long Swamp

*Bluff
Bay*

*Wickhams
Cay*

Ft. Shirley

16

*Fat Hogs
Bay*

*Beef
Island*

*Road
Harbour*

35

*Paraquita
Bay*

*Buck
Island*

TO VIRGIN
GORDA

Sir Francis Drake Channel

◢ **Alice in Wonderland**
↘

◢ **Blonde Rock**
◢ **Painted Wall**
◢ **RMS Rhone**

0 _____ 2 miles
0 _____ 3 km

N
↑

TO PETER
ISLAND

$$–$$$ ⌂ **Maria's Hotel by the Sea.** Perched on the edge of Road Harbour, next to a large government building and the cruise-ship dock, this simple hotel is an easy walk to restaurants in town. The small rooms are minimally decorated with white rattan furniture, floral-print bedspreads, and murals painted by local artists. All rooms have balconies, some with harbor views. ⌧ *Waterfront Dr. (Box 206),* ☎ *284/494–2595,* ℻ *284/494–2420. 20 rooms. Restaurant, bar, air-conditioning, kitchenettes, pool. AE, MC, V. EP.*

$$–$$$ ⌂ **Village Cay Resort.** This pleasant, compact hotel looks out on Road Harbour and several marinas. It's popular with yachters and those who love to shop and dine. Rooms are decorated in rattan furniture and tropical prints. Some units have cathedral ceilings and harbor views; others are quite small. After trotting to town and back, you can have a swim and then head for the bar. ⌧ *Wickham's Cay I (Box 145),* ☎ *284/494–2771,* ℻ *284/494–2773. 18 rooms. Restaurant, bar, air-conditioning, pool. AE, MC, V. EP.*

$$ ⌂ **Hotel Castle Maria.** You can spend all the money you save here at the nearby in-town attractions. And these very simple accommodations have everything most folks need: a refrigerator and cable TV; some rooms also have full kitchenettes, balconies, and air-conditioning. Refresh yourself either in the bar or the freshwater pool. ⌧ *Waterfront Dr. (Box 206),* ☎ *284/494–2553,* ℻ *284/494–2111. 30 rooms. Bar, pool. AE, MC, V. EP.*

OUTSIDE ROAD TOWN

$$$–$$$$ ⌂ **Frenchman's Cay Hotel.** This small, casual collection of one- and two-bedroom condos overlooks Drake's Channel. Each unit includes a full kitchen, a dining area, and a sitting room—ideal for families or couples. Rooms are done in neutral colors, with cream-color curtains and bedspreads and tile floors. Ceiling fans and pleasant breezes keep things cool. There's a small pool and a modest-size artificial beach that's sandy to the water's edge but rocky offshore (snorkelers will enjoy the reef here). The alfresco bar and dining room are breeze-swept and offer simple fare. ⌧ *Frenchman's Cay (Box 1054, West End),* ☎ *284/495–4844,* ℻ *284/495–4056. 9 units. Restaurant, bar, kitchenettes, fans, pool, tennis court, beach, snorkeling. AE, MC, V. EP.*

$$$–$$$$ ⌂ **Long Bay Beach Resort.** Spectacularly set on a gentle 1-mi-long (1½-
★   km-long) arc of white sand, this resort is one of Tortola's best. Beachfront accommodations include cozy tropical hideaways set on stilts and spacious deluxe units with marble-top wet bars and showers and roomy dressing areas with Italian tiles. Hillside choices all have balconies and lovely views and range from small rooms with Jacuzzis to studios with comfortable seating areas to roomy one- and two-bedroom villas with full kitchens. Floral prints and rattan furniture are used throughout. The casual Beach restaurant offers all-day dining inside and around the beachside pool, and the ☞ **Garden Restaurant** serves gourmet dinners in a romantic, candlelit setting. A rustic 9-hole, par-3, pitch-and-putt golf course completes the complex. ⌧ *Long Bay (Box 433, Road Town),* ☎ *284/495–4252 or 800/729–9599,* ℻ *284/495–4677. 72 rooms, 10 suites, 20 villas. 2 restaurants, 2 bars, air-conditioning, 2 pools, 3 tennis courts, beach, snorkeling, shops. AE, MC, V. EP.*

$$$–$$$$ ⌂ **Sugar Mill Hotel.** The owners of this small, out-of-the-way hotel know what they're doing—they were food and travel writers before they opened the Sugar Mill more than two decades ago. Their savvy has paid off: many visitors return year after year. The reception area, bar, and restaurant are in the ruins of an old sugar mill, and the walls throughout are hung with bright Haitian artwork. Guest houses are scattered up a hill; the rooms are simply decorated in soft pastels and have rattan furnishings. A small circular swimming pool is set into the hillside

In case you want to see the world.

At American Express, we're here to make your journey a smooth one. So we have over 1,700 travel service locations in over 130 countries ready to help. What else would you expect from the world's largest travel agency?

do more

Travel

Call 1 800 AXP-3429 or visit
www.americanexpress.com/travel

In case you want to be welcomed there.

We're here to see that you're always welcomed at establishments everywhere. That's why millions of people carry the American Express® Card – for peace of mind, confidence, and security, around the world or just around the corner.

do more

Cards

To apply, call 1 800 THE-CARD or visit www.americanexpress.com

In case you're running low.

We're here to help with more than 190,000 Express Cash locations around the world. In order to enroll, just call American Express at 1 800 CASH-NOW before you start your vacation.

do more **AMERICAN EXPRESS**

Express Cash

And in case you'd rather be safe than sorry.

We're here with American Express® Travelers Cheques. They're the safe way to carry money on your vacation, because if they're ever lost or stolen you can get a refund, practically anywhere or anytime. To find the nearest place to buy Travelers Cheques, call 1 800 495-1153. Another way we help you do more.

do more

Travelers Cheques

©1999 American Express

and at the tiny beach lunches and light dinners are served, in season, on a shady terrace. The ☞ **Sugar Mill Restaurant** is well known on the island. ⊠ *Apple Bay (Box 425, Road Town),* ☎ *284/495–4355,* FAX *284/495–4696. 16 rooms, 4 suites, 1 villa. 2 restaurants, 2 bars, air-conditioning, pool, beach, snorkeling. AE, MC, V. EP.*

$$$–$$$$ ⊡ **The Villas at Fort Recovery Estates.** This cozy complex has all the
★ ingredients for a good Caribbean vacation: grounds full of tropical flowers; a remote, beachside setting around the remnants of a Dutch fort; and friendly, helpful management. All suites and the four-bedroom villa have excellent views (sliding glass doors open onto patios or balconies that face Drake's Channel) and fully equipped kitchens. Living rooms (not air-conditioned) can be used as a bedroom for one child. A gourmet kitchen provides room-service dinners, which are served course by course and accompanied by candlelight. There are exercise and yoga classes, massages, and VCRs and videos for rent. ⊠ *Waterfront Dr. (Box 239, Road Town),* ☎ *284/495–4354 or 800/367–8455 (direct to hotel),* FAX *284/495–4036. 14 suites, 1 villa. Pool, massage, kitchenettes, beach, snorkeling, baby-sitting. AE, MC, V. EP.*

$$–$$$ ⊡ **Ole Works Inn.** Nestled in the hillside across the road from one of Tortola's most beautiful beaches is this rustic but appealing inn—owned by local recording star Quito Rhymer. A steeply pitched roof, wood, and island stonework add a contemporary flair to what was once an old sugar mill. Simply decorated rooms have ceiling fans, air-conditioning, and refrigerators. The Honeymoon Suite has an indoor swing for two. ⊠ *Cane Garden Bay (Box 560, Road Town),* ☎ *284/495–4837,* FAX *284/495–9618. 15 rooms, 3 suites. MC, V. EP.*

$$–$$$ ⊡ **Sebastian's on the Beach.** The best rooms here are the eight small ones that open right onto the beach. They're airy and white, simply decorated with floral-print curtains and bedspreads, and have either terraces or balconies and great water breezes and views (the ocean lulls you to sleep). Tiny bathrooms have only small showers. The other 18 rooms are very basic, lack views, and can be noisy. Some of these are across the street and are considerably cheaper than the beach rooms. The casual restaurant looks out over the water; at lunch you can order fresh salads, grilled vegetables, and a variety of soups and sandwiches; for dinner, the menu includes grilled fish, lobster, and steak. ⊠ *Apple Bay (Box 441, Road Town),* ☎ *284/495–4212,* FAX *284/495–4466. 26 rooms. Restaurant, bar, snack bar, fans, beach. AE. EP.*

$$–$$$ ⊡ **Tamarind Club Hotel and Villas.** This small, out-of-the-way resort on the northeast side of the island is charming and intimate. It's tucked into a valley not too far from East End and about a ½-mi (¾-km) inland from the beach at Josiah's Bay. The ten units are built around a courtyard and a pool that has a swim-up bar. All rooms have ceiling fans; some are air-conditioned. The largest, the Honeymoon Suite, has its own private patio. There are also three two-bedroom villas. ⊠ *Josiah's Bay (Box 441, Road Town),* ☎ *284/495–2477 or 888/744–3376,* FAX *284/495–2858. 9 rooms, 1 suite, 3 2-bedroom villas. Restaurant, bar, fans, pool. MC, V. EP.*

Private Homes and Villas

Areana Villas (⊠ Box 263, Road Town, ☎ 284/494–5864, FAX 284/494–7626) represents the island's top-of-the-line properties. Homes offer accommodations for 2 to 10 people in one- to five-bedroom villas, decorated in soothing pastels. Many have swimming pools, Jacuzzis, and glazed terra-cotta courtyards. On Long Bay, Areana works with **Sunset House and Villas,** an exquisite hideaway whose first guest was Britain's Princess Alexandra (but you needn't be royalty to receive the royal treatment here). The company also works with Equinox House, also on Long Bay, a handsome three-bedroom estate set amid lavish tumbling gardens. Rates vary

but range from expensive (\$\$\$) to very expensive (\$\$\$\$) in season.
Mount Sage Villas (✉ Sage Mountain Rd. [Box 821], Road Town, ☎ 284/495–9567), near the highest peak on Tortola, is a bit of a drive down to the beaches, but views and breezes are spectacular.

Campground

$　🏕 **Brewers Bay Campground.** Both prepared and bare sites are on Brewers Bay, one of Tortola's prime snorkeling spots. Check out the ruins of the distillery that gave the bay its name. There are public bathrooms but no showers. ✉ *Brewers Bay (Box 185, Road Town),* ☎ *284/494–3463. 10 prepared and 18 bare sites. Restaurant, bar, beach, windsurfing, baby-sitting. No credit cards.*

Dining

On Tortola, seafood is plentiful, and although other fresh ingredients are scarce, the island's chefs are an adaptable lot, who apply creative genius to whatever the weekly supply boat delivers. Contemporary American dishes prepared with a Caribbean influence are very popular. The fancier, more expensive restaurants have dress codes: long pants and collared shirts for men, and elegant, casual resort wear for women.

CATEGORY	COST*
\$\$\$\$	over \$35
\$\$\$	\$25–\$35
\$\$	\$15–\$25
\$	under \$15

per person for a three-course meal, excluding drinks and service; there's no sales tax in the BVI

Road Town

AMERICAN/CASUAL

\$\$–\$\$\$\$　✕ **The Pub.** At this lively waterfront spot, tables are arranged along a terrace facing a small marina and Road Town harbor. Hamburgers, salads, and sandwiches are typical lunch offerings. In the evening you can also choose grilled fish, steak, chicken, sautéed conch, or barbecued ribs. There's entertainment here weekends and almost always a spirited dart game. ✉ *Waterfront Dr.,* ☎ *284/494–2608. Reservations not accepted. AE, MC, V. No lunch Sun.*

\$–\$\$　✕ **Pusser's Road Town Pub.** Almost everyone who visits Tortola stops here at least once to have a bite to eat and to sample the famous Pusser's Rum Painkiller (fruit juices and rum). The menu includes cheesy pizza, such pub grub as shepherd's pie and fish 'n chips, and deli sandwiches. ✉ *Waterfront Dr.,* ☎ *284/494–3897. AE, MC, V.*

CARIBBEAN

\$\$\$–\$\$\$\$　✕ **Callaloo.** Windows open to the breezes at this romantic second-floor
★　　restaurant that overlooks a small marina at the ☞ **Prospect Reef Resort.** The West Indian–influenced menu includes cracked jerk conch and pumpkin crepes for appetizers, as well as spicy callaloo pepper pot and sweet potato soups. For the main course, try Caribbean beef Wellington (wrapped in sweet potatoes and spinach) or blackened swordfish with a mango salsa. Rum cheesecake and Tia Maria tiramisù are dessert specialties. ✉ *Waterfront Dr.,* ☎ *284/494–3311. Reservations essential. AE, MC, V. No lunch.*

\$\$–\$\$\$\$　✕ **C and F Restaurant.** Crowds head to this casual spot for the best
★　　barbecue in town (chicken, fish, and ribs), fresh local fish prepared your way, and excellent curries. Sometimes there's a wait for a table, but it's worth it. The restaurant is just outside Road Town, on a side street past the Moorings and just past Riteway. ✉ *Purcell Estate,* ☎ *284/494–4941. Reservations not accepted. AE, MC, V. No lunch.*

ECLECTIC

$–$$$$ ✕ **Virgin Queen.** The sailing and rugby crowd gathers here to play darts, drink beer, and eat Queen's Pizza—a crusty, cheesy pie topped with sausage, onions, green peppers, and mushrooms—which some say is the best pizza in the Caribbean. Also on the menu is excellent West Indian and English fare: salt fish, barbecued ribs with beans and rice, bangers and mash, shepherd's pie, and chili. ✉ *Fleming St.,* ☎ *284/ 494–2310. Reservations not accepted. No credit cards. Closed Sun.*

$–$$ ✕ **Tavern in the Town.** Birds and bougainvillea brighten the garden setting of this English-style pub. Aside from mixed grills and fish-and-chips, you can also order hamburgers and such entrées as duck in orange and rum sauce and garlic shrimp. There's cozy indoor dining, too. ✉ *Waterfront Dr.,* ☎ *284/494–2790. MC, V. Closed Sat.*

ITALIAN

$$–$$$$ ✕ **Spaghetti Junction.** This cozy indoor spot is popular with the boating crowd. Penne with a spicy tomato sauce, spinach-mushroom lasagna, and capellini with shellfish are house specialties here, but the menu also includes more traditional Italian fare (veal or chicken parmigiana, pasta, etc.). The sun-dried tomatoes in the Caesar salad are a nice twist. ✉ *Waterfront Dr.,* ☎ *284/494–4880. MC, V. Closed Sept. and holidays. No lunch.*

$–$$ ✕ **Capriccio di Mare.** The owners of the well-known ☞ Brandywine
★ Bay restaurant also run this authentic Italian outdoor café. People stop by in the morning for an espresso and a fresh pastry, and all day long for a cappuccino or a tiramisù, delicious toast Italiano (grilled ham and Swiss cheese sandwiches), fresh salads, bowls of perfectly cooked linguine or penne with a variety of sauces, and crispy tomato and mozzarella pizzas. Drink specialties include the Mango Bellini, an adaptation of the famous Bellini cocktail served by Harry's Bar in Venice. ✉ *Waterfront Dr.,* ☎ *284/494–5369. Reservations not accepted. No credit cards. Closed Sun. Closes at 9:30 PM Mon.–Sat.*

MEXICAN

$$–$$$$ ✕ **Lime 'n' Mango.** A long open-air veranda is the romantic setting for this popular restaurant in the ☞ Treasure Isle Hotel. The menu features local specialties and, surprisingly, authentic Mexican cuisine. Try the conch fritters, salt fish cakes, or Jamaican calamari for an appetizer. The fajitas—chicken, beef, or vegetarian—are the best Mexican entrée; they arrive at your table sizzling in a hot iron frying pan, with a side basket of warm tortillas. The coconut shrimp is also popular. There's a West Indian barbecue here Saturday night. ✉ *Waterfront Dr.,* ☎ *284/494–2501. AE, MC, V.*

SEAFOOD

$$$–$$$$ ✕ **The Captain's Table.** Select the exact lobster you want from the lobster pool here, and be careful not to fall in—the pool is in the floor right in the middle of the dining room. The menu also includes traditionally prepared escargot, fresh local fish, grilled lobster, filet mignon with béarnaise sauce, duckling with berry sauce, and creative daily specials. Ceiling fans keep the dining room cool, but there are also tables on a breezy terrace overlooking the harbor. ✉ *Columbus Centre, Wickham's Cay I,* ☎ *284/494–3885. AE, MC, V. No lunch Sat.–Sun.*

$$–$$$$ ✕ **The Fishtrap.** Dine alfresco at this laid-back restaurant, which serves grilled local lobster, several local catches-of-the-day, steaks, and chicken. The lunch menu includes burgers and salads as well as a few Mexican items. ✉ *Columbus Centre, Wickham's Cay I,* ☎ *284/494–3626. AE, MC, V. No lunch Sun.*

Outside Road Town

AMERICAN/CASUAL

$$–$$$ ✕ **Pusser's Landing.** Yachters flock to this waterfront restaurant. Downstairs, belly up to the large, outdoor mahogany bar or choose a waterside table for drinks, sandwiches, and light dinners. Head upstairs for quieter alfresco dining and a delightfully eclectic menu that includes homemade black bean soup, freshly grilled local fish, pasta, and pub favorites like shepherd's pie. Tuesday is all-you-can-eat shrimp night. ⊠ *Soper's Hole,* ☎ *284/495–4554. AE, MC, V.*

CARIBBEAN

$$–$$$$ ✕ **The Apple.** This small, inviting restaurant is in a little West Indian house. Soft candlelight creates a relaxed atmosphere in which to partake of fish steamed in lime butter, conch or whelks in garlic sauce, or other local seafood dishes. There's a traditional West Indian barbecue and buffet every Sunday evening from 7 until 9, and coconut chips and conch fritters are served at happy hour weekdays from 5 until 7. ⊠ *Little Apple Bay,* ☎ *284/495–4437. AE, MC, V. No lunch.*

$$–$$$ ✕ **Mrs. Scatliffe's.** The best West Indian cooking on the island is here, according to many knowledgeable Tortolans (though some bemoan, "She's gone Continental"). Lunch and dinner are served on the upstairs terrace of Mrs. Scatliffe's home. The food is freshly prepared (vegetables come from the family garden); the baked chicken in coconut is meltingly tender. After dinner, live entertainment is often provided by family members. ⊠ *Carrot Bay,* ☎ *284/495–4556. Reservations essential. No credit cards.*

$$–$$$ ✕ **Myett's.** Right in the middle of Cane Garden Bay Beach, this two-
★   level restaurant and bar is hopping day and night. Chowder made with fresh Anegada lobsters is the house specialty. The menu includes everything from hamburgers to fruit platters and vegetarian dishes to grilled shrimp, lobster, steak, and tuna. Sunday there's an all-day barbecue buffet and a live reggae band. ⊠ *Cane Garden Bay,* ☎ *284/495–9649. Reservations not accepted. AE, MC, V.*

$$–$$$ ✕ **Quito's Gazebo.** This rustic beachside bar and restaurant is owned and operated by Quito Rhymer, a multitalented BVI recording star who plays the guitar and sings Calypso ballads and love songs Tuesday, Thursday, Friday, and Sunday; a reggae band performs Saturday. The menu is Caribbean with an emphasis on fresh fish. Try the conch stew or the curried chicken. A Caribbean buffet is featured on Sunday night, and Friday is fish-fry night. The atmosphere is so convivial that by the time you finish dinner, you're likely to find yourself swapping yarns with some colorful local personalities. ⊠ *Cane Garden Bay,* ☎ *284/495– 4837. MC, V. Closed Mon.*

CONTEMPORARY

$$$–$$$$ ✕ **Garden Restaurant.** Relax over dinner in this dimly lit, intimate, open-air restaurant at ☞ **Long Bay Beach Resort.** The extensive menu changes daily: Appetizers might include escargot and Portobello mushrooms in pastry or Caesar salad with passion-fruit croutons; and the list of entrées might feature broiled swordfish steak with pecan-lime butter, duck breast with Grand Marnier sauce, or beef tenderloin with red-pepper salsa. Pecan pie and rum cheesecake are among the dessert specialties. ⊠ *Long Bay,* ☎ *284/495–4252. AE, MC, V. No lunch.*

$$$–$$$$ ✕ **Skyworld.** The longtime owner-chef of the well-known Upstairs
★   restaurant took over this mountaintop aerie several years ago, bringing his superb menu with him. Come at sunset and watch the western horizon go ablaze with color, then settle back in the casually elegant dining room to feast. The superbly cooked filet mignon with peaches and port wine sauce is truly exceptional. Other specialties include a

delicious lobster au gratin appetizer, grilled local fish, roast duck, and key lime pie. ⊠ *Ridge Rd.*, ☎ *284/494–3567. AE, MC, V.*

$$$–$$$$ ✕ **Sugar Mill Restaurant.** Candles gleam, and the background music is peaceful in this well-known, romantic restaurant. Inside a 360-year-old mill that's part of their ☞ **Sugar Mill Hotel,** owners Jeff and Jinx Morgan never disappoint. Well-prepared selections on the à la carte menu, which changes nightly, include pasta and vegetarian entrées. Crab bisque with crab rolls or Caribbean sweet-potato soup are good starters. House favorite entrées include the Jamaican jerk pork roast, the regimental beef curry with *poppadoms* (Indian popovers), marinated roast duck, and fresh local fish with spicy creole sauce. ⊠ *Apple Bay,* ☎ *284/ 495–4355. AE, MC, V.*

ENGLISH

$$–$$$ ✕ **The Last Resort.** Actually on Bellamy Cay, just off Beef Island (free ferry service is provided to and from Trellis Bay/Beef Island), this spot features an English buffet, complete with pumpkin soup, prime rib, and Yorkshire pudding, as well as vegetarian selections. This is also the site of the longest-running show in the BVI. For more than 20 years, guests have been laughing at the inimitable cabaret humor and ribald ditties of owner Tony Snell, the BVI's answer to Benny Hill. ⊠ *Bellamy Cay,* ☎ *284/495–2520. AE, MC, V.*

ITALIAN

$$$–$$$$ ✕ **Brandywine Bay.** For the best in romantic dining, don't miss this
★ hillside gem. Candlelit outdoor tables have a sweeping view of neighboring islands. Owner-chef Davide Pugliese prepares foods the Tuscan way: grilled with lots of fresh herbs. The remarkable menu can include homemade mozzarella, foie gras, grilled local wahoo, and grilled veal chop with ricotta and sun-dried tomatoes; it always includes duck with an exotic fruit sauce. The wine list is excellent, and the lemon tart and the tiramisù are irresistible. ⊠ *Sir Francis Drake Hwy., east of Road Town,* ☎ *284/495–2301. Reservations essential. AE, MC, V. Closed Sun. No lunch.*

SEAFOOD

$$$–$$$$ ✕ **Conch Shell Point.** This peaceful, alfresco restaurant sits on a point
★ overlooking boat-studded Trellis Bay on Beef Island, just off Tortola's east end. The menu features fish fresh out of the local waters. Tender swordfish steaks, mahimahi, and grouper fillets are popular choices and can be prepared grilled, blackened, or panfried with a variety of light sauces. Duck, chicken, and steaks are also available. ⊠ *Beef Island, East End, just past airport,* ☎ *284/495–2285. AE, MC, V. Closed Mon.*

Beaches

Beaches in the BVI have less development than those on St. Thomas or St. Croix—and fewer people. Try to get out on a dive-snorkeling boat or a day-trip sailing vessel at least once during your stay. This is often the best way to reach the most virgin Virgin beaches, which are on deserted islands. Tortola's north side has several perfect, palm-fringed white sand beaches that curl around turquoise bays and coves. Nearly all are accessible by car (preferably one with four-wheel-drive), albeit down bumpy roads that corkscrew precipitously. Facilities run the gamut, from absolutely none to a number of beachside bars and restaurants and places to rent water-sports equipment.

If you want to surf, the area of **Apple Bay** (⊠ North Shore Rd.), which includes **Little Apple** Bay and **Capoon's Bay,** is the spot—although the beach itself is pretty narrow. Sebastian's, the very casual hotel here, caters to those in search of the perfect wave. Good waves are never a sure thing, but you're more apt to catch one in January and February.

The water at **Brewers Bay** (⊠ Brewers Bay Rd. W or Brewers Bay Rd. E) is good for snorkeling and there's a campground and beach bar here. The beach and its old sugar mill and rum-distillery ruins are just north of Cane Garden Bay (up and over a steep hill), just past Luck Hill. There's another entrance just east of Skyworld.

Cane Garden Bay (⊠ Cane Garden Bay Rd.) rivals St. Thomas's Magens Bay in beauty. Exceptionally calm, crystalline waters and a silky stretch of sand make this enticing beach one of Tortola's most popular getaways. It's the closest beach to Road Town—one steep uphill and downhill drive—and is one of the BVI's best-known anchorages. (Unfortunately, it can be very crowded when cruise ships are in town.) You can rent sailboards and such, star-gaze from the bow of a boat, and nosh or sip at a variety of places, including Quito's Gazebo (*see also* Dining, *above, and* Nightlife, *below*).

Elizabeth Beach (⊠ Ridge Rd.) is a wide sandy stretch lined with palm trees, accessible by walking down a private road. The undertow can be severe here in winter. **Josiah's Bay** (⊠ Ridge Rd.) is another favored place to hang ten, although in winter the undertow is often strong. The wide and oft-deserted beach is a nice place for a quiet picnic.

The scenery at **Long Bay, Beef Island** (⊠ Beef Island Rd.) draws superlatives: You can catch a glimpse of Little Camanoe and Great Camanoe islands, and if you walk around the bend to the right, you can see little Marina Cay and Scrub Island. Long Bay is also a good place to find interesting seashells. Take the Queen Elizabeth II Bridge to Beef Island and watch for a small dirt turnoff on the left before the airport. Follow the road that curves along the east side of the dried-up marsh flat; don't drive directly across the flat as you can damage it.

Long Bay West (⊠ Long Bay Rd.) is a stunning, 1-mi-long (1½-km-long) stretch of white sand. Have your camera ready for snapping the breathtaking approach. Although Long Bay Resort sprawls along part of it, the entire beach is open to the public. The water is not as calm here as at Cane Garden or Brewers Bay, but it's still swimmable.

After bouncing your way to the beautiful **Smuggler's Cove** (⊠ Belmont Rd.), you'll really feel as if you've found a hidden piece of the island, although you probably won't be alone on weekends. There's a fine view of Jost Van Dyke Island, and the snorkeling is good. About the only thing you'll find moving at **Trunk Bay** (⊠ Ridge Rd.) is the surf. It's directly north of Road Town, midway between Cane Garden Bay and Beef Island, and to reach it you have to hike down a *ghut* (gully) from the high Ridge Road.

Outdoor Activities and Sports

Participant Sports

FISHING

The deep-sea fishing here is so good that tournaments draw competitors from around the world for the largest bluefish, wahoo, and shark. You can bring your catch back to your hotel's restaurant, and the staff will prepare it for you for dinner. For a few hours of reel fun, try **Blue Ocean Adventures** (⊠ Romasco Pl., Road Town, ☎ 284/494–2872) or **Pelican Charters Ltd.** (⊠ Prospect Reef, ☎ 284/496–7386).

HORSEBACK RIDING

If you've ever wanted to ride a horse along a deserted beach, now's your chance. Or you can head up to Tortola's ridges for spectacular views. The **Ellis Thomas Riding School** (⊠ Sea Cows Bay, ☎ 284/494–4442) teaches riding and also has trips through scenic hills and along sandy beaches. **Shadow Stables** (⊠ Ridge Rd., ☎ 284/494–2262) offers small group rides down onto the shore or up into the hills.

SAILING

The BVI are among the world's most popular sailing destinations. They're close together and surrounded by calm waters, so it's fairly easy to sail from one anchorage to the next. If you know how to sail, you can charter a bareboat (perhaps for your entire vacation); if you're unschooled, you can hire a boat with a captain or learn to sail. **Catamaran Charters** (⊠ Village Cay Marina, Road Town, ☎ 284/495–6661) charters catamarans with or without captains. **BVI Yacht Charters** (⊠ Inner Harbour Marina, Road Town, ☎ 284/494–4289) offers 38-ft to 51-ft sailboats for charter. Their boats come with or without a captain, whichever you prefer. **Full Sailing School** (⊠ Maya Cove, ☎ 284/494–0512) offers beginner and advanced sailing lessons. **The Moorings** (⊠ Wickham's Cay II, Road Town, ☎ 284/494–2501 or 800–535-7289), considered one of the best bareboat operations in the world, has a large fleet of well-maintained, mostly Beneteau yachts. Hire a captain or sail the boat yourself. If you prefer a power boat, call **The Power Co.** (⊠ Fat Hog's Bay, East End, ☎ 284/495–1979) for both bareboat and captained charters.

SCUBA DIVING AND SNORKELING

Clear waters and numerous reefs mean that the BVI have some of the best scuba diving and snorkeling opportunities in the Caribbean. **Alice in Wonderland** is a deep dive south of Ginger Island with a wall that slopes gently from 15 ft to 100 ft. It features huge mushroom-shape coral, hence its name. Crabs, lobsters, and shimmering fan corals make their home in the tunnels, ledges, and overhangs of **Blonde Rock,** a pinnacle that goes from just 15 ft below the surface to 60 ft deep. It's between Dead Chest and Salt Island. When the currents aren't too strong, **Brewer's Bay Pinnacle** (from 20 ft down to 90 ft) is a great dive site that teems with sealife. *The Chikuzen,* sunk northwest of Brewer's Bay in 1981, is a 246-ft vessel in 75 ft of water; it's home to thousands of fish, colorful corals, and big rays. At **The Indians,** near Pelican Island, colorful corals decorate canyons and grottoes created by four large, jagged pinnacles that rise 50 ft from the ocean floor.

In 1867, the **RMS *Rhone,*** a 310-ft-long royal mail steamer, split in two when it sank in a devastating hurricane. It's so well preserved that it was used in the movie *The Deep.* You can see the crow's nest and bowsprit, the cargo hold in the bow, and the engine and enormous propeller shaft in the stern. Its four parts are at various depths from 30 to 80 ft (nearby Rhone Reef is only 20–50 ft down). Get yourself some snorkeling gear and hop a dive boat to this wreck, off Salt Island (just across the channel from Road Town) and part of the BVI National Parks Trust. Every dive outfit in the BVI runs superlative scuba and snorkel tours here. For timid snorkelers, simple and safe flotation devices are available, and the scuba supervisors will keep an eye on you. The **Painted Walls** is a shallow dive site where corals and sponges create a kaleidoscope of colors on the walls of four long gullies. It's just northeast of Dead Chest.

Baskin' in the Sun (⊠ Prospect Reef, ☎ 284/494–2858) has beginner and advanced diving courses and daily trips. **Underwater Safaris** (⊠ The Moorings, ☎ 284/494–3235) offers resort and advanced diving courses and scheduled day and night dives.

TENNIS

Tortola's tennis facilities range from simple, untended, concrete courts to professionally maintained surfaces where organized tournaments and socials are hosted. Listed below are facilities available to the public; some have restrictions for nonguests.

Frenchman's Cay (⊠ West End, ☎ 284/495–4844) has an artificial-grass court with a pretty view of Sir Francis Drake Channel. Those who patronize the hotel or restaurant can use the court free of charge; for others, there's an hourly fee. Although the court is lighted, there's no pro available to be your guiding light, so to speak.

At the **Moorings-Mariner Inn** (⊠ Road Town, ☎ 284/494–2332) hotel, marina, and Treasure Isle Hotel guests have free access to the one all-weather hard court. But the lack of lights and a pro staffer may leave you in the dark.

Prospect Reef Resort (⊠ Road Town, ☎ 284/494–3311) guests can play free by day (there's a fee for lights) on any of six hard-surface courts; nonguests pay by the hour. You can make an appointment with the island's most famous pro, Mike Adamson.

WINDSURFING

The winds are so steady here that some locals use sailboards to get from island to island. Two of the best spots for sailboarding are Nanny Cay and Trellis Bay on Beef Island. **Boardsailing BVI** (⊠ Nanny Cay, ☎ 284/495–0422; ⊠ Trellis Bay, Beef Island, ☎ 284/495–2447) rents equipment and offers private and group lessons.

Spectator Sports

BASKETBALL

The NBA games are a national passion and folks also play pretty good basketball here. Die-hard fans can catch games at the New Recreation Grounds on Monday, Wednesday, Friday, or Saturday between May and August. For information, contact the **BVI Tourist Board** (☞ Visitor Information *in* British Virgin Islands A to Z, *below*).

CRICKET

Fans of this sport are fiercely loyal and are an exuberant crowd at cricket matches. They're held at the New Recreation Grounds, next to the J. R. O'Neal Botanic Gardens, weekends February–April.

SOFTBALL

If you enjoy watching softball, you can catch local games on weekend evenings at the Old Recreation Grounds between Long Bush Road and Lower Estate Road. The season runs February–August.

Shopping

The BVI aren't really a shopper's delight, but you can find some interesting items, particularly artwork. Don't be put off by an informal shop entrance. Some of the best finds in the BVI lie behind shabby doors.

Areas

Most of the shops and boutiques on Tortola are clustered on and off Road Town's Main Street and at the **Wickham's Cay** shopping area adjacent to the marina. There's also an ever-growing number of art and clothing stores at **Soper's Hole** in West End.

Specialty Stores

ART

Caribbean Fine Arts Ltd. (⊠ Main St., Road Town, ☎ 284/494–4240) carries a wide range of Caribbean art, including original watercolors, oils, and acrylics, as well as signed prints, limited-edition serigraphs, and turn-of-the-century sepia photographs.

Fluke's (⊠ Trellis Bay, East End, ☎ no phone) is the place to come for unique island maps, appealing prints, and colorful T-shirts.

Islands Treasures (⊠ Soper's Hole, ☎ 284/495–4787) sells elaborate model ships; coffee-table books on the Caribbean; maps and prints; and watercolors, paintings, pottery, and sculpture by island artists.

Sunny Caribbee Art Gallery (⊠ Main St., Road Town, ☎ 284/494–2178) has one of the largest displays in the Caribbean of paintings, prints, and watercolors by artists from all of the Caribbean islands.

CLOTHES AND TEXTILES

Arawak (⊠ On the dock at Nanny Cay, ☎ 284/494–5240) carries gifts, batik sundresses, sportswear and resort wear for men and women, accessories, and children's clothing.

Caribbean Handprints (⊠ Main St., Road Town, ☎ 284/494–3717) creates Caribbean-themed silk-screened fabric and sells it by the yard or in all forms of clothing and beach bags.

Domino (⊠ Main St., Road Town, ☎ 284/494–5879) showcases a colorful array of comfortable, light cotton clothing—including selections from Indonesia—as well as island jewelry and gift items.

The Pusser's Company Store (⊠ Main St. and Waterfront Rd., Road Town, ☎ 284/494–2467; ⊠ Soper's Hole Marina, ☎ 284/495–4603) features nautical memorabilia, ship models, marine paintings, an entire line of clothes and gift items bearing the Pusser's logo, handsome decorator bottles of Pusser's rum, Caribbean books, and a new line of stormproof luggage.

Sea Urchin (⊠ Waterfront, Columbus Centre, Road Town, ☎ 284/494–2044; ⊠ Mill Mall, Road Town, ☎ 284/494–4108; ⊠ Soper's Hole Marina, ☎ 284/495–4850) is the source for local books, sunglasses, and islandwear—print shirts and shorts, slinky swimsuits, cover-ups, sandals, and T-shirts.

Turtle Dove Boutique (⊠ Flemming St., Road Town, ☎ 284/494–3611) is one of the best shops in the BVI for international swimwear and silk and linen dresses, as well as gifts and accessories for the home.

Violet's (⊠ Wickham's Cay I, ☎ 284/494–6398) features a collection of beautiful silk lingerie and a small line of designer dresses.

Zenaida's of West End (⊠ Frenchman's Cay, ☎ 284/495–4867) displays the fabric finds of Argentine Vivian Jenik Helm, who travels through South America, Africa, and India in search of batiks, hand-painted and hand-blocked fabrics, and interesting weaves that can be made into *pareos* (women's wraps) or wall hangings. The shop also sells unusual bags, belts, sarongs, scarves, and ethnic jewelry.

FOODSTUFFS

Ample Hamper (⊠ Village Cay Marina, Wickham's Cay I, ☎ 284/494–2494; ⊠ Soper's Hole Marina, ☎ 284/495–4684) has a good selection of cheeses, wines, fresh fruits, and canned goods from the United Kingdom and the United States. You can have the management here provision your yacht or rental villa.

Fort Wine Gourmet (⊠ Main St., Road Town, ☎ 284/494–3036) carries a sophisticated variety of gourmet items and fine wines and champagnes, including Petrossian caviar and Hediard goods from France.

Gourmet Galley (⊠ Wickham's Cay II, Road Town, ☎ 284/494–6999) sells wines, cheeses, fresh fruits and vegetables, and provides full provisioning for yachtspeople and villa renters.

GIFTS

Buccaneer's Bounty (⊠ Main St., Road Town, ☎ 284/494–7510) sells a delightful assortment of greeting cards, pirate memorabilia, nautical and tropical artwork, books on seashells and the islands, and Christmas ornaments.

Caribbean Corner Spice House (⊠ Soper's Hole, ☎ 284/495–4498) sells exotic herbs and spices and homemade jams, jellies, hot sauces, and natural soaps. You'll find Cuban cigars here, too.

J. R. O'Neal, Ltd. (⊠ Main St., Road Town, ☎ 284/494–2292) stocks the shelves of its somewhat hidden shop with fine crystal, Royal Worcester china, a wonderful selection of hand-painted Italian dishes, handblown Mexican glassware, ceramic housewares from Spain, and woven rugs and tablecloths from India.

The Sunny Caribbee Herb and Spice Company (⊠ Main St., Road Town, ☎ 284/494–2178), in a brightly painted West Indian house, packages its own herbs, teas, coffees, vinegars, hot sauces, natural soaps, skin and suntan lotions, and exotic concoctions—Arawak Love Potion and Island Hangover Cure, for example. You'll also find Caribbean books and art and hand-painted decorative accessories.

JEWELRY

Columbian Emeralds (⊠ Wickham's Cay I, Road Town, ☎ 284/494–7477), a Caribbean chain catering to the cruise-ship crowd, is the source for duty-free genuine emeralds plus other gems, gold jewelry, crystal, and china.

Felix Gold and Silver Ltd. (⊠ Main St., Road Town, ☎ 284/494–2406) may have an unimpressive site, but its handcrafted jewelry is exceptional. Choose from island or nautical themes or have something custom-made out of sterling silver or 14-karat gold.

Samarkand (⊠ Main St., Road Town, ☎ 284/494–6415) handcrafts charming gold and silver pendants, earrings, bracelets, and pins—many with an island theme. You'll also find genuine Spanish pieces of eight (coins—old Spanish pesos of eight *reals*—from sunken galleons).

PERFUMES AND COSMETICS

Flamboyance (⊠ Main St., Road Town, ☎ 284/494–4099; ⊠ Soper's Hole Marina, ☎ 284/495–5946) carries a wide selection of designer fragrances and upscale cosmetics.

Nightlife and the Arts

Nightlife

Like any good sailing destination, Tortola has watering holes that are popular with salty and not-so-salty dogs alike. Many offer entertainment; check the weekly *Limin' Times* for current schedules. The local beverage is a Painkiller, an innocent-tasting mixture of fruit juices and rums. It goes down smoothly but packs quite a punch, so give yourself a moment before you order another.

Bing's Drop In Bar. This rollicking local hangout has a DJ nightly in season. ⊠ *Fat Hog's Bay, East End,* ☎ *284/495–2627.*

Bomba's Surfside Shack. By day, this little shack—covered with everything from crepe paper leis to license plates to colorful graffiti—looks like a pile of junk; by night, it's one of Tortola's liveliest spots and one of the Caribbean's most famous beach bars. Sunday at 4 there's always some sort of live music, and Wednesday at 8 the locally famous Blue Haze Combo shows up to play everything from reggae to top-40 tunes. Every full moon, bands play all night long and people flock here from all over. ⊠ *Apple Bay,* ☎ *284/495–4148.*

Fish Trap. Karaoke fans head here Friday evening, taking turns at amusing the crowds. ⊠ *Columbus Centre, Wickham's Cay I,* ☎ *284/ 494–3626.*

Jolly Roger. An ever-changing array of local, U.S., and down-island bands play everything from rhythm and blues to reggae to country to good old rock and roll Friday and Saturday starting at 8. ⊠ *West End,* ☎ *284/495–4559.*

Myett's. Local bands play here Friday, Saturday, and Sunday evenings (and sometimes Monday evenings, too), and there's usually a lively dance crowd. ⊠ *Cane Garden Bay,* ☎ *284/495–9543.*

The Pub. Here you'll find an all-day happy hour on Friday, guitarist Reuben Chinnery on Friday and Saturday, and late-night local bands on occasion. ⊠ *Waterfront St., Road Town,* ☎ *284/494–2608.*

Pusser's Deli. Thursday is nickel-beer night, and crowds gather here for courage (John Courage, that is) by the pint. Other nights try Pusser's famous mixed drinks—Painkillers—and snack on the excellent pizza. ⊠ *Waterfront St., Road Town,* ☎ *284/494–4199.*

Pusser's Landing. The schedule at Pusser's varies nightly, but you can usually count on some kind of live music (it could be reggae, rock, or a steel band) on Friday and Saturday evenings and Sunday afternoons. ⊠ *Soper's Hole, West End,* ☎ *284/495–4554.*

Quito's Gazebo. BVI recording star Quito Rhymer sings island ballads and love songs, accompanied by the guitar at this rustic beachside bar-restaurant (☞ *also* Dining, *above*). Solo shows are on Sunday, Tuesday, and Thursday nights at 8:30; Friday and Saturday, Quito and the band—The Edge—pump out a variety of tunes. ⊠ *Cane Garden Bay,* ☎ *284/495–4837.*

Sebastian's. There's often live music here on Saturday and Sunday, and you can dance under the stars. ⊠ *Apple Bay,* ☎ *809/495–4214.*

The Arts

Classics in the Atrium. Musical artists from around the world perform here October–February each year. Past artists have included Britain's premier a cappella group, Black Voices; New Orleans jazz pianist Ellis Marsalis; and Keith Lockhart and the Serenac Quartet (from the Boston Pops Symphony). ⊠ *The Atrium at the H. Lavity Stoutt Community College, Paraquita Bay,* ☎ *284/494–4994.*

Exploring Tortola

Tortola doesn't have many historical sights, but it does have lots of beautiful natural scenery. Although you could explore the island's 10 square mi (26 square km) in a few hours, opting for such a whirlwind tour would be a mistake. Life in the fast lane has no place amid some of the Caribbean's most breathtaking panoramas and beaches. Also, the roads are extraordinarily steep and twisting, making driving quite demanding. The best strategy is to explore a bit of the island at a time. For example, you might try Road Town (the island's main town) one morning and a drive to Cane Garden Bay and West End (a little town on, of course, the island's west end) the next afternoon. Or you might consider a visit to East End, a *very* tiny town located exactly where its name suggests. The north shore is where you'll find all of the best beaches.

Numbers in the margin correspond to points of interest on the Tortola map.

Sights to See

❷ Ft. Burt. The most intact historic ruin on Tortola was built by the Dutch in the early 17th century to safeguard Road Harbour. It sits on a hill at the western edge of Road Town and is now the site of a small hotel and restaurant. The foundations and magazine remain, and the structure offers a commanding view of the harbor. ⊠ *Waterfront Dr.,* ☎ *no phone.* 🎟 *Free.* ☉ *Daily dawn–dusk.*

4 Ft. Recovery. The unrestored ruins of the 17th-century Dutch fort, 30 ft in diameter, sit amid a profusion of tropical greenery on the Villas at Fort Recovery Estates grounds. There's not much to see here, and there are no guided tours, but you're welcome to stop by and poke around. ☒ *Waterfront Dr.,* ☏ *284/485–4467.* ☑ *Free.*

5 Frenchman's Cay. On this little island connected by a causeway to Tortola's western end, there's a marina and a captivating complex of pastel West Indian–style buildings with shady balconies, shuttered windows, and gingerbread trim that house art galleries, boutiques, and restaurants. **Pusser's Landing** is a lively place where you can stop for a cold drink (many are made with Pusser's famous rum) and a sandwich and watch the boats come and go from the harbor.

3 J. R. O'Neal Botanic Gardens. Take a walk through this 2¾-acre showcase of lush tropical plant life. There are sections devoted to prickly cacti and succulents, hothouses for ferns and orchids, gardens of medicinal herbs, and plants and trees indigenous to the seashore. From the tourist board office in Road Town (☞ Visitor Information *in* British Virgin Islands A to Z, *below*), cross Waterfront Drive and walk one block over to Main Street and turn right. Keep walking until you see the BVI High School. The gardens are on your left. ☒ *Botanic Station,* ☏ *284/494–4997.* ☑ *Free.* ☉ *Mon.–Sat. 9–4:30.*

9 Mt. Healthy National Park. The remains of an 18th-century sugar plantation are here. The windmill structure has been restored, and you can see the ruins of a mill, a factory with boiling houses, storage areas, stables, a hospital, and many dwellings. This is a nice place to picnic. ☒ *Ridge Rd.,* ☏ *no phone.* ☑ *Free.* ☉ *Daily dawn–dusk.*

6 North Shore Shell Museum. On Tortola's north shore, this casual museum has a very informal exhibit of shells, unusually shaped driftwood, fish traps, and traditional wooden boats. ☒ *North Shore Rd.,* ☏ *284/495–4714.* ☑ *Free.* ☉ *Daily dawn–dusk.*

1 Road Town. The laid-back capital of the BVI is on the south side of Tortola and looks out over Road Harbour. It takes only an hour or so to stroll down Main Street and along the waterfront, checking out the traditional pastel-painted West Indian buildings with high-pitched, corrugated-tin roofs, bright shutters, and delicate fretwork trim. For hotel and sightseeing brochures and the latest information on everything from taxi rates to ferry-boat schedules, stop in the BVI Tourist Board (☞ Visitor Information *in* British Virgin Islands A to Z, *below*). Or just choose a seat on one of the benches in Sir Olva Georges Square, on Waterfront Drive, and watch the people come and go from the ferry dock and customs office across the street.

7 Sage Mountain National Park. At 1,716 ft, Sage Mountain is the highest peak in the BVI. From the parking area, a trail will lead you in a loop not only to the peak itself (and extraordinary views) but also to the island's small rain forest, sometimes shrouded in mist. Most of the forest was cut down over the centuries to clear land for sugarcane, cotton, and other crops, as well as pastureland and stands of timber; in 1964 this park was established to preserve what rain forest remained. Up here you can see mahogany trees, white cedars, mountain guavas, elephant-ear vines, mamey trees, and giant bulletwoods, to say nothing of such birds as mountain doves and thrushes. Take a taxi from Road Town or drive up Joe's Hill Road and make a left onto Ridge Road toward Chalwell and Doty villages. The road dead-ends at the park. ☒ *Ridge Rd.,* ☏ *no phone.* ☑ *Free.*

8 Skyworld. Drive up here and climb the observation tower for a stunning, 360-degree view of numerous islands and cays. On a clear day, you can even see St. Croix (40 mi/64½ km away) and Anegada (20 mi/32 km away). ⊠ *Ridge Rd.*, ☎ *no phone.* ⊡ *Free.*

VIRGIN GORDA

Virgin Gorda, with its mountainous central portion connected by skinny necks of land to southern and northern appendages—on a map it looks like the slightest breeze would cause the whole island to splinter apart—is quite different from Tortola. The pace is even slower here, and Virgin Gorda receives less rain, so some areas are more arid and home to scrub brush and cactus. Goats and cattle own the right of way, and the unpretentious friendliness of the people is winning.

Lodging

Virgin Gorda's charming hostelries appeal to a select, appreciative clientele. Repeat business is extremely high here. Visitors who prefer Sheratons, Marriotts, and the like may feel they get more for their money on other islands, but the peace and pampering offered on Virgin Gorda are priceless to the discriminating traveler. For price categories, *see* the chart *under* Lodging *in* Tortola, *above.*

Hotels and Inns

$$$$ 🏨 **Biras Creek Hotel.** A longtime guest purchased Biras Creek several
★ years ago and made it so classy that it's accepted by the exclusive Relais & Chateaux family of hotels. Units are in cottages, and each has a bedroom and a living room with terra-cotta floor tiles and a decor of soft Caribbean colors and fabrics. Off the bath is an enclosed garden shower that's open to the sky. Although entrances are discreetly hidden among the trees, many of the cottages are just feet from the water's edge. Bike paths and trails lead to the beaches and the outstanding ☞ **Biras Creek** restaurant. General manager Jamie Holmes brings his special touch and years of Caribbean hotel experience to this 140-acre hideaway. The hilltop, open-air, bar-restaurant area is made of stonework and has stunning views of North Sound. A "Sailaway" package includes two nights on a private yacht. ⊠ *North Sound (Box 54),* ☎ *284/494–3555 or 800/223–1108,* 🖷 *284/494–3557. 33 suites, 1 villa. 2 restaurants, bar, air-conditioning, pool, 2 tennis courts, hiking, beach, snorkeling, windsurfing, boating, bicycles, shop. AE, MC, V. FAP.*

$$$$ 🏨 **Bitter End Yacht Club and Marina.** This family-oriented, convivial
★ resort-cum-marina is accessible only by boat. Accommodations range from comfortable hillside or beachfront villas to live-aboard yachts. Your day can include as many or as few activities as you wish: snorkeling and diving trips to nearby reefs, cruises, windsurfing lessons, excursions to local attractions, and lessons at the well-regarded Nick Trotter Sailing School. When the sun goes down, the festivities continue at ☞ **The Clubhouse,** an open-air restaurant-bar overlooking North Sound. ⊠ *North Sound (Box 46),* ☎ *284/494–2746,* 🖷 *284/494–4756. 95 rooms. 2 restaurants, bar, pool, beach, dive shop, snorkeling, windsurfing. AE, MC, V. FAP.*

$$$$ 🏨 **Little Dix Bay.** Relaxed elegance is the hallmark here. The resort sits
★ amid the mangroves, along the curve of a crescent beach. Duplexes with hexagonal units and quadraplex cottages are tucked among the trees and on a little hill. Interiors have handsome fieldstone walls and are decorated in Caribbean prints. About half the rooms are air-conditioned. Lawns are beautifully manicured; the reef-protected beach is long and silken; and the candlelight dining in an open, peak-roof pavilion is a

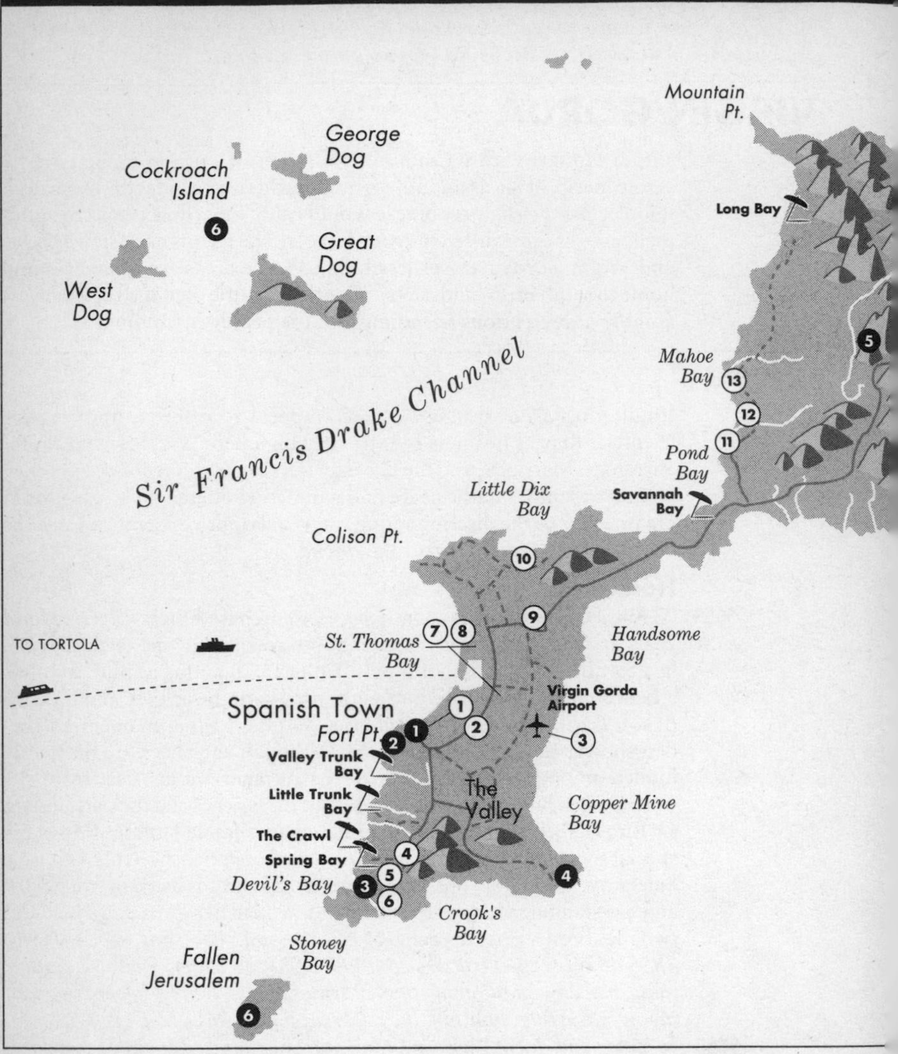

Lodging

Biras Creek Hotel, **16**

Bitter End Yacht Club and Marina, **17**

Guavaberry Spring Bay Vacation Homes, **4**

Leverick Bay Hotel, **14**

Little Dix Bay, **10**

Mango Bay Resort, **12**

Olde Yard Inn, **9**

Paradise Beach Resort, **13**

Virgin Gorda Villa Rentals, **15**

Dining

The Bath and Turtle, **1**

Biras Creek, **16**

Chez Bamboo, **2**

The Clubhouse, **17**

The Crab Hole, **7**

The Flying Iguana, **3**

Giorgio's Italian Restaurant, **11**

Little Dix Bay Pavilion, **10**

Mad Dog's, **5**

Olde Yard Inn, **9**

Pusser's at Leverick Bay, **14**

Sip and Dip Grill, **9**

Teacher Ilma's, **8**

Top of the Baths, **6**

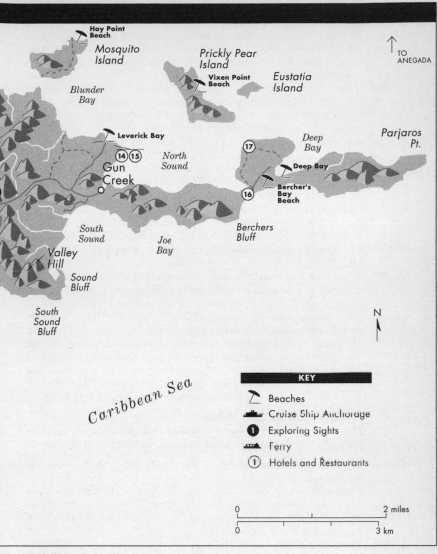

KEY

Beaches
Cruise Ship Anchorage
1 Exploring Sights
Ferry
(1) Hotels and Restaurants

0   2 miles
0   3 km

Exploring
The Baths, **3**
Coastal Islands, **6**
Copper Mine Point, **4**
Little Fort
National Park, **2**
Spanish Town, **1**
Virgin Gorda Peak
National Park, **5**

memorable experience. This resort is popular with honeymooners and older couples who have been coming for years. The ☞ **Little Dix Bay Pavilion** is an unforgettable setting for any meal. ⊠ *Little Dix Bay (Box 70)*, ☎ *284/495–5555*, FAX *284/495–5661. 94 rooms, 4 suites. 3 restaurants, 2 bars, 7 tennis courts, beach, snorkeling, windsurfing, library, children's programs. AE, MC, V. EP, MAP.*

$$$ ⊞ **Olde Yard Inn.** Owners Charlie Williams and Carol Kaufman have
★   cultivated a friendly, refreshing atmosphere at this quiet retreat just outside Spanish Town. Classical music plays in the bar, and books line the walls of the octagonal library cottage. Guest rooms are cozy and very simply furnished (in warmer months, request a room with air-conditioning). You can make arrangements for day-sails and scuba diving excursions, and you can swim in the large pool and work out or get a massage in the health club. There are also two excellent restaurants: the ☞ **Olde Yard Inn** for French-accented dinners and the ☞ **Sip and Dip Grill,** for poolside lunches. The inn isn't on the beach, but free transportation is provided to nearby Savannah Bay. ⊠ *The Valley (Box 26)*, ☎ *284/495–5544 or 800/653–9273 (direct to hotel)*, FAX *284/495–5986. 14 rooms, 1 suite. 2 restaurants, bar, pool, croquet, shop, library. AE, MC, V. EP.*

$$–$$$ ⊞ **Leverick Bay Hotel.** The hillside rooms at this hotel are decorated in pastels and original artwork. All have refrigerators, balconies, and views of North Sound; four two-bedroom condos are also available. A Spanish colonial–style main building houses the ☞ **Pusser's at Leverick Bay** restaurant and a store (also operated by Pusser's of Tortola). The resort's office has books, games, and tennis rackets that you can borrow. A restaurant, a bar, several shops, a pool, a beauty salon, a tiny beach, a dive shop, a coin-operated laundry, and a market are just down the hill. ⊠ *Leverick Bay (Box 63)*, ☎ *284/495–7421*, FAX *284/ 495–7367. 16 rooms, 4 condos. Refrigerators. AE, D, MC, V. EP.*

Private Homes and Villas

Those craving seclusion would do well at a villa or even a private home. Both offer comfortable lodgings with full kitchens and maid service.

$$$–$$$$ ⊞ **Mango Bay Resort.** Sparkling white villas framed by morning glories and frangipanis, handsome contemporary Italian decor, and a gorgeous ribbon of golden sand that all but vanishes at high tide make this an idyllic family retreat. Even for Virgin Gorda it's a study in isolation. ⊠ *Mahoe Bay (Box 1062)*, ☎ *284/495–5672*, FAX *284/495–5674. 5 villas. Beach. No credit cards.*

$$$–$$$$ ⊞ **Paradise Beach Resort.** These one-, two-, and three-bedroom beachfront suites and villas have a handsome Caribbean-style decor, pastel color schemes, and outdoor showers. Four-wheel-drive vehicles are included in the daily rate. ⊠ *Mahoe Bay (Box 534)*, ☎ *284/495–5871. 9 units. Beach. No credit cards.*

$$–$$$$ ⊞ **Guavaberry Spring Bay Vacation Homes.** It's hard to say what's more unusual about these one- and two-bedroom units: their shape (hexagonal) or their location (perched on stilts and scattered about a hillside). Regardless, you're so close to chirping birds and breezes through leaves, you feel as if you're in a tree house. It's just a short walk from the cottages down to the tamarind-shaded beach and not far from the mammoth boulders and cool basins of the famed Baths, which adjoin this property. Eleven private houses are also rentable. ⊠ *The Valley (Box 20)*, ☎ *284/495–5227. 12 1-bedroom units, 9 2-bedroom units. Beach. No credit cards.*

$$–$$$$ ⊞ **Virgin Gorda Villa Rentals.** This company manages the adjacent Leverick Bay Hotel, so it's perfect for those who want to be close to some activity. Many villas have private swimming pools; all are well main-

tained and have spectacular views. ⊠ *Leverick Bay (Box 63),* ☏ *284/ 495–7421. 21 villas, from studios to 3-bedrooms. AE, D, MC, V.*

Dining

Restaurants on Virgin Gorda range from simple to elegant. Hotels that are accessible only by boat will arrange transport in advance upon request for nonguests who wish to dine at their restaurants. It's wise to make dinner reservations almost everywhere. The fancier, more expensive restaurants have dress codes: long pants and collared shirts for men and elegant casual resort wear for women. For price categories, *see* the chart *under* Dining *in* Tortola, *above.*

AMERICAN/CASUAL

$$–$$$ ✕ **Pusser's at Leverick Bay.** This bilevel restaurant at the ☞ Leverick Bay Hotel looks out over picturesque North Sound. The upstairs is slightly less casual and more expensive, with a menu that includes grilled steak, chop, and chicken dishes. Below, the Beach Bar offers light fare—hamburgers, salads, pizzas—all day and a nightly theme menu. Tuesday is pizza-and-beer night; Thursday is $1 Heineken night. ⊠ *Leverick Bay,* ☏ *284/495–7369. AE, MC, V.*

$$–$$$ ✕ **Top of The Baths.** At the entrance to The Baths, this popular restaurant serves food all day long, starting at 8 AM. Tables are outside on a terrace or in an open-air pavilion; all have stunning views of the Sir Francis Drake Channel. Hamburgers, salads, and sandwiches are offered at lunch. Conch seviche and lentil soup are among the dinner appetizers. Entrées include Cornish hen with wild rice, grilled swordfish with fresh rosemary sauce, and local lobster. For dessert, you can choose from such delectables as lemon cheesecake and pecan pie. ⊠ *The Valley,* ☏ *284/495–5497. AE, MC, V.*

$$ ✕ **The Bath and Turtle.** You can really sit back and relax at this infor-
★ mal patio tavern with a friendly staff—although the TV noise can be a bit much. Burgers, well-stuffed sandwiches, pizzas, pasta dishes, and daily specials round out the casual menu. Live entertainers perform on Wednesday and Sunday nights. ⊠ *Virgin Gorda Yacht Harbour,* ☏ *284/ 495 5239. MC, V.*

$$ ✕ **The Flying Iguana.** In this charming restaurant's comfortable lounge, lifelike stuffed or colorfully painted wood iguanas are perched in the plants and local artwork is displayed. The open-air dining room looks out over Virgin Gorda's tiny airport to the sea. Sandwiches and thick, juicy hamburgers are served for lunch. The dinner menu includes a pasta special, grilled chicken, and steaks. ⊠ *The Valley, at the airport,* ☏ *284/495–5277. AE, MC, V.*

$–$$ ✕ **Sip and Dip Grill.** The pool at the ☞ Olde Yard Inn is the setting
★ for this pleasant, informal lunch spot. Come for the grilled fish, pasta salads, chilled soups, and ice cream. Sunday evening there's a barbecue and live entertainment. ⊠ *The Valley,* ☏ *284/495–5544. Reservations not accepted. AE, MC, V. No dinner Mon.–Sat.*

$ ✕ **Mad Dog's.** Piña coladas are *the* thing at this breezy bar just outside The Baths. The menu includes great BLTs, hot dogs, and burgers. ⊠ *The Valley, just before you reach the entrance to The Baths,* ☏ *284/ 495–5830. Reservations not accepted. MC, V. No dinner.*

CAJUN/CREOLE

$$–$$$ **Chez Bamboo.** This pleasant little hideaway isn't really that hard to find: Just look for the building with the purple and green latticework. Candles on the dining-room tables and the patio create a mellow atmosphere in which to enjoy such dishes as conch gumbo, Chez B's bouillabaisse, and leg of lamb *pistou* (baked with a crust of pistachio nuts). Stop by Friday night for live jazz. ⊠ *Across from, and a little* *north of, Virgin Gorda Yacht Harbour,* ☎ *284/495–5752. Reservations not accepted. AE, MC, V. Closed Mon. No lunch.*

CARIBBEAN/CREOLE

$$–$$$$ ✕ **Teacher Ilma's.** A delightful local atmosphere and delicious native-style family dinners—including goat, grouper or snapper, pork, and chicken—are givens at the restaurant in this small house. ✉ *The Valley,* ☎ *284/ 495–5355. Reservations essential. No credit cards. No lunch.*

$–$$ ✕ **The Crab Hole.** This homey hangout serves callaloo soup, salt fish, stewed goat, curried chicken roti, rice and peas, and green bananas. ✉ *The Valley,* ☎ *284/495–5307. No credit cards.*

CONTEMPORARY

$$$$ ✕ **Biras Creek.** This hilltop restaurant at the ☞ **Biras Creek Hotel** is
★   built of island stone and has a signature turret roof. The setting is stunning: broad steps lead up to an open-air lounge and restaurant with beautiful views of North Sound. The gourmet menu changes daily to accommodate resort guests. Appetizers might be chilled yellow-pepper soup, conch fritters with papaya sauce, or avocado and lobster salad. Roast duck breast with plum sauce, grilled swordfish with bacon and caper sauce, pan-seared snapper with a ginger beurre blanc, and a roast breast of pheasant are some of the enticing entrées offered. Delightful desserts include key lime pie with raspberry sauce, a warm treacle tart, and a rich chocolate brownie with chocolate sauce. Dinner ends with Biras Creek's signature offering of Stilton and port. ✉ *North Sound,* ☎ *284/494–3555. Reservations essential. AE, MC, V.*

$$$$ ✕ **Little Dix Bay Pavilion.** For an elegant evening at the ☞ **Little Dix**
★   **Bay** resort, you can't do better than this—the candlelight in the main open-air pavilion is enchanting, the menu sophisticated, the service attentive. The dinner menu changes daily, but there's always a fine selection of superbly prepared seafood, meat, and vegetarian entrées—gingered duck breast with Pacific Rim vegetables, black Angus rib eye with horseradish and mustard sauce, pan-seared snapper with christophene ratatouille. The breakfast and lunch buffets here shine. ✉ *Spanish Town,* ☎ *284/495–5555, ext. 174. AE, MC, V.*

$$$–$$$$ ✕ **Olde Yard Inn.** Dinner at the ☞ **Olde Yard Inn** is a charming, civilized affair. The intimate dining room is suffused with gentle classical melodies and the scent of herbs; a cedar roof covers the breezy space, which is decorated with old-style Caribbean charm. The French-accented cuisine includes lamb chops with mango chutney, chicken breast in a rum cream sauce, grilled fish, steaks, and lobster. Chocolate mousse, cheesecake, and key lime pie are sweet endings. ✉ *The Valley, north of the marina,* ☎ *284/495–5544. AE, MC, V.*

ITALIAN

$$$–$$$$ ✕ **Giorgio's Italian Restaurant.** Gaze out at the stars and listen to the water lap against the shore while dining on veal scaloppine, filet mignon with mushrooms, fresh local fish, or penne with garlic and tomatoes. Lunch fare at this pleasant, casual establishment includes pizzas and sandwiches. ✉ *Mango Bay, 10 mins north of Yacht Harbour,* ☎ *284/495–5684. MC, V.*

SEAFOOD

$$$ ✕ **The Clubhouse.** The ☞ **Bitter End Yacht Club**'s open-air, waterfront restaurant is a favorite rendezvous for the sailing set—busy day and night. At the lavish buffets you also get your choice of an entrée for breakfast, lunch, and dinner. Dinner selections include grilled swordfish or tuna, chopped sirloin, scallops, and shrimp. ✉ *Bitter End Yacht Club, North Sound,* ☎ *284/494–2746. AE, MC, V.*

Beaches

The best beaches are most easily reached by water, although they are also accessible on foot, usually after a moderately strenuous hike of 10 to 15 minutes. Either way, your persistence is amply rewarded. Anybody going to Virgin Gorda must experience swimming or snorkeling among its **unique boulder formations** (Lee Rd.). But why go to **The Baths** (☞ Exploring Virgin Gorda, *below*), which is usually crowded, when you can catch some rays just to the north at **Spring Bay Beach,** which is a gem, and a little farther north at the **Crawl**? Both are easily reached from The Baths on foot via Lee Road or by swimming.

From Biras Creek or Bitter End on the north shore, you can walk to **Bercher's Bay Beach** and along the windswept surf. Footpaths from Bitter End and foot and bike paths from Biras Creek also lead to **Deep Bay,** a calm, well-protected swimming beach. Mosquito Island's **Hay Point Beach** is a broad band of white sand accessible only by boat or by a path from a little dock on the island's east side.

Leverick Bay (⊠ Leverick Bay Rd.) is a small, busy beach-cum-marina that fronts a resort restaurant and pool. Don't come here to be alone, but do come if you want a lively little place and a break from the island's noble quiet. The view of Prickly Pear Island is also a plus, and there's a dive facility right here to motor you out to beautiful Eustatia Reef just across North Sound.

It's worth heading out to **Long Bay** (⊠ Plum Tree Bay Rd., near Virgin Gorda's northern tip, past the Diamond Beach Club), for the snorkeling (Little Dix Bay resort has outings here). The drive takes about half an hour after the turnoff from North Sound Road, and a dirt road makes up part of the route.

For a wonderfully private beach close to Spanish Town, try **Savannah Bay** (⊠ North Sound Rd.). It may not always be completely deserted, but it's a lovely long stretch of white sand. Prickly Pear Island has a calm swimming beach at **Vixen Point Beach.**

Outdoor Activities and Sports

Participant Sports

FISHING

The sportfishing here is so good that anglers from around the world fly in for the annual tournaments. **Walford Ferrington** (⊠ Leverick Bay, North Sound, ☎ 284/495–7612) will pick you up almost anywhere on Virgin Gorda and take you out on his 24-ft speedboat for half- or full-day fishing jaunts.

SAILING

BVI waters are calm and a terrific place to learn to sail. The **Nick Trotter Sailing School** (⊠ Bitter End Yacht Club, North Sound, ☎ 284/494–2745) offers both beginner and advanced courses.

SCUBA DIVING AND SNORKELING

The combination of clear waters, numerous reefs, and interesting shipwrecks means that the BVI have some of the best scuba diving and snorkeling opportunities in the Caribbean. For details on a few of the many breathtaking sites, *see* Scuba Diving and Snorkeling *under* Outdoor Activities and Sports *in* Tortola, *above.* Also, note that the North Sound has some terrific snorkeling spots. The **Bitter End Yacht Club** (⊠ Bitter End Yacht Club, North Sound, ☎ 800/872–2392) offers a number of snorkeling trips. Contact **DIVE BVI** (⊠ Virgin Gorda Yacht Harbour, ☎ 284/495–5513) for expert diving instruction, certification, and day trips.

The North Sound is a good place to learn to windsurf: it's protected, so you can't be easily blown out to sea. The **Bitter End Yacht Club** (☞ Scuba Diving and Snorkeling, *above*) gives lessons and rents equipment.

Spectator Sports

CRICKET

You can catch a cricket match at the **Recreation Grounds** in Spanish Town February–April. Contact the tourist office (☞ Visitor Information *in* British Virgin Islands A to Z, *below*) for specific information on game dates and times.

Shopping

Most boutiques are within hotel complexes. Two of the best are at Biras Creek and Little Dix Bay. Other properties—the Bitter End, Leverick Bay, and the Olde Yard Inn—have small but equally select boutiques, and there's a more than respectable and diverse scattering of shops in the bustling yacht harbor complex in Spanish Town.

ART

Thee Artistic Gallery (✉ Virgin Gorda Yacht Harbour, ☎ 284/495–5104) features Caribbean jewelry, 14-karat-gold nautical jewelry, maps, collectible coins, and crystal.

CLOTHING

DIVE BVI (✉ Virgin Gorda Yacht Harbour, ☎ 284/495–5513) sells books about the islands as well as sportswear, sunglasses, and beach bags.
Island Silhouette in Flax Plaza (✉ Near Fischer's Cove Beach Hotel, ☎ no phone) is the place to go for resort wear hand-painted by Virgin Gorda artists, and locally made tie-dyed T-shirts.
Next Wave (✉ Virgin Gorda Yacht Harbour, ☎ 284/495–5623) sells bathing suits, T-shirts, and canvas tote bags.
Pavilion Gift Shop (✉ Little Dix Bay Hotel, ☎ 284/495–5555) has the latest in resort wear for men and women, as well as jewelry, books, and expensive T-shirts.
Pelican's Pouch Boutique (✉ Virgin Gorda Yacht Harbour, ☎ 284/495–5477) is where you'll find a large selection of swimsuits plus coverups, T-shirts, and accessories.
Pusser's Company Store (✉ Leverick Bay, ☎ 284/495–7369) has a trademark line of rum products, gift items, and sportswear.
Tropical Gift Collections (✉ The Baths, ☎ 284/495–5380) specializes in locally made handicrafts, including hats, bags, and pottery. Island spices are also for sale.

FOODSTUFFS

Bitter End's Emporium (✉ North Sound, ☎ 284/494–2745) is the place for such edible treats as local fruits, cheeses, and bakery goods.
Commissary and Ship Store (✉ The Valley, ☎ 284/495–5555) offers daily specials prepared by Little Dix Resort chefs as well as assorted cheeses, canned goods, wines, and gourmet items.
Wine Cellar and Bakery (✉ Virgin Gorda Yacht Harbour, ☎ 284/495–5250) bakes bread, rolls, muffins, and cookies and has sandwiches and sodas to go.

GIFTS

Palm Tree Gallery (✉ Leverick Bay, ☎ 284/495–7479) sells attractive handcrafted jewelry, paintings, and one-of-a-kind gift items, as well as games and books about the Caribbean.
The Reeftique (✉ Bitter End, North Sound, ☎ 284/494–2745) carries a variety of gift items, including island crafts and jewelry, clothing, and nautical odds and ends with the Bitter End logo.

HANDICRAFTS

Virgin Gorda Craft Shop (✉ Virgin Gorda Yacht Harbour, ☎ 284/495–5137) features the work of island artisans, and carries West Indian jewelry and crafts styled in straw, shells, and other local materials. It also stocks clothing and paintings by Caribbean artists.

Nightlife

Andy's Chateau de Pirate's Pub (✉ The Valley, ☎ 284/495-5252) hops with disco Friday, Saturday, and Sunday nights.

The Bath and Turtle (✉ Virgin Gorda Yacht Harbour, ☎ 284/495-5239), one of the liveliest spots on Virgin Gorda, hosts island bands on Thursday and Sunday from 8 PM until midnight.

Bitter End Yacht Club (✉ North Sound, ☎ 284/494-2746) features local bands several nights a week in season. Call for schedules.

Chez Bamboo (✉ Across from Virgin Gorda Yacht Harbour, ☎ 284/495-5752) is the place to go to listen to jazz on Friday nights.

Little Dix Bay (✉ Little Dix Bay, ☎ 284/495-5555) presents elegant live entertainment several nights a week in season.

Pusser's at Leverick Bay (✉ Leverick Bay, ☎ 284/495-7370) has live bands on Saturday night and Sunday afternoon.

Rock Cafe (✉ The Valley, ☎ 284/495-5177) showcases local talent several nights a week, usually on weekends.

Sip and Dip Grill (✉ Olde Yard Inn, ☎ 284/495-5544) has a live local band at their Sunday night barbecue.

Exploring Virgin Gorda

One of the most effective ways to see Virgin Gorda is by sailboat. There are few roads, and most byways don't follow the scalloped shoreline. The main route sticks resolutely to the center of the island, linking The Baths at the tip of the southern extremity with Gun Creek and Leverick Bay at North Sound and providing exhilarating views. The craggy shoreline, scissored with grottoes and fringed by palms and the island's trademark boulders, has a primitive beauty. If you drive, you can hit all the sights in one day. The best plan is to explore the area near your hotel (either The Valley or North Sound) first, then take one day to drive to the other end. Stop to climb Gorda Peak, in the center of the island.

Numbers in the margin correspond to points of interest on the Virgin Gorda map.

Sights to See

❸ The Baths. At Virgin Gorda's most celebrated sight, giant boulders are scattered about the beach and in the water. Some are almost as large as houses and form remarkable grottoes. Climb between these rocks to swim in the many pools. Early morning and late afternoon are the best times to visit if you want to avoid crowds. (If it's privacy you crave, follow the shore northward to quieter bays—**Spring**, the **Crawl**, **Little Trunk**, and **Valley Trunk**—or head south to **Devil's Bay**.) ✉ *Lee Rd.,* ☎ *no phone.* 🖸 *Free.*

❻ Coastal Islands. You can easily reach the quaintly named islands of **Fallen Jerusalem** and the **Dog Islands** by boat. They're all part of the BVI National Parks Trust, and their seductive beaches and unparalleled snorkeling opportunities display the BVI at their beachcombing, hedonistic best. ☎ *No phone.* 🖸 *Free.*

❹ Copper Mine Point. Here you'll see a tall, stone shaft silhouetted against the sky and a small stone structure that overlooks the sea. These are the ruins of a copper mine established 400 years ago and worked first by the Spanish, then by the English until the early 20th century. ⊠ *Copper Mine Rd.,* ☎ *no phone.* 🎫 *Free.*

❷ Little Fort National Park. This 36-acre wildlife sanctuary has the ruins of an old fort. Giant boulders like those at The Baths are scattered throughout the park. ⊠ *Spanish Town Rd.,* ☎ *no phone.* 🎫 *Free.*

❶ Spanish Town. Virgin Gorda's main settlement, on the island's southern wing, is a peaceful village so tiny that it barely qualifies as a town at all. Also known as the Valley, Spanish Town is home to a marina, a cluster of shops, and a couple of car-rental agencies. Just north of town is the ferry slip. At the **Virgin Gorda Yacht Harbour** you can stroll along the dock and do a little shopping.

❺ Virgin Gorda Peak National Park. There are two trails at this 265-acre park, which contains the island's point highest point at 1,359 ft. Small signs on North Sound Road mark both entrances; sometimes, however, the signs are missing, so keep your eyes open for a set of stairs that disappears into the trees. It's about a 15-minute hike, from either entrance, up to a small clearing, where you can climb a ladder to the platform of a wooden observation tower and a spectacular 360-degree view. ⊠ *North Sound Rd.,* ☎ *no phone.* 🎫 *Free.*

JOST VAN DYKE

Named after an early Dutch settler, Jost Van Dyke is a small island northwest of Tortola and is *truly* a place to get away from it all. Mountainous and lush, the 4-mi-long (6½-km-long) island—home to only about 140 people—has one tiny resort, some rental houses, a campground, and fewer than a dozen informal eateries. With only a handful of cars and a single road, the island makes you feel as if you've stepped back in time. This is one of the Caribbean's most popular anchorages, and there's a disproportionately large number of informal bars and restaurants, which have helped earn Jost its reputation as the "party island" of the BVI.

Lodging

For price categories, *see* the chart *under* Lodging *in* Tortola, *above.*

$$$ 🏨 **Sandcastle.** This six-cottage hideaway is on a ½-mi (¾-km) stretch of white-sand beach at remote White Bay. There's "nothing" to do here, except relax in a hammock, read, walk, swim, and enjoy sophisticated cuisine by candlelight in the ☞ **Sandcastle** restaurant. You can also make arrangements for diving, sailing, and sportfishing trips. ⊠ *White Bay,* ☎ *284/495–9888,* 📠 *284/495–9999. 6 cottages. Restaurant, bar, beach, shop. MC, V. EP.*

$$$ 🏨 **Sandy Ground Estates.** The eight privately owned one- and two-bedroom houses here are tucked into the foliage along the edge of a beach at the east end of Jost Van Dyke. Each one is architecturally different, and interiors range from spartan to stylish. The fully equipped kitchens can be prestocked if you supply a list of groceries (a good idea as supplies are limited on the island), and there are four very casual restaurants on the other side of the hill—a long walk away. ⊠ *Sandy Ground,* ☎ *284/494–3391. 8 houses. Beach. No credit cards. EP.*

$ ⛺ **White Bay Campground.** On remote White Bay beach, this simple campground has bare sites, equipped tent sites (with electricity and a lamp), and screened cabins. The owners will take you on nature walks and can arrange island tours and sailing and diving trips. ⊠ *White Bay,* ☎ *284/495–9312. 8 bare sites, 4 prepared sites, 4 cabins. Restaurant, bar, beach. No credit cards.*

Dining

Restaurants on Jost Van Dyke are informal (some serve meals family style at long tables) but charming. The island is a favorite charter stop, and you're bound to hear people exchanging stories about the previous night's anchoring adventures. Most restaurants don't take reservations, and in all cases dress is casual. For price categories, *see* the chart *under* Dining *in* Tortola, *above.*

ECLECTIC

$$$ ✕ **Sandcastle.** Candlelit dinners in the tiny beachfront dining room of the ☞ Sandcastle cottage complex are four-course, prix-fixe affairs. The menu changes but can include a West Indian pumpkin or curried apple soup; curried shrimp or three-mustard chicken; and, for dessert, rum bananas or key lime pie. Reservations are requested by 4 PM. Sandwiches are served at lunch at the Soggy Dollar Bar, famous as the purported birthplace of the lethal Painkiller drink. ✉ *White Bay,* ☎ *284/ 495–9888. MC, V.*

$$–$$$ ✕ **Abe's Little Harbour.** Specialties at this informal, popular spot include fresh lobster, conch, and spare ribs. During most of the winter season, there's a pig roast every Wednesday night. ✉ *Little Harbour,* ☎ *no phone (boaters can use VHF Channel 16). No credit cards.*

$$–$$$ ✕ **Foxy's Tamarind.** One of the true hot spots in the BVI—and a "must
★   stop" for yachters from the world over—Foxy's hosts the madcap Wooden Boat Race every May and throws big parties on New Year's Eve, April Fools' Day, and Halloween. This lively place serves local dishes and terrific barbecue, and it makes a rum punch that's all its own. Foxy himself plays the guitar and delights in creating calypso ditties about his guests. Next door is Foxy's Store, which sells clothing, sundries, souvenirs, and cassettes of Foxy performing. ✉ *Great Harbour,* ☎ *284/495–9258. AE, MC, V. No lunch.*

$–$$$ ✕ **Club Paradise.** The dinner menu at this casual beachfront establishment includes grilled local fish such as mahimahi, red snapper, and grouper; grilled steak; and barbecued chicken and ribs. Hamburgers, West Indian conch stew, and curried chicken are the luncheon fare. ✉ *Great Harbour,* ☎ *284/495–9267. No credit cards.*

$–$$$ ✕ **Harris' Place.** Owner Harris Jones is famous for his pig-roast buffets and Monday night Lobstermania. Harris' Place is a great spot to rub elbows with locals and the charter-boat crowd. ✉ *Little Harbour,* ☎ *284/495–9302. AE, MC, V.*

$–$$$ ✕ **Sydney's Peace and Love.** Here you'll find great lobster, barbecue, and a sensational (for the BVI) jukebox. The cognoscenti sail here for dinner since there's no beach—meaning no irksome sand fleas. ✉ *Little Harbour,* ☎ *284/495–9271. No credit cards.*

$–$$ ✕ **Happy Laurry.** Hamburgers, cheeseburgers, and honey-dipped fried chicken are the specialties at this beachfront spot. ✉ *Great Harbour,* ☎ *284/495–9259. No credit cards.*

Beaches

White Bay, on the south shore, west of Great Harbour, has a long stretch of white sand. Just offshore, the little islet known as **Sandy Cay** is a gleaming scimitar of white sand, with marvelous snorkeling.

PETER ISLAND

A dramatic, hilly island with wonderful anchorages and beautiful beaches, Peter Island is about 5 mi (8 km) directly south across the Sir Francis Drake Channel from Road Town, Tortola. Set amid the string of small islands that stream from the southern tip of Virgin Gorda, the island is an idyllic hideaway replete with white sand beaches, stunning views, and the Peter Island Resort. You can sail here on your own craft or take a launch from the Peter Island dock just east of Road Town, Tortola ($15 each way or free if you're coming for dinner; just mention that you have a reservation).

Lodging

For price categories, *see* the chart *under* Lodging *in* Tortola, *above.*

$$$$ 🏨 **Peter Island Resort and Yacht Harbour.** Owned and run by the
★   Amway Hotel Corporation, this is an elegant retreat. Fifty-two guest rooms, in four-unit cottages tucked amid beds of radiant tropical flowers, are either on the beach or near the pool. Beachfront units are beautiful stone-and-wood structures with French doors that open onto a lovely stretch of sand. The less expensive ocean-view and garden-terrace rooms look across the pool toward the hills and Tortola. A spectacular hilltop villa, the Crow's Nest, has four bedrooms, a living room, a state-of-the-art kitchen, a dining room, a terrace, an inner courtyard, an entertainment system, domestic help, vehicles, and a private pool. There's lots to do here: facilities include (but *truly* aren't limited to) a tennis program run by Peter Burwash, a water-sports center, mountain bicycles, a 20-station fitness trail, and a 5-star PADI dive facility. After a dinner in the ☞ **Tradewinds Restaurant,** you can often dance under the stars. Those seeking seclusion take note: some of the resort's beaches are on bays that are popular charter-boat anchorages. ✉ *Sprat Bay (Box 211, Road Town, Tortola),* ☎ *284/495–2000 or 800/346–4451,* FAX *284/495–2500. 52 rooms, 3 villas. 2 restaurants, 2 bars, pool, 4 tennis courts, basketball, exercise room, beach, dive shop, windsurfing, mountain bikes, laundry service, helipad. AE, MC, V. FAP.*

Dining

For price categories, *see* the chart *under* Dining *in* Tortola, *above.*

ECLECTIC

$$$$ ✕ **Tradewinds Restaurant.** The ☞ **Peter Island Resort**'s open-air dining room (on really hot days there's air-conditioning, however) overlooks the Sir Francis Drake Channel and is an enchanting dinner setting. The à la carte menu offers mostly Continental selections with subtle Caribbean touches; Saturday night is buffet night. After dinner, dance under the stars to soft, rhythmic tunes performed by local musicians three or four nights a week in season. ✉ *Sprat Bay,* ☎ *284/ 495–2000. Reservations essential. AE, MC, V. No lunch.*

$$$–$$$$ ✕ **Deadman's Bay Bar and Grill.** The resort's casual grill on the beach serves lunches of ribs, burgers, grilled fish, and a bountiful salad bar. Sunday lunch features a lavish West Indian buffet and a steel band. A dinner with a choice of grilled local fish, steak, or chicken is served most evenings. Try one of the many delicious frozen tropical drinks. ✉ *Sprat Bay,* ☎ *284/495–2000. Reservations essential. AE, MC, V.*

Beaches

Palm-fringed **Dead Man's Bay,** considered by many to be one of the world's 10 most romantic beaches, is just a short hike from the dock. Snorkeling is good at both ends of the beach, and you'll find a bar and restaurant for lunch. If you feel like taking a hike instead of heading down to Dead Man's Bay, follow the road up, and when it levels off bear right and head down to the other side of the island and secluded **White Bay.**

ANEGADA

Anegada lies low on the horizon about 14 mi (22½ km) north of Virgin Gorda. Unlike the hilly volcanic islands in the chain, this is a flat coral and limestone atoll. Nine mi (14 km) long and 2 mi (3 km) wide, the island rises no more than 28 ft above sea level. In fact, by the time you're able to see it, you may have run your boat onto a reef. (More than 300 captains, unfamiliar with the waters, have done so since exploration days; note that bareboat charters don't allow their vessels to head here without a trained skipper.) Although the reefs are a sailor's nightmare, they (and the shipwrecks they've caused) are a scuba diver's dream. Snorkeling, especially in the waters around Loblolly Bay on the north shore, is also a transcendent experience. You can float in shallow, calm, totally reef-protected water just a few feet from shore and see one coral formation after another, each shimmering with a rainbow of colorful fish. Such watery pleasures are complemented by ever-so-fine, ever-so-white sand (the northern and western shores have long stretches of the stuff) and the occasional beach bar (stop in for burgers, Anegada lobster, or a frosty beer). The island's population of about 150 lives primarily in a small, south-side village called the Settlement. Many local fisherfolk are happy to take visitors out bonefishing.

Lodging

For price categories, *see* the chart *under* Lodging *in* Tortola, *above.*

$$$$ 🏨 **Anegada Reef Hotel.** If you favor laid-back living (meaning, among other things, absolutely no schedules), this is the spot for you. Pack a bathing suit and a few warmer garments for the evening, and you're good to go. The hotel's 16 simply furnished rooms are laid out in motel fashion. It has its own narrow strip of beach, but beach lovers will want to spend their days on the deserted beaches at the other side of the island; you can ask to be dropped off with a picnic lunch or be picked up and returned to the hotel for lunch. Snorkeling and diving are popular activities, as are deep-sea fishing or bonefishing in the flats. Cool down with a drink in the outdoor bar, and be sure to try the island's famous lobster—freshly grilled in the ☞ **Anegada Reef** restaurant. ✉ *Setting Point,* ☎ *284/495–8002,* FAX *284/495–9362. 16 rooms. Restaurant, bar, beach. No credit cards. FAP.*

$$ 🏨 **Neptune's Treasure.** This little guest house offers four simple double and single rooms that are very basically furnished. However, all have private baths. There's a restaurant, ☞ **Neptune's Treasure,** and a little gift shop on the premises. ✉ *Between Pomato and Saltheap points,* ☎ *284/495–9439. 4 rooms. Restaurant, beach. AE, MC, V. EP.*

$ ⛺ **Anegada Beach Campground.** The tents (8×10 ft or 10×12 ft) here are pitched in a marvelously serene setting. Sites cost $7 per person, per night. ✉ *The Settlement,* ☎ *284/495–9466. Restaurant, bar, beach. No credit cards.*

Dining

There are between 3 and 10 restaurants open at any one time, depending on the season and also on whim. Check when you're on the island. For price categories, *see* the chart *under* Dining *in* Tortola, *above.*

SEAFOOD

$$$ ✕ **Anegada Reef Hotel.** Seasoned yachters gather nightly at the ☞ **Anegada Reef Hotel**'s bar-restaurant to converse and dine with the hotel guests. Dinner is by candlelight and always includes famous Anegada lobster, steaks, and chicken—all prepared on the large grill by the little open-air bar. ⊠ *Setting Point,* ☎ *284/495–8002. Reservations essential. No credit cards.*

$$–$$$ ✕ **Neptune's Treasure.** The owners catch, cook, and serve the seafood (lobster is a specialty) at this casual bar and restaurant in the ☞ Neptune's Treasure guest house. ⊠ *Between Pomato and Saltheap points,* ☎ *284/495–9439. AE.*

$$–$$$ ✕ **Pomato Point.** This relaxed restaurant-bar is on a narrow beach, a short walk from the Anegada Reef Hotel. Entrées include steak, chicken, lobster, and fresh-caught seafood. Owner Wilfred Creque displays various island artifacts, including shards of Arawak pottery and 17th-century coins, cannonballs, and bottles. ⊠ *Pomato Point,* ☎ *284/495–8038. Reservations essential. No credit cards.*

$–$$$ ✕ **Big Bamboo.** Ice-cold beer, island drinks, burgers, and grilled lobster entice a steady stream of barefoot diners to this beach bar for lunch. Dinner is by request. ⊠ *Loblolly Bay,* ☎ *284/495–2019. AE.*

Shopping

Anegada Reef Hotel Boutique (⊠ Setting Point, ☎ 284/495–8002) has a bit of everything: resort wear, hand-painted T-shirts, locally made jewelry, books, and one-of-a-kind gifts. **Pat's Pottery** (⊠ Nutmeg Point, ☎ 284/495–8031) sells bowls, plates, cups, candlestick holders, original watercolors, and more.

OTHER BRITISH VIRGIN ISLANDS

Cooper Island

This small hilly island on the south side of the Sir Francis Drake Channel, about 8 mi (13 km) from Road Town, Tortola, is popular with the charter-boat crowd. There are no roads (which doesn't really matter because there aren't any cars), but you will find a beach restaurant, a casual little hotel, a few privately owned houses (some of which are available for rent), and great snorkeling at the south end of Manchioneel Bay.

Dining and Lodging

For price categories on this island and the others discussed below, *see* the charts *under* Lodging *and* Dining *in* Tortola, *above.*

$$–$$$ ✕🏠 **Cooper Island Beach Club.** Two West Indian–style cottages—set back from the beach among the palm trees—house 12 no-frills units with a living area, a small but complete kitchen, and a balcony. A stay here takes you back to the basics: you use rainwater that has been collected in a cistern, and you can't use any appliances because electricity is so limited (who needs pressed clothes and blow-dried hair anyway?). There's plenty of "civilization," however, at the on-site bar, which fills nightly with boaters. The restaurant is also popular with the boating crowd (if you don't have your own vessel, note that ferry service from Road Town is available only to hotel guests). It serves great ratatouille (it's a main course at lunch, an appetizer at dinner); grilled fish, chicken, and steak; and conch creole. For lunch, there are hamburgers, conch fritters, and pasta salad. Reservations are essential. ⊠ *Machioneel Bay (Box 859, Road Town, Tortola),* ☎ *413/659–2602 or 800/542–4624; no phone to restaurant (boaters can use VHF Channel 16). 12 rooms. Restaurant, beach, dive shop. AE, MC, V. EP.*

Guana Island

Guana Island is very quiet and, because the whole thing is owned by the resort, *very* private. There are *no* public amenities, and access is limited (the hotel sends a private launch to pick up its guests on Beef Island). If you arrive on your own boat, the only place you're allowed is on the beach.

Dining and Lodging

$$$$ ✕🏠 **Guana Island.** The hotel complex is atop a hill, a 10-minute walk from the beach, and the views of neighboring islands are stunning. Fifteen comfortable guest rooms are in seven houses that are scattered throughout the grounds. The houses are decorated in Caribbean style, with rattan furniture, and each has its own porch. You can observe more than 50 species of birds on this island, and the terrain is a verdant collection of tropical plants ringed by six deserted beaches. Guests mingle during cocktail hour, and often choose to dine together at several large tables in the main house, but there are small tables if you prefer a more intimate meal. ✉ *Hilltop (Box 32, Road Town, Tortola),* ☎ *284/494–2354,* 🕾 *284/495–2900. 15 rooms. Restaurant, ceiling fans, tennis court, croquet, hiking. No credit cards. FAP.*

Little Thatch Island

Just west of Tortola is Little Thatch Island, a petite private island with an elegant hideaway.

Dining and Lodging

$$$$ ✕🏠 **Little Thatch Island.** When you want to be pampered and don't care about the price (the cost per day is $8,250 for 1–4 guests, and $9,500 for 5–10 guests), this stunning hilltop hideaway can be all yours. The four octagonal, one-bedroom cottages have Douglas Fir roofs and broad terraces. Three of the four have handsome, outdoor (but exceedingly private), stonework showers. Rattan furnishings are of the highest quality and are extremely comfortable. Views from the open-air living room, the dining room, and the pool are breathtaking. A gourmet chef prepares all your meals, and unobtrusive staff members provide impeccable service, seeing to your every need. ✉ *Box 861, Road Town, Tortola,* ☎ *284/495–9227.* 🕾 *284/495–9212. Pool, beach, windsurfing, boating. AE, MC, V. FAP*

Necker Island

Necker Island, just north of Virgin Gorda, is yet another private isle. Accommodations here are luxurious, but you can only stay if you rent the whole island.

Lodging

$$$$ 🏠 **Necker Island.** You and as many as 23 friends can lease the whole island, including its five beaches, many walks, tennis courts, luxurious villa with 10 spacious guest rooms, and two Balinese cottages. The common living area is anything but common: The huge room is lined with doors that open to the breezes. Here and there are oversize couches and chairs; these are surrounded by tropical potted plants, artwork, and sculptures. Bedrooms have slate floors, stonework walls, and stunning views. A chef prepares gourmet meals for you in the state-of-the-art kitchen; a full staff takes care of everything else. ✉ *Box 1091, The Valley, Virgin Gorda,* ☎ *284/494–2757,* 🕾 *284/494–4396. Pool, 2 tennis courts, exercise room, beaches, boating. AE, MC, V.*

Marina Cay

Beautiful little Marina Cay is in Trellis Bay, not far from Beef Island. Sometimes you can see it and its large J-shape coral reefs—a most dramatic sight—from the air during the approach to the airport on Beef Island. With only 6 acres, this islet is considered small even by BVI stan-

dards. There's a restaurant, Pusser's Store, and a six-unit hotel here.
Ferry service is free from the dock on Beef Island.

Dining and Lodging

$$$ ✕⌂ **Marina Cay Hotel and Restaurant.** The tiny island's only hotel has
four double rooms and two suites, all with lovely views of the water
and neighboring islands. Each has its own porch. The restaurant's menu
ranges from fish and lobster to steak, chicken, and barbecued ribs.
Pusser's Painkiller Punch is the house specialty. There's free ferry ser-
vice from the Beef Island dock for anyone visiting the island (call for
ferry times, which vary with the season). ✉ *West side of Marina Cay
(Box 76, Road Town, Tortola)*, ☎ 284/494–2174, FAX 284/494–4775.
4 rooms, 2 villas. Restaurant, bar, beach. AE, DC, MC, V. EP.

BRITISH VIRGIN ISLANDS A TO Z

Arriving and Departing

BY AIRPLANE

Both the Beef Island/Tortola and Virgin Gorda airports are classic
Caribbean—always sleepy. Sometimes the Beef Island terminal gets
crowded before departures, and lines at service desks move slowly when
this happens; give yourself at least an hour. There's no nonstop ser-
vice from the continental United States to the BVI; connections are usu-
ally made through San Juan, Puerto Rico, or St. Thomas, USVI. Airlines
that serve both San Juan and St. Thomas include: **American** (☎ 284/
495–1122), **Continental** (☎ 340/777–8190), and **Delta** (☎ 340/774–
9300). **Air St. Thomas** (☎ 284/495–5935) flies between St. Thomas and
Virgin Gorda. Regularly scheduled flights between the BVI and most
other Caribbean islands are provided by **LIAT** (☎ 284/495–2577).
Many Caribbean islands can also be reached through **Gorda Aero Ser-
vice** (☎ 284/495–1571), a charter service on Tortola.

From the Airport: At the Beef Island/Tortola airport, taxi drivers usu-
ally hover at the exit from customs. Fares are officially set; they're not
negotiable and are lower per person when there are several passengers.
Figure about $15 for up to three people and $5 for each additional
passenger for the 20-minute ride to Road Town, and about $20–$30
for the 45-minute ride to West End. Expect to share your taxi, and be
patient if your driver searches for people to fill his cab—only a few
flights land each day, and this could be your driver's only run. You can
also call the **BVI Taxi Association** (☎ 284/495–1982).

On Virgin Gorda call **Mahogany Rentals and Taxi Service** (☎ 284/495–
5469). If you're staying anywhere on Virgin Gorda's North Sound, you
can fly to Beef Island/Tortola and catch the nearby North Sound Ex-
press (☞ Getting Around, *below*), or you can fly to Virgin Gorda and
take a taxi to North Sound. From here a hotel launch will meet you,
but you must have made arrangements with your hotel before your ar-
rival. Don't get nervous if your land taxi leaves you by yourself on a
deserted dock and tells you to wait for your skipper—someone *will*
show up. If your destination is Leverick Bay, your land taxi will take
you there directly.

BY BOAT

Ferries connect St. Thomas, USVI, with Tortola and Virgin Gorda. **Inter-
Island Boat Services'** *Sundance II* (☎ 284/495–4166) connects St.
John and West End, Tortola, daily. **Native Son, Inc.** (☎ 284/495–4617)
operates three ferries (*Native Son, Oriole,* and *Voyager Eagle*) and has
daily service between St. Thomas and Tortola (West End and Road
Town). The *Nubian Princess* (☎ 284/495–4999) operates between
Red Hook, St. Thomas; Cruz Bay, St. John; and West End, Tortola,

daily. **Smiths Ferry Services** (☎ 284/495–4495 or 284/494–2355) operates between downtown St. Thomas and Road Town and West End daily. **Speedy's Ferries** (☎ 284/495–5240) runs between Virgin Gorda, Tortola, and St. Thomas on Tuesday, Thursday, and Saturday.

Electricity
Electricity is 110 volts, the same as it is in North America. The electricity is quite reliable.

Emergencies
Clinics: On Virgin Gorda, there's a clinic in Spanish Town, or The Valley (☎ 284/495–5337). There's also a clinic on Virgin Gorda at North Sound (☎ 284/495–7310). **General emergencies:** ☎ 999. **Hospital: Peebles Hospital** (☎ 284/494–3497) is in Road Town, on Tortola. **Pharmacies:** In Road Town, try **J. R. O'Neal Drug Store** (☎ 284/494–2292) or **Lagoon Plaza Drug Store** (☎ 284/494–2498). In Spanish Town, Virgin Gorda, the pharmacies are **Island Drug Centre** (☎ 284/495–5449) and **Medicure** (☎ 284/495–5479).

Festivals and Seasonal Events
In March, catch the breathtaking displays of local foliage at the **Horticultural Society Show** at the Botanical Gardens (☎ 284/494–4557). In April, join in the fun at the **Virgin Gorda Festival,** which culminates with a parade on Easter Sunday. Also in April, glimpse the colorful spinnakers as sailing enthusiasts from around the world gather for the internationally known **BVI Spring Regatta.** May is the time for partying at **Foxy's Wooden Boat Regatta** on Jost Van Dyke. In August, try your hand at sportfishing as anglers from around the globe compete to land the largest catch at the **BVI Sportfishing Tournament.** Also in August, you can participate in two weeks of joyful revelry during Tortola's **BVI Summer Festival.** If you've always wanted to escape to the islands and live on a boat, then the November **BVI Boat Show** is for you. To compete in sailing races and games, drop in on Virgin Gorda's North Sound during the last six weeks of the year for the **Bitter End Yacht Club's Competition Series,** including the Invitational Regatta. For the best in local *fungi* bands (bands that make music using household items—washboards, spoons, and the like—as instruments), stop by the **Scratch/Fungi Band Fiesta** in December (☎ 284/494–2629).

Getting Around
AIRPLANES
Gorda Aero Service (☞ Arriving and Departing, *above*) flies between Tortola and Anegada on Monday, Wednesday, and Friday and offers charter flights between Tortola, Virgin Gorda, and Anegada as well as to other Caribbean islands.

BUSES
There's bus service on Tortola. For information about rates and schedules, call **Scato's Bus Service** (☎ 284/494–2365). Taking the bus is a great way to meet locals, albeit at a bumpy snail's pace. Look for an eight-passenger van with Scato's name on the front, and wave your hand when you see it. The fare ranges from $2 to $10, depending on where you're going. Rates are determined by the driver, and they vary, since the bus can pick you up anywhere and drop you anywhere.

CAR RENTALS
Driving in the BVI is on the left side of the road. Main roads are, for the most part, well paved, but there are exceptionally steep hills and sharp curves; driving demands your complete attention. Basically, a main road encircles the island and several roads cross it, almost always through mountainous terrain. Speed limits (rarely enforced) are 20 mph in town and 40 mph outside town. Gas costs about $2 a gallon. You'll

need a temporary BVI license, available at the rental car company for
$10 with a valid license from another country.

On Tortola, **Avis** (☎ 284/494–3322) rents four-wheel-drive vehicles
and cars in Road Town. **Budget** has two offices (✉ Wickham's Cay I,
Road Town, ☎ 284/494–2639; ✉ Wickham's Cay II, Road Town, ☎
284/494–5150) and rents both cars and four-wheel-drive vehicles.
Hertz (✉ West End, ☎ 284/495–4405) also rents four-wheel-drive vehicles and cars. On Virgin Gorda, **Mahogany Rentals and Taxi Service**
(✉ Spanish Town, ☎ 284/495–5469) rents four-wheel-drive vehicles
and compact cars. **Speedy's** (✉ Spanish Town, ☎ 284/495–5240)
provides four-wheel-drive vehicles and compact cars.

FERRIES

Speedy's Fantasy (☎ 284/495–5240) makes the run between Road
Town, Tortola, and Spanish Town, Virgin Gorda, daily. **North Sound
Express** (☎ 284/495–2271) boats run daily between Virgin Gorda's
North Sound and Beef Island/Tortola. The **Peter Island Ferry** (☎ 284/
495–2000) runs daily between Peter Island's private dock on Tortola
(just east of Road Town) and Peter Island. **Jost Van Dyke Ferry Service** (☎ 284/494–2997) makes the Jost Van Dyke–Tortola run several
times daily.

TAXIS

Your hotel staff will be happy to summon a taxi for you. Rates aren't
published so you should negotiate the fare with your driver before you
start your trip. It's cheaper to travel in groups as there's a minimum
fare to each destination, which is the same whether you are one, two,
or three people. The taxi number is also the license plate number. On
Tortola, there are **BVI Taxi Association** stands in Road Town near the
ferry dock (☎ 284/494–7519), at Wickham's Cay I (☎ 284/494–
2322), and at the Beef Island/Tortola airport (☎ 284/495–1982). You
can also usually find a taxi at the ferry dock at Soper's Hole, West End,
where ferries arrive from St. Thomas.

Andy's Taxi and Jeep Rental (✉ The Valley, ☎ 284/495–5511) offers
taxi service from one end of Virgin Gorda to the other. **Mahogany Rentals
and Taxi Service** (✉ The Valley, ☎ 284/495–5469) also provides taxi
service all over Virgin Gorda.

Guided Tours

To do some chauffeured sightseeing of Tortola, get in touch with the
BVI Taxi Association (☞ Getting Around, *above*); the minimum is
three persons. **Travel Plan Tours** (☎ 284/494–2872) can arrange island
tours, boat tours, and yacht charters from its Tortola base. To arrange
tours on Virgin Gorda, contact **Andy's Taxi and Jeep Rental** (☞ Getting Around, *above*) and **Mahogany Rentals and Taxi Service** (☞ Getting Around, *above*).

Language, Culture, and Etiquette

English is the official language, and it's often spoken with a West Indian accent and with a few idiomatic expressions. If someone says they're
"just limin," it means they're hanging out. If you ask for an item in a
store, and the shopkeeper replies "It's finished" then the shop has tem-
porarily run out. Islanders are religious, and churches fill up on Sunday. You're welcome to attend services, but be sure to dress up. If you
encounter any rudeness, you probably didn't begin the conversation
properly: Only after courteous exchanges ("Hello, how are you today?"
and "Not too bad, and how are you?") can you get down to the business of buying groceries, ordering lunch, or hiring a taxi.

Money Matters

CURRENCY

The currency is the U.S. dollar. Any other currency must be exchanged at a bank. On Tortola you'll find a **Barclays Bank** (✉ Wickham's Cay I, ☎ 284/494–2171) near the waterfront in Road Town. The **Chase Manhattan Bank** (✉ Wickham's Cay I, ☎ 284/494–2662) is also near Road Town's waterfront and has an ATM machine. On Virgin Gorda **Barclay's Bank** (✉ Virgin Gorda Yacht Harbour, ☎ 284/495–5271) isn't far from the ferry dock in Spanish Town.

SERVICE CHARGES, TAXES, AND TIPPING

There's a 7% government tax on hotel rooms; service charges range from 5% to 15%. Tip porters and bellhops $1 per bag. Sometimes a service charge (10%) is included on restaurant bills; it's customary to leave another 5% if you liked the service. If no charge is added, 15% is the norm. Cabbies normally aren't tipped because most own their cabs; add 10%–15% if they exceed their duties. There's no sales tax in the BVI. The departure tax is $10 by plane and $5 by boat.

Opening and Closing Times

Banks usually have hours Monday–Thursday 9–2:30 and Friday 9–2:30 and 4:30–6. **Post offices** are open weekdays 9–5 and Saturday 9–1. **Stores** are generally open Monday–Saturday 9–5.

HOLIDAYS

New Year's Day, Commonwealth Day (Mar. 13), Good Friday (Apr. 21), Easter Monday (Apr. 24), Whit Monday (June 12), Sovereign's Birthday (June 17), Territory Day (July 1), BVI August Festival Days (Aug. 6–11), St. Ursula's Day (Oct. 25), Birthday of Heir to the Throne (Nov. 20), Christmas, Boxing Day (Dec. 26).

Passports

U.S. and Canadian citizens need a valid passport or a birth certificate with a raised seal along with a government-issued photo ID. Visitors from all other countries need a valid passport.

Precautions

Although crime is almost nonexistent, use common sense: don't leave your camera on the beach while you take a dip or your wallet on a hotel dresser when you go for a walk. The fruit (which resembles small green apples) from the manchineel tree is poisonous, and the sap can blister skin badly. These trees are found all over the Caribbean, and those on resort property or trails are usually marked. No-see-ums (fleas) can be a bother at twilight, especially along the beaches. Use insect repellent, if there's no wind to blow them away.

Telephones and Mail

The area code for the BVI is 284; when you make calls from North America, you need only dial the area code and the number. From the United Kingdom, you must dial 001 and then the area code and the number. To call anywhere in the BVI once you've arrived, dial all seven digits. A local call from a pay phone costs 25¢, but such phones are often on the blink. An alternative is a Caribbean phone card, available in $5, $10, and $20 denominations. It's sold at most major hotels and many stores and can be used to call all over the Caribbean and to access USADirect from special phone-card phones. For credit card or collect long-distance calls to the United States, use a phone-card telephone or look for special **USADirect** phones, which are linked directly to an AT&T operator. For access dial 800/872–2881, or dial 111 from a pay phone and charge the call to your MasterCard or Visa. USADirect and pay phones can be found at most hotels and in towns.

There are post offices in Road Town on Tortola and in Spanish Town on Virgin Gorda. (Note that postal service in the BVI isn't very efficient.) Postage for a first-class letter to the United States, Canada, or the United Kingdom is 35¢; for a postcard, 20¢. For a small fee, **Rush It** in Road Town (☎ 284/494–4421) and in Spanish Town (☎ 284/495–5821) offers most U.S. mail and UPS services (via St. Thomas the next day). If you wish to write to an establishment in the BVI, include the specific island in the address; there are no postal codes.

Visitor Information

Information about the BVI is available through the **British Virgin Islands Tourist Board** (✉ 370 Lexington Ave., Suite 1605, New York, NY 10017, ☎ 212/696–0400 or 800/835–8530) or **British Virgin Islands Information Offices** (✉ 1804 Union St., San Francisco, CA 94123, ☎ 415/775–0344; 800/232–7770 nationwide). British travelers can write or visit the **BVI Information Office** (✉ 110 St. Martin's La., London WC2N 4DY, ☎ 0171/240–4259).

On Tortola there's a **BVI Tourist Board Office** at the center of Road Town near the ferry dock, just south of Wickham's Cay I (✉ Box 134, Road Town, Tortola, ☎ 284/494–3134). It's open weekdays 9–5. The **Virgin Gorda BVI Tourist Board** is in Virgin Gorda Yacht Harbour in Spanish Town (☎ 284/495–5181). It's open weekdays 9–5.

Finally, a travel companion that doesn't snore on the plane or eat all your peanuts.

When traveling, your MCI WorldCom Card is the best way to keep in touch. Our operators speak your language, so they'll be able to connect you back home—no matter where your travels take you. Plus, your MCI WorldCom Card is easy to use, and even earns you frequent flyer miles every time you use it. When you add in our great rates, you get something even more valuable: peace-of-mind. So go ahead. Travel the world. MCI WorldCom just brought it a whole lot closer.

You can even sign up today at www.mci.com/worldphone or ask your operator to make a collect call to 1-410-314-2938.

EASY TO CALL WORLDWIDE

1 Just dial the WorldPhone access number of the country you're calling from.
2 Dial or give the operator your MCI WorldCom Card number.
3 Dial or give the number you're calling.

Australia ◆	
To call using OPTUS	1-800-551-111
To call using TELSTRA	1-800-881-100
Bahamas/Bermuda	1-800-888-8000
British Virgin Islands	1-800-888-8000
Costa Rica ◆	0-800-012-2222
Denmark	8001-0022
Norway ◆	800 19912
India	000-127
For collect access	000 126
United States/Canada	1-800-888-8000

For your complete WorldPhone calling guide, dial the WorldPhone access number for the country you're in and ask the operator for Customer Service. In the U.S. call 1-800-431-5402.

◆ Public phones may require deposit of coin or phone card for dial tone.

EARN FREQUENT FLYER MILES

US AIRWAYS
DIVIDEND MILES

MCI WorldCom, its logo and the names of the products referred to herein are proprietary marks of MCI WorldCom, Inc. All airline names and logos are proprietary marks of the respective airlines. All airline program rules and conditions apply.

The first thing you need overseas is the one thing you forget to pack.

FOREIGN CURRENCY DELIVERED OVERNIGHT

Chase Currency To Go® delivers foreign currency to your home by the next business day*

It's easy—before you travel, call 1-888-CHASE84 for delivery of any of 75 currencies

Delivery is free with orders of $500 or more

Competitive rates— without exchange fees

You don't have to be a Chase customer—you can pay by Visa® or MasterCard®

 CHASE

THE RIGHT RELATIONSHIP IS EVERYTHING.®

1•888•CHASE84
www.chase.com

*Orders must be placed before 5 PM ET. $10 delivery fee for orders under $500.
©1999 The Chase Manhattan Corporation. All rights reserved. The Chase Manhattan Bank. Member FDIC.

4 PORTRAITS OF THE VIRGIN ISLANDS

BEACH PICNIC

AS THE BOAT from St. Thomas neared St. John, it occurred to me again that I might have made a serious mistake leaving behind my ham. You could say, after all, that our entire trip had been based on that ham. In our family, the possibility of renting a house for a week on St. John had been kicking around for years; Abigail and Sarah were so strongly for it that I sometimes referred to them as "the St. John lobby." We had been on St. John briefly during the week we'd spent on St. Thomas, only a short ferry ride away. St. Thomas is known mainly for recreational shopping—its principal town, Charlotte Amalie, had already been a tax-free port for a century and a half when the United States bought St. Thomas and St. John and St. Croix from Denmark toward the end of the five or six thousand years of human history now thought of as the pre-credit-card era—and what I remember most vividly about our week there was trying to explain to Abigail and Sarah that the mere existence of a customs exemption of $800 per person does not mean that each person is actually required to spend $800. ("I happen to know of a man who was permitted to leave even though he had purchased only $68.50 worth of goods. He is now living happily in Metuchen, New Jersey.") I was rather intent on getting the point across because according to what I could see from the shopping patterns on St. Thomas, our family would ordinarily have been expected to buy $3,200 worth of perfume—enough perfume, I figured, to neutralize the aroma of a fair-sized cattle feedlot.

What Abigail and Sarah remembered most vividly were rumless piña coladas—it was their first crack at rumless piña coladas—and the spectacular beaches on St. John. The beaches are accessible to everyone through inclusion in the Virgin Islands National Park, which covers nearly three quarters of the island, and, just as important, going to the beach is pretty much

all there is to do—a state of affairs that Abigail and Sarah would think of as what ham purveyors call Hog Heaven. We had talked about it a lot, but the conversation usually ended with a simple question: What would we eat?

The question went beyond the dismal food we had come to expect in Virgin Islands restaurants. (On St. Thomas, the restaurants had seemed to specialize in that old Caribbean standby, Miami frozen fish covered with Number 22 sunblock, and my attempts to find some native cooking had resulted mainly in the discovery of bullfoot soup.) In a house on St. John, we would presumably have our own kitchen, but we'd be dependent on the ingredients available in the island stores. Our only previous experience in that line—in the British Virgin Islands, where we had once rented a house when Abigail was a baby—had produced the shopping incident that I have alluded to ever since when the subject of Caribbean eating comes up. On a shopping trip to Roadtown, the capital, Alice ordered a chicken and asked that it be cut up. When we returned from our other errands, we found that the butcher had taken a frozen chicken and run it through a band saw, producing what looked like some grotesque new form of lunch meat.

The memory of that chicken caused a lot of conversations about St. John rentals to fizzle and die. Then, during one of the conversations, my eye happened to fall on a country ham that was hanging in our living room. Maybe I'd better explain the presence of a ham in our living room; Abigail and Sarah seem to think it requires an explanation whenever they bring friends home for the first time. Now and then, we have arranged to buy a country ham from Kentucky. The ham often arrives with a wire attached to it, and since we have a couple of stalking cats, I put the ham out of their reach by attaching the wire to a living room beam in what seems to be a natural hanging place—a spot where we once briefly considered hanging a philodendron. The first time I hung a ham in

---

The individual customs exemption has been increased from $800 to $1,200.

the living room, Alice pointed out that some of the people expected at a sort of PTA gathering about to be held at our house didn't know us well enough to see the clear logic involved in the ham's presence, so I put a three-by-five card of the sort used in art galleries on a post next to the ham. The card said, "Country ham. 1983. J. T. Mitchum. Meat and wire composition." Since then, I've found that even without the card many guests tend to take the country ham as a work of art, which, at least in the view of people who have eaten one of Mr. Mitchum's, it is.

Contemplating that ham, I found my resistance to renting a house in St. John melting away. We could take the ham along to sustain us, in the way a band of Plains Indians, living in happier times, would have brought their newly killed buffalo to the next camp site. We would bring other provisions from the neighborhood. We would not be dependent on frozen chicken lunch meat. We made arrangements to rent a house for a week on St. John.

Then I left the ham at home. Not because it slipped my mind. A country ham is not the sort of thing you simply forget. Alice had argued that it was terribly heavy, that it was more than we needed, that she didn't feel like making biscuits on St. John (because the American Virgin Islands are U.S. territory, the federal law against eating country ham without biscuits applies). I finally agreed, although I couldn't resist pointing out that the remark about its being more than we needed was directly contradicted by the number of times I've heard people who have just finished off a plateful of country ham and biscuits say, "That's exactly what I needed."

I don't mean we arrived in St. John empty-handed. I had brought along an extra suitcase full of provisions. There were some breakfast necessities—tea and the seven-grain bread that Alice likes in the mornings and, of course, a dozen New York bagels. We also had smoked chicken breasts, a package of a Tuscan grain called farro, a couple of packages of spaghetti, sun-dried tomatoes, a package of pignoli nuts, an Italian salami, several slices of the flat Italian bread called focaccia that a man near our house makes every morning, a jar of olive paste, and what Alice usually refers to as her risotto kit—arborio rice, fresh Parme-

san cheese, olive oil, wild mushrooms, a head of garlic, a large onion, and a can of chicken broth. Better safe than sorry.

FINDING A PLACE to rent had turned out to be relatively simple. St. John is organized on the premise that a lot of visitors will want to rent a house. The only hotels of any size on the island are Caneel Bay, one of the first of the resorts that the Rockefellers built for those who feel the need of being cosseted for a few days in reassuringly conventional luxury, and a new resort called the Virgin Grand, a touch of flash that is always mentioned in the first 30 seconds of any discussion about whether the island is in danger of being ruined by development.

The de facto concierges of St. John are a dozen or so property managers, each of whom presides over a small array of houses that seem to have been built with renting in mind—which is to say that you can usually count on your towels being of a uniform color and you don't have to toss somebody else's teddy bears off the bed to go to sleep. Most of the houses are tacked onto the side of a hill—the side of a hill is about the only place to build a house on St. John, which has so many ups and downs that its old Indian name was probably Place Where You're Always in First Gear—and have decks whose expansive views are measured by how many bays are visible. Our house was a simple but cheery two-bedroom place with what I would call a one-and-a-sliver-bay view. It had a kitchen more than adequate for the preparation of an arrival supper of grilled smoked-chicken sandwiches on focaccia. As I ate one, I tried to keep in mind that out there in the dark somewhere people were probably eating Miami frozen fish with sunblock. We weren't safe yet.

I think it was the phrase "fresh fish" that gave me the first hint that sustaining life on St. John might be easier than I had anticipated. For years, the American Virgin Islands have been known for being surrounded by fish that never seem to make it onto a plate. The first sunny news about fresh fish came accompanied by a small black cloud: local fishermen, I was told, showed up on Tuesday and Thursday mornings on a dock behind the customs shed in Cruz Bay, the one place on St. John that more or less passes as a town, but some of the coral-feeding fish they catch had lately been carrying a disease called ciguatera, which attacks your central nervous system. There was conflicting information around on the subject of ciguatera. I met people in St. John who said that they don't hesitate to eat coral-feeders, and I met someone who said she had been horribly ill from eating one kingfish. I met someone who said that in Japan ciguatera, which isn't detectable by taste or smell, is avoided by putting the fish in a bucket of water with a quarter and discarding it if the quarter tarnishes. I decided to pass. The phrase "attacks your central nervous system" tends to dull my appetite; also, I kept wondering what all those American quarters were doing in Japan.

IT TURNED OUT, though, that a store in Cruz Bay called Caribbean Natural Foods sold fresh deep-water fish like tuna—not to speak of soy sauce and rice wine and sesame oil for the marinade. Caribbean Natural Foods was one of two or three small but ambitious food stores that had opened since our previous visit to St. John, and among them the island had available California wine and Tsingtao beer and Silver Palate chocolate sauce and Ben & Jerry's ice cream (including my daughters' favorite flavor, Dastardly Mash) and New York bagels and real pastrami and a salad identified as "tortellini with walnut pesto sauce and sour cream." I suppose there are old St. John hands who grumble that the world of exotic beers and gourmet ice cream was what they were trying to get away from, but there must be a lot of regular visitors who feel like celebrating the expansion of available foodstuffs with an appropriately catered parade.

Leading the parade would be people serious about picnics. On St. John, the pleasantness of beaches tends to vary roughly in direct proportion to how hard it is to get there. Anyone who chooses a beach on St. John because it has a convenient parking lot or a commissary or a marked underwater trail or plenty of changing rooms may find himself thinking at some point in the afternoon that he should have paid more attention to what his mother said about the rewards that come to those willing to make a little extra effort. (A difficult road, though, is not an absolute guarantee of peacefulness: someone who has been reading a novel on what seemed like an out-of-the-way beach may look up from his book and find that 20 boats of one sort or another have materialized in a line across the bay, prepared to disgorge a small but expensively outfitted invasion force.) Once you're settled in at the beach, the prospect of going back to Cruz Bay for lunch can provoke the great bicultural moan: "*Quel schlep!*" I don't know what people used to do about lunch at a beach like Francis Bay, where a beach-lounger can watch pelicans as they have a go at the flying fish and a snorkeler with a little patience can usually spot a giant sea turtle. By the time we got there, you could reach into the ice chest for a seafood-salad sandwich and a bottle of Dos Equis.

At Salt Pond, a spectacular beach on the more remote eastern end of the island, we did leave for lunch one day in order to go to Hazel's, where Hazel Eugene, whose wanderings after she left St. Lucia included New Orleans, was said to serve what she sometimes called Caribbean Creole cooking. Hazel's turned out to be on the ground floor of a sort of aqua house that had goats wandering around the back and a neighbor who seemed to be the island's leading collector of auto bodies. Its signs identified it as SEABREEZE: GROCERY, RESTAURANT, BAR, and while we were there Hazel would occasionally leave the kitchen to pour a couple of shots or to fill a shopping list that might consist of a box of Kraft Macaroni & Cheese dinner, a bottle of rum, and a beer for the ride home. She also waited on tables, and in that role she began a lot of sentences with "I could do you . . ." as in "I could do you some of my fried chicken with cottage fries" or "I could do you some codfish fritters and some of my special pumpkin soup to start." Hazel did us all of that, plus some blackened shark and some seafood creole and some puffed shrimp and some chicken curry and a plate of assorted root vegetables that tasted an awful lot better than they sounded or looked. When it was over, I was just about ready to admit that I might have sold St. John short.

I don't mean I regretted bringing along the extra suitcase. Hazel's was too far to drive at night. Places to eat dinner were limited, although at least one restaurant in Cruz

Bay, the Lime Inn, had fish from the Caribbean, of all places, and served it grilled, without even a dash of sunblock on the side. And, of course, we had one dress-up evening in the main dining room at Caneel Bay. What was being sold there, I realized, was simulation of membership in the most prominent country club in town—at a cost that might seem considerable but is, I assume, nothing compared to the kick of the real club's annual dues. The food is of the sort that is described by the most enthusiastic members as "not highly seasoned," and the waiters, playing the role of old club retainers, serve it in a manner so true to the rituals of the upper-middle-class past that you even get a little tray of olives and carrot sticks to nibble on while you're waiting for your shrimp cocktail. The night we were there, the menu offered a marinated conch appetizer as the single reminder that we were on an island rather than in one of the better suburbs, and it listed some California wines as the single reminder that we hadn't found ourselves, willy-nilly, in 1954.

All of which means that we often ate dinner at the place with a one-and-a-sliver-bay view—grilled tuna with some pasta on the side, a great meal of spaghetti with garlic and oil and sun-dried tomatoes, and, finally, the fruits of Alice's risotto kit. It occurred to me, as we ate the risotto and talked about risotto in Milan, that behind our shopping there may have been an unconscious desire to create the Italian West Indies. In fact, I informed those at the table, it hadn't been a bad try—although it might have been improved by bringing along a little more focaccia for the picnics.

Back home, we decided that surviving on St. John had been easy enough to merit a return engagement. A few months later we heard that Hazel had closed her restaurant and taken her talent for Caribbean Creole cooking elsewhere. It was a blow, but not a blow severe enough to change our minds about going back. After all, we still had the country ham.

— Calvin Trillin

ME? THE DAD?
ON A SPRING-BREAK CRUISE?

ON A PERFECT MORNING in the British Virgin Islands, I am sitting alone in the cockpit when two young fellows, who are rowing by not quite as accidentally as they would like it to appear, rest on their oars long enough to ask me where my crew and I are headed.

"Norman Island," I answer pleasantly, albeit untruthfully.

Our actual destination is Trellis Bay, at the other end of the BVI from Norman Island. But over the past few days I've learned that evasive tactics are sometimes necessary when you are cruising with a college-age daughter and a few of her girlfriends. I've learned that if I were to be truthful to all the young men who have taken an interest in where we were going to anchor each night, there wouldn't be any room for us to anchor.

Besides, even though the girls had been polite to these particular two young fellows when we'd talked to them a shore on the preceding evening, I'd seen Kris roll her eyes in that meaningful way I'd come to understand means "total dweebs." And I'd heard one of the other girls label them with an even more damning epithet: "high school boys."

The idea for a spring-break cruise with my daughter had been mine. I wanted to share with her one of the things I enjoy most—visiting tropical waters aboard a sailboat when everyone at home is complaining about how cold the weather is. I wanted to do it in a way that would make her feel she was the focus of our adventure, not just tagging along. And I wanted some time to get caught up with how her life was going—not, of course, by asking her, which, as most parents know, is a singularly unenlightening method of intelligence gathering, but by taking advantage of the small confines of a boat to listening in on her conversations with her friends.

Even though the idea had been mine, Kris was keen on it from the start. That's one of the reasons I was so looking forward to it. She was finally beyond the age when

kids consider the ideal distance between parent and offspring on vacation to be two or three states. Either that, or she was wise enough to see that spring break in the Virgin Islands is worth a certain amount of sacrifice.

But she did have one concern. After I explained that I'd pay all expenses except her friends' airfare, she said she feared that most of her friends, who were "poor college students," probably would not be able to afford the price of a ticket to the Caribbean. That fear lasted about 24 hours, after which she called me and asked, "How many people did you say was the maximum I could bring?"

We finally signed on two: Carol, whose enrollment in a sailing course at school left me in constant fear that she would ask me to demonstrate a knot I would not remember how to tie; and Missy, who, apparently somewhat dubious about details of the cruise ending up in print, throughout the week made such statements as "Don't quote me on this, but has anybody seen my eyeliner?"

The boat I chartered was a Bénéteau 41S, from Sunsail, which is based at Soper's Hole, at the west end of Tortola. With three double cabins plus the main saloon, the beamy French design could have accommodated more. In fact, based on charters by college-age groups I've seen over the years, the typical number aboard a 41-ft boat is about a dozen—with the crew sleeping all over the deck and, in at least one instance I remember, in the dinghy. But I was glad we were only four, because knowing that my crew had little sailing experience and not knowing how enthusiastic they would be about galley chores, I'd hired a paid captain for a few days, to be followed for a few days after that by a paid cook.

The captain, a young local named David, worked out well. He had what seems to me the most important quality of a paid hand—the ability to get along pleasantly with strangers on a small boat (although he himself admitted that with our crew he didn't find it a particularly tough assignment).

He ably handled the girls' sailing instruction for the first few days and was also handy to have aboard whenever I had a question about the boat's systems. His knowledge actually added a half-day to the time we could spend cruising, because we didn't have to be checked out before Sunsail let us go off on our own. David checked us out while we were under way. And his presence allowed us to solve a few small problems that might otherwise have required me to spend more of the cruise than I cared to reading service manuals.

He had local knowledge that we benefited from immediately. He showed us, almost within sight of the dock, a great day anchorage on Little Thatch Island, which he said most people overlooked because they were in a hurry to get either into or away from Soper's Hole. As the less fortunate waited for their pre-cruise briefings, we let the chain rattle out over a white sand bottom that proved an excellent spot for introducing the girls to snorkeling, windsurfing, and, eventually, lunch as prepared by "The Dad," as I was to overhear various young men call me throughout the week.

And, as we motored into The Bight at Norman Sound just before sunset on that first day, and David said, "Look at how those boats are turned every which way; I'm going to be poppin' my head out the hatch all night," his presence allowed me the pleasant realization that I just might be sleeping better than I usually do on a charter.

At Gorda Sound, on Virgin Gorda, the ferry service that runs between the Bitter End Resort and Tortola made it simple for us to get David back home and pick up the cook whom Sunsail had assigned to us. She was an Englishwoman named Val, whom, to my great relief, the girls got along with splendidly, and not just, as they hinted, because it meant that I would no longer be cooking.

Again, Val's ability to get along with strangers was her best quality. Not counting, of course, her willingness to do all the dish washing. None of our crew were gourmets, and none of us had spent a lifetime being the one expected to cook, so I can't really judge those aspects of having a professional aboard, which my wife and about half the human race have told me can make the difference between a true vacation and simply moving the work load to a new venue. But I do know that at the end of the time we had planned to keep her, our crew decided we needed to convince Val to stay until the end of the cruise.

The crew, I am happy to report, were themselves a joy to have aboard. As I've said, they arrived with little experience, but they set about everything they did—learning how to steer a course, set a sail, handle the dinghy, wash their hair in a rainsquall—with nearly as much enthusiasm as they exhibited when getting ready to go ashore on the evenings when young men were likely to be present.

Of course, we did have our small differences. My inability to appreciate some of their music left me with the uncomfortable feeling that I might be—well, getting old. And they didn't care much for some of my music either. Not even what they called the classical stuff, such as Jimmy Buffett. But mostly what we had was one of the most pleasant cruises I can remember.

IT WAS PLEASANT introducing my daughter and her friends to places I'd visited and enjoyed a dozen times before: the sea caves on Norman Island, where rumors still persist of buried treasure; The Baths, on Virgin Gorda, where cathedral light and the ocean's swell bounce gently back and forth beneath church-size rocks; Cane Garden Bay, on Tortola, where the evening sun turned the palm trees golden; Sandy Cay, which has a beach as beautifully white as the image its name conjures up; the Bitter End Yacht Club in North Sound, on Virgin Gorda, where (I'd never really noticed before) the boys are; and Foxy's Tamarind Bar, on Jost Van Dyke, where in the afternoon, while we were picking out lobsters for our end-of-the-cruise evening meal ashore, Foxy himself played his guitar for us and told us how he had planned to travel to America and become a big star—and would have, too, he said, if he hadn't learned at the last moment that in order to board the airplane he would be required to wear shoes.

It was pleasant sailing with a crew whose neophyte's enthusiasm helped me remember what it was like to feel a boat come alive in my hands for the first time. Yet a crew so unafraid that they delighted in taking turns at the wheel when the wind attempted to put us on our ear during a beat up Sir Francis Drake Channel. And a crew that by the end of the week, as we reached across a gentle blue sea from Jost Van Dyke to Little Thatch for one more quick swim and a tidying up before heading back into Soper's Hole, had become so competent that I had nothing to do but what I fancy myself as doing best—serving in a supervisory capacity.

Most of all, it was pleasant to think that if Kris and her friends were still as enthusiastic about their spring-break cruise when they got back to school as they were when I saw them off at the airport, she might occasionally remember it was an adventure she had shared with her dad.

Oh, and if those guys from the sailing team who sat up in our cockpit half the night are still looking for the steering wheel that somebody removed from their boat, I don't know anything about it.

— Bob Payne

EXPLORING THE WATERS OF THE VIRGIN ISLANDS

THERE ARE MOMENTS in a person's life when things seem to change forever. One such moment occurred 20 years ago, when I first arrived in the Virgin Islands and immediately shoved off from St. Thomas to "fetch Tortola" on a small, ketch-rigged sailboat. I still remember that sun-kissed passage as if it happened yesterday: tacking up through the Narrows, the sweet trades rustling my hair, I sensed the boat dip and curtsy in the Caribbean Sea and found myself grinning like a child. The palm-fringed islands seemed to wave in welcome, and I realized that a part of me would never be the same.

Of course, such memories can be dangerous. Father Time tends to burnish them into a romantic brilliance they don't deserve. So I recently bareboated a 44-ft Oceanis sloop with some snow-weary friends to see if the magic was still there. It was. On the second evening I saw it clearly reflected on the smiling face of Russ Tate, an old landlubbing friend of mine from Massachusetts. He had been totally bewitched by the day's sail. We'd seen porpoises and flying fish—even a huge manta ray just astern of our transom. We had briskly sailed past colorful sunbathers, blowing snorkelers, bubbling scuba divers and streaking windsurfers. But what most impressed Russ was our final tranquil anchorage on Tortola's northeast tip. It was as if we had sailed onto a tropical movie set. Seagulls wheeled and cackled above. Pelicans humorously dive-bombed for their small silvery prey at the harbor entrance. Ashore, an exuberant rooster crowed. The smell of frangipani, wood smoke, and coconut oil wafted gently across the water.

The next morning, Russ was already sitting in the cockpit when I arose at first light. "Tell me about it, Gary," he said, a strange light of intense interest in his eyes. "Tell me about this boat, that reef, and every single thing in between." "Okay," I said with a smile, "The first thing you should know is . . ."

Riding the Waves

With a sailing fleet of several hundred boats, based mostly on St. Thomas, Tortola, and Virgin Gorda, access to Virgin Island attractions is remarkably easy—year-round and from all directions. You can sail independently on a bareboat charter or aboard a fully crewed boat with an experienced captain and cook. The Virgin Islands can match every sailor's wish list: sunny days in the 70°F to 80°F range; dependable trade winds of 12 to 20 knots from the east–southeast; varied, exotic scenery; protected anchorages that are free and slip and mooring rentals that are affordable; tides of less than 2 ft and generally predictable currents; short passages between islands; and easy access to onshore sights. (Note that St. Croix is an exception because it sits alone, 40 mi south of the group.)

A bareboat, no matter how luxurious, is bare of crew. You have to sail it yourself, just like you have to drive a rental car yourself. For the duration of the charter, the boat is your responsibility. A crewed charter is similar to renting a chauffeur-driven limousine. The captain and crew cater to your every whim and do all the heavy lifting. Your sole responsibility is to relax. Bare-boating offers skilled sailors a lot of freedom, but it carries with it serious responsibility and considerable physical effort. A crewed charter, on the other hand, is like having your own ocean-going resort. It is, however, less private and more expensive than bareboating, and, although the captain will make every effort to carry out your requests, the ship's navigation and routing are his sole right and responsibility.

Bareboat Charters

If you're an experienced sailor and are on a budget, bareboating is the way to go. If you don't have the experience to handle a boat, don't try to fake it. Each company has a "check out" orientation during which they carefully determine your competence.

Most sailors select a boat and make reservations at least six months in advance for high-season charters (earlier to guarantee holiday dates). Cruising in style costs about the same as staying in a mid-range resort. Prices vary depending on how many people you have to share the costs, whether or not you do some of your own provisioning, the kinds of activities (fishing, shopping, diving) you include, what type of optional equipment (e.g., refrigeration) the boat has, and the boat's age or reputation.

You can charter an older (note that it's prudent to ask for a boat in charter service for less than five years), smaller boat for less than $2,000 a week or you can pay more than $6,000 for a fully outfitted 50 footer that can accommodate a crowd. The most popular size is 42 feet. Remember: Mother Ocean will be just as awe-inspiring from the deck of a modest boat as from a mega-yacht.

Crewed Charters

Deciding on which boat to charter isn't as important as deciding on a captain and crew with whom to charter. Some crews love kids; others won't allow them aboard. Some vessels specialize in gourmet cooking, others in rail-down competitive sailing. Still others cater to scuba divers, retired couples, or gay and lesbian passengers. It's best to seek out the assistance of a charter yacht broker, a sea-going travel agent who specializes in fully crewed chartering.

How do you find a good broker? Well, a good broker always attends the annual Caribbean yacht "viewing" shows on St. Thomas and Tortola and has been aboard the vessels he or she represents. The very best brokers are on a first-name basis with their captains. Good brokers are also interested in ensuring that you have the vacation of a lifetime, so you'll rebook with them next year; bad brokers are interested primarily in selling you on any boat so that they can collect their commission.

Brokers' services include an interview to determine your vacation expectations, budget, and other pertinent information. This is generally followed by a mailing of brochures on recommended boats and another conversation with the broker to help you narrow the selection. Brokers can be adept at matching a crew's personalities with your needs and at helping with island travel arrangements, including air and hotel. They also coordinate with the crew all the details of the actual charter contract:

special food and beverage preferences, any special occasions to be celebrated during the voyage, etc.

U.S.-flagged vessels and U.S. captains operating in the USVI (or picking up passengers from U.S. ports) must be licensed by the U.S. Coast Guard. Crewed charters in the BVI are usually (but not always) operated by people with British Yacht Masters' Tickets. In either case, besides confirming the boat's and crew's status with a broker, you can verify their good standing by contacting voluntary associations in both U.S. and British territories (e.g., the Virgin Islands Charteryacht League or the Charter Yacht Society of the BVI).

Like bareboat charters, the costs for a crewed charter depend on the type and size of vessel; the level of crew service is another factor. One mega-yacht on St. Thomas charges $26,000 per day. However, for a party of six on a well-found 50-ft sloop, figure on $1,200 to $1,800 per person per week. A couple can expect to pay between $1,600 and $2,300 each for a top-of-the-line 41 footer—not bad considering that you're getting the most private, most exclusive, catered vacation in the world. (A 15% tip is appreciated for captain and crew.)

Day-Sails

The easiest, cheapest, and least complicated way to get to sea is on a multi-passenger day-sail boat. Most charter for around $75 per person for a full day (including snorkel gear, lunch, snacks, and beverages). You can also find cheaper half-day or sunset cruises. There are two main types of boats: private "six-pack" yachts that carry as many as six passengers, and multi-passenger vessels that can take up to 100 people.

The advantage of a six-pack vessel is one of intimacy. If you charter it with several friends, chances are you'll have it all to yourself, so it's like having your own private yacht for a day. The captain and crew are often highly interesting Caribbean sea gypsies, and at the end of the day you may feel as if you've evolved from paying guest to new-found friend. Of course, there's no denying that the enthusiasm of a large group of sun-drenched mariners is infectious on multi-passenger boats. If, however, you hate crowds, loud music, and boisterous sing-alongs, perhaps a more laid-back six-pack boat would be the best choice.

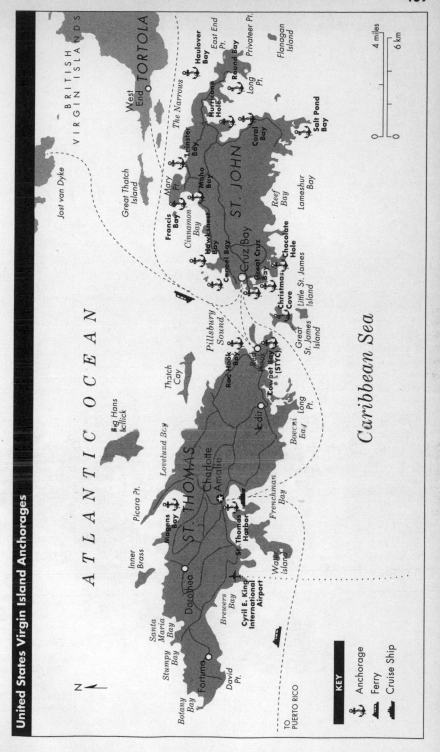

United States Virgin Island Anchorages

N

BRITISH VIRGIN ISLANDS

Jost van Dyke

A T L A N T I C   O C E A N

Great Thatch Island

Mary Pt.

TORTOLA

West End

The Narrows

Haulover Bay

East End Pt.

Round Bay

Long Pt.

Privateer Pt.

Flanagan Island

Hurricane Hole

Leinster Bay

Coral Bay

Salt Pond Bay

Francis Bay

Maho Bay

Cinnamon Bay

Hawksnest Bay

Trunk Bay

Cruz Bay

ST. JOHN

Great Cruz

Chocolate Hole

Reef Bay

Lameshur Bay

Christmas Cove

Little St. James Island

Great St. James Island

Great Thatch Island

Big Hans Lollick

Inner Brass

Santa Maria Bay

Stumpy Bay

Botany Bay

Picara Pt.

Loveland Bay

Magens Bay

Thatch Cay

Pillsbury Sound

Red Hook Bay

Red Hook

Tow'pet Bay (STYC)

Long Pt.

Bovoni Bay

Redir

ST. THOMAS

Charlotte Amalie

St. Thomas Harbor

Frenchman Bay

Water Island

Brewers Bay

Cyril E. King International Airport

Dorothea

David Pt.

Fortuna

Caribbean Sea

TO PUERTO RICO

4 miles

6 km

KEY

⚓ Anchorage

Ferry

Cruise Ship

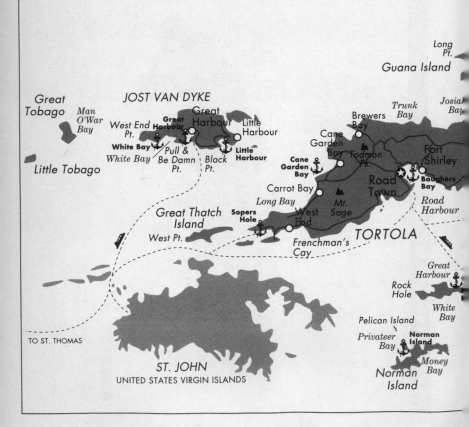

ATLANTIC

Long
Pt.

Guana Island

*Great
Tobago*

*Man
O'War
Bay*

JOST VAN DYKE

*Great
Harbour*

*Trunk
Bay*

*Josiah
Bay*

Brewers
Bay

West End
Pt.

**Great
Harbour**

Little
Harbour

Cane
Garden
Bay

Fort
Shirley

White Bay

White Bay

Pull &
Be Damn
Pt.

**Little
Harbour**

*Black
Pt.*

**Cane
Garden
Bay**

Todman
Pk.

*Great
Tobago*

Little Tobago

Carrot Bay

Road
Town

Baughers
Bay

*Road
Harbour*

Great Thatch
Island

**Sopers
Hole**

Long Bay

West
End

*Mt.
Sage*

TORTOLA

West Pt.

*Frenchman's
Cay*

*Great
Harbour*

Rock
Hole

*White
Bay*

Pelican Island

*Privateer
Bay*

**Norman
Island**

TO ST. THOMAS

ST. JOHN
UNITED STATES VIRGIN ISLANDS

*Money
Bay*

Norman
Island

West End Pt.

Bones Bight

Loblolly Bay

Table Bay

Flamingo Pond

Red Pond

Anegada Reef Hotel ⚓

The Settlement ⊙

ANEGADA
(15 miles north of Necker Is.)

Lower Bay

Budrock Pond

Horse Shoe Reef

White Bay

O C E A N

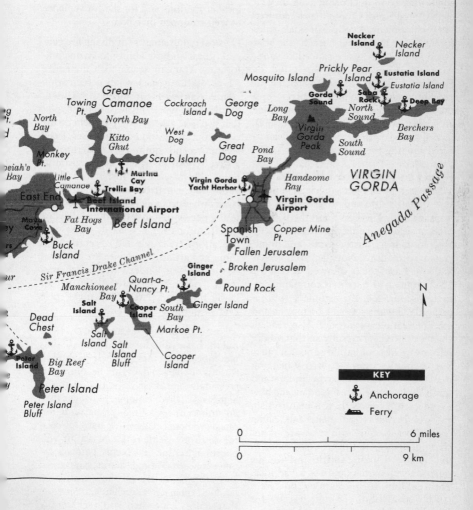

Necker Island ⚓ Necker Island

Prickly Pear Island ⚓

Mosquito Island

Eustatia Island ⚓ Eustatia Island

Gorda Sound ⚓

Saba Rock ⚓ Deep Bay ⚓

Great Camanoe

Towing Pt.

North Bay

Cockroach Island

George Dog

Long Bay

North Sound

Berchers Bay

North Bay

North Bay

Kitto Ghut

West Dog

Great Dog

Pond Bay

Virgin Gorda Peak

South Sound

Monkey Pt.

Scrub Island

VIRGIN GORDA

eiah's Bay

Little Camanoe

Marina Cay ⚓

Trellis Bay

Virgin Gorda Yacht Harbor ⚓

Handsome Bay

East End

Beef Island International Airport ⚓ ⛴

Virgin Gorda Airport

Anegada Passage

Fat Hogs Bay

Beef Island

ey Mas Cove ⚓

Spanish Town

Copper Mine Pt.

Buck Island

Fallen Jerusalem

Sir Francis Drake Channel

Broken Jerusalem

ur

Manchioneel Bay ⚓

Quart-a-Nancy Pt.

Ginger Island ⚓

Round Rock

Dead Chest

Salt Island ⚓

Cooper Island ⚓

South Bay

Ginger Island

ey ⚓

Salt Island

Salt Island Bluff

Markoe Pt.

Peter Island ⚓

Big Reef Bay

Cooper Island

Peter Island

N ↑

Peter Island Bluff

KEY	
⚓	Anchorage
⛴	Ferry

0 — 6 miles
0 — 9 km

Powerboats

Another interesting way to see the islands is by small rental powerboat. Although this requires some basic seamanship skills, you don't have to be a salty dog to give it a whirl. Many people are pleasantly surprised at how affordable this option is. A 40-hp, outboard-driven, open, 18-ft boat can rent for less than $150 a day; a 22-footer goes for around $300 a day. Most companies (but not all) require you to top off the fuel tanks at the end of the day—remember, marine fuel is expensive here. A small deposit is usually required, as is a major credit card. Some companies restrict rentals to persons 25 and older. Hint: Slow boats are cheaper, safer, and just as much fun as the fast ones. All U.S. boats come with good anchoring gear, as well as all United States Coast Guard–required safety equipment. A couple of safety rules to remember: Don't ever "beach" the boat even momentarily, since sand (like sandpaper) scratches and isn't very good for Fiberglas hulls. In shallow water, be especially careful not to nick the prop—and thus lose your deposit. Watch your engine gauges (for overheating or low oil pressure), as well as the color of the water ahead to avoid running the boat aground.

Points to Ponder on the Seas

Whatever type of boat you charter, make sure that it's allowed to go where you want it to go. The USVI and the BVI are parts of separate countries with distinctly different marine, customs, tax, and immigration regulations. Not all charter vessels in the BVI are legally allowed to visit the USVI. Some BVI bareboat companies actively discourage their customers from entering USVI waters. Check on marine and other regulations in advance. Also, read all charter contracts carefully so that you're fully aware of your liability and insurance responsibilities from the start. When you head out be sure that you understand which VHF channels are important and how to use each properly. If you plan to fish, check on permit requirements and fishing restrictions. Be sure you're aware of anchoring, diving, and other restrictions as well. Finally, drinking and driving—on the water as well as the land—is a bad idea. The legal limit for recreational boaters is .10 blood alcohol content; it's .04 for USCG-licensed captains. (Indeed, such captains cannot drink *any* alcohol within four hours of stepping aboard their vessels.)

Below the Waves

Reefs, wrecks, and rife vegetation make the islands as interesting underwater as above. Convenient anchorages, conditions suitable to different levels of ability, and a plethora of dive shops add to the appeal of scuba diving and snorkeling here.

Scuba Diving

Scuba divers are required to show certification of training—a C-card—to rent air tanks, get air refills, and join others on guided dives virtually anywhere in the world. If you're an old hand, then diving on your own—off a boat or from a beach—is just a matter of renting filled air tanks. Even experienced divers, however, often hire guides, if only for their knowledge of local attractions and for the convenience of well-equipped dive boats.

Physical requirements for diving are general fitness and the ability to swim comfortably. You can accomplish the entire 32- to 40-hour open-water certification course in as few as three days of vacation, but it's hard work. Professionals suggest that you take a two-part approach: do the classroom study and pool exercises (basic swimming and equipment skills) through a dive school or a YMCA program at home. Then, with a transfer form from your home instructor, certified Virgin Islands dive instructors will lead you through four open-water dives and check your qualifications for a C-card. Most dive operations are connected to retail/rental shops and are affiliated with the National Association of Underwater Instructors (NAUI) or the Professional Association of Diving Instructors (PADI). The latter is most evident in the Virgin Islands.

All certification courses stress diver safety. But the basic rules for safe diving are simple; fools ignore them at their own peril. Serious diving accidents are becoming increasingly rare these days, thanks to the high level of diver training. However, they *do* still occur occasionally. Surfacing too rapidly without exhaling—or going too deep for too long—can result in an air embolism or a case of the bends. Fauna is another concern. Though sharks, barracuda, and moray eels are on the most-feared list, more often it's sea urchins and fire coral that cause pain when you accidentally bump them. Part of any scuba-training program is a review of sea life and the importance of respecting the new world you're exploring. Dive professionals recognize the value of protecting fragile reefs and ecosystems in tropical waters, and instructors emphasize look-don't-touch diving (the unofficial motto is: take only pictures, leave only bubbles). Government control and protection of dive sites is increasing, especially in such heavily used areas as the Virgin Islands.

Many hotels promote a package deal or have a direct line to a nearby dive shop. But, be aware that the experience could be discouraging, particularly if you find a bored instructor handing out ill-fitting equipment and sloppy advice. There are several simple questions to ask yourself and the staff to assess a dive operation. Are the facilities neat, clean, and businesslike? Are the boats custom-built for diving? Is the rental equipment in good shape? Are the instructors interested in providing you with a quality dive experience and not constantly trying to sell you another dive gadget? Do they repair their own gear in their own workshop? Do they dive frequently, and are all dives guided? Are they safety conscious and rescue trained? Do they know (without the slightest hesitation) where the nearest hyperbaric chamber is—and how to get there fast? Is the boat captain properly licensed, and does the vessel have a tank of oxygen aboard? Is the information on the dive sites precise and specific? Is the staff friendly, knowledgeable, and helpful? The answers to all these questions should be "yes."

Snorkeling

Scuba diving always requires advance planning; snorkeling, on the other hand, can be a far more casual affair. There's no heavy, expensive, complicated equipment involved. There's usually no need for a boat, since many of the finest snorkel sites are adjacent to a beach. Because most tropical marine life lives fairly near the water's surface, there's no link between the depth of a dive and your enjoyment. Many avid water-sports enthusiasts progress from swimming to snorkeling to scuba—and then gradually drift back to snorkeling. The Silent World is even quieter without the hiss of a two-stage regulator.

Few places on this planet are as convenient to snorkel as the Virgin Islands, and many dive shops rent snorkeling gear and offer some training. It can't hurt to go in know-

ing a few tricks, though: To see whether or not a mask fits, hold it up to your face and breath in gently through your nose. It should stick there for a moment. If not, try another. Fins should fit well: if they're too loose they'll fall off, and if too tight they'll give you blisters. Usually, any snorkel with a mouthpiece that doesn't leak is OK.

To prevent your mask from fogging, spit in it and rub the saliva on the inside of the lens. (A drop of ordinary dishwashing liquid or a commercial "mask defogger" also works.) Warning: It's difficult to walk in fins. Some people walk into the water backwards with them; a better idea is to put them on while sitting in shallow water. Practice clearing your snorkel (with a sharp blow of air) in very shallow water, bracing yourself with your hands on clear sand. This will help you develop confidence before venturing into deeper waters.

The dangers of snorkeling are few and easily avoided. As when scuba diving, don't touch red or reddish brown coral; for that matter, don't touch *any* coral. Don't put your hands into dark holes—unless you want to play "patty cake" with a defensive moray eel. Ignore sharks and barracudas unless they act particularly aggressive; if so, retreat calmly without excessive splashing. Don't wear shiny jewelry. Never snorkel alone, at dusk, or at night. Avoid areas with heavy surf or strong currents.

Snorkel as far away from boats as is practical. Avoid busy harbors, dock areas, or navigational channels. If you hear a motorized vessel approaching, resurface immediately and clasp both hands together over your head. This makes you clearly visible and means "Diver Okay." (Waving your hands rapidly back and forth over your head means "Diver in trouble. Need Help!") In addition, make sure you don't get hit by one boat while watching another. Sound direction can be confusing underwater. Finally towing a floating dive flag is you best protection against being run down.

— Gary Goodlander

Longtime Virgin Islands resident Gary Goodlander has lived aboard sailing craft for much of his life and currently resides with his wife and daughter on his 38-ft S&S sloop *Wild Card* in Cruz Bay, St. John. He's a freelance marine journalist for *SAIL, Yachting World,* and other publications and is the author of both *Chasing the Horizon* and *Sea Dogs, Clowns & Gypsies.*

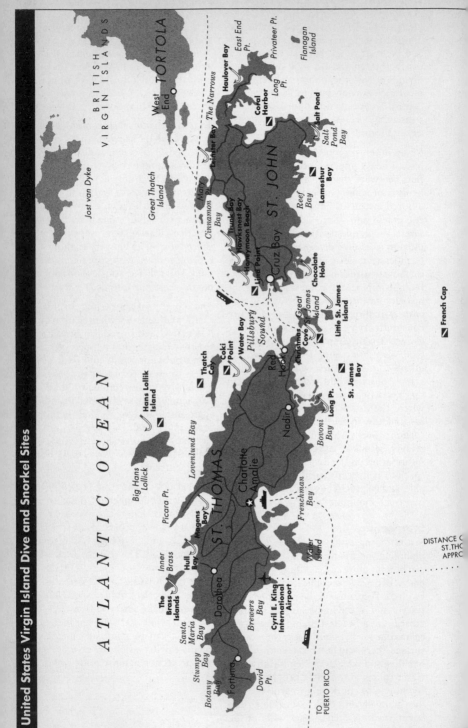

United States Virgin Island Dive and Snorkel Sites

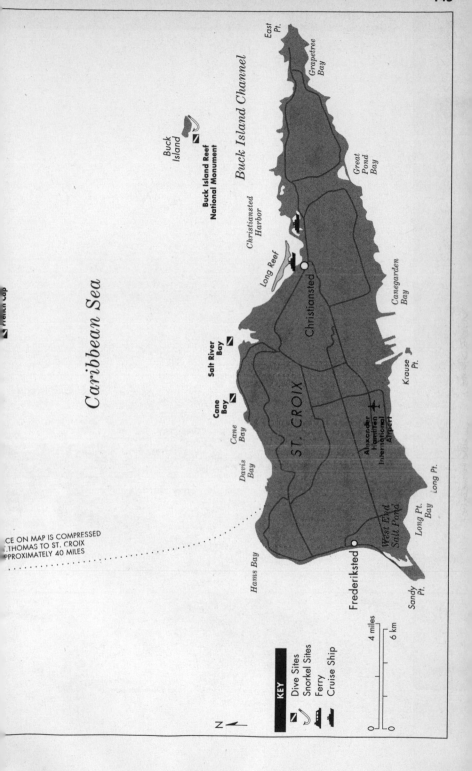

Caribbean Sea

French Cap

CE ON MAP IS COMPRESSED
THOMAS TO ST. CROIX
PPROXIMATELY 40 MILES

Buck Island Channel

East Pt.

Grapetree Bay

Great Pond Bay

Buck Island

Buck Island Reef National Monument

Christiansted Harbor

Long Reef

Christiansted

Canegarden Bay

Salt River Bay

Cane Bay

Cane Bay

Krause Pt.

Davis Bay

ST. CROIX

Alexander Hamilton International Airport

Hams Bay

Long Pt. Bay

Long Pt.

West End Salt Pond

Frederiksted

Long Pt. Bay

Sandy Pt.

N

KEY
Dive Sites
Snorkel Sites
Ferry
Cruise Ship

4 miles
6 km

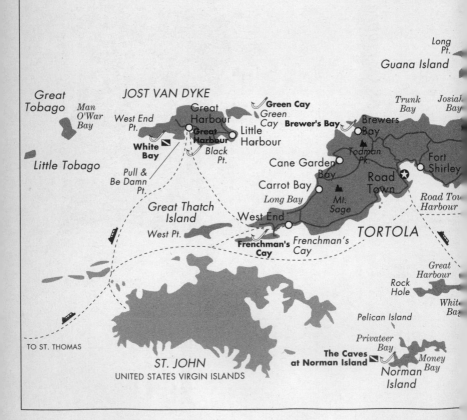

ATLANTIC

Long
Pt.

Guana Island

Great
Tobago

Man
O'War
Bay

JOST VAN DYKE

West End
Pt.

Great
Harbour

Green Cay

Green
Cay

Trunk
Bay

Josiah
Bay

Brewer's Bay

Brewers
Bay

**Great
Harbour**

Little
Harbour

**White
Bay**

Black
Pt.

Cane Garden
Bay

Todman
Pk.

Fort
Shirley

Little Tobago

Pull &
Be Damn
Pt.

Carrot Bay

Long Bay

Mt.
Sage

Road
Town

Road Tow
Harbour

Great Thatch
Island

West End

West Pt.

**Frenchman's
Cay**

Frenchman's
Cay

TORTOLA

Great
Harbour

Rock
Hole

Whit
Bay

Pelican Island

Privateer
Bay

**The Caves
at Norman Island**

Money
Bay

TO ST. THOMAS

ST. JOHN

UNITED STATES VIRGIN ISLANDS

Norman
Island

West End Pt.

Bones Bight

Flamingo Pond *Red Pond*

Loblolly Bay

Table Bay

The Settlement

ANEGADA
(15 miles north of Necker Is.)

Lower Bay

Budrock Pond

Horse Shoe Reef

Wreck of the Rokus

White Bay

O C E A N

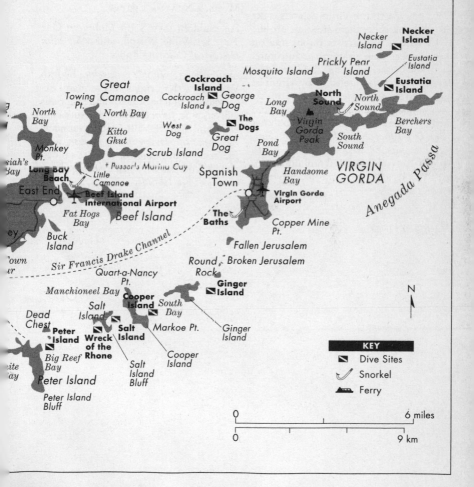

Necker Island

Necker Island

Prickly Pear Island

Eustatia Island

Mosquito Island

Eustatia Island

North Sound

North Sound

Berchers Bay

Great Camanoe

Towing Pt.

Cockroach Island

Cockroach Island

George Dog

Long Bay

North Bay

North Bay

Virgin Gorda Peak

South Sound

The Dogs

Kitto Ghut

West Dog

Great Dog

Pond Bay

North Bay

Scrub Island

Monkey Pt.

VIRGIN GORDA

siah's Bay

Pusser's Marina Cay

Spanish Town

Handsome Bay

Long Bay Beach

Little Camanoe

Beef Island International Airport

East End

Virgin Gorda Airport

Anegada Passage

Fat Hogs Bay

The Baths

Beef Island

Copper Mine Pt.

Buck Island

Fallen Jerusalem

own r

Sir Francis Drake Channel

Quart-a-Nancy Pt.

Round Rock

Broken Jerusalem

Manchioneel Bay

Cooper Island

South Bay

Ginger Island

Dead Chest

Salt Island

Peter Island

Salt Island

Markoe Pt.

Ginger Island

Wreck of the Rhone

Big Reef Bay

Cooper Island

Peter Island

Salt Island Bluff

Peter Island Bluff

N

KEY	
◥	Dive Sites
ᶜ	Snorkel
⛴	Ferry

0 — 6 miles

0 — 9 km

FURTHER READING

If you have the time before your trip, read James Michener's *Caribbean;* it will enhance your visit. *Don't Stop the Carnival* by Herman Wouk is a classic Caribbean book, though some of its 1950s perspectives seem rather dated. In *Coming About: A Family Passage at Sea* author Susan Tyler Hitchcock details the adventure of a lifetime—one in which she and her family sail for nine months and 3,500 mi in the Bahamas and the Caribbean; the book offers an intimate look at the islands and is also a wonderful meditation on marriage and family.

Once you get to the Virgin Islands, take time to book-shop; there are some prolific USVI writers and artists publishing on every subject from pirates to architecture. Look for books, art prints, and cards by Mapes de Monde, published by Virgin Islands native son Michael Paiewonsky, who splits his time between Rome and the USVI. Mapes de Monde also publishes *The Three Quarters of the Town of Charlotte Amalie* by local historian Edith Woods. It's richly printed and illustrated with Woods's fine pen-and-ink drawings.

Photography buffs will want to look for the book of internationally known St. Croix photographer Fritz Henle. For BVI history buffs, Vernon Pickering's *Concise History of the British Virgin Islands* is a wordy but worthy guide to the events and personalities that shaped the region. Pickering also produces the *Official Tourist Handbook* for the BVI. Pick up a copy of *A Place Like This: Hugh Benjamin's Peter Island,* the charming and eloquent personal account of the Kittitian's past two decades in the British Virgin Islands. The book was written in collaboration with Richard Myers, a New York writer.

For children there's *Up Mountain One Time* by Willie Wilson, and a *St. John Historical Coloring Book.*

For linguists, *What a Pistarckle!* by Lito Valls gives the origins of the many expressions you'll be hearing, and historians will enjoy *St. John Backtime* by Ruth Hull Low and Rafael Valls, and *Eyewitness Accounts of Slavery in the Danish West Indies* by Isidor Paiewonsky. For sailors, Simon Scott has written a *Cruising Guide to the Virgin Islands.*

INDEX

NOTES

Mon. Sage Mountain National Park
Mon. Shopping in Road Town
Fri. Smuggler's Cove and snorkelling
Tues. Day sail - or rent our own
       Mt. Healthy National Park
Wed. Cane ~~Mary~~ Garden Bay   495 9660 (sailing)

Sugar Mill Restaurant - Apple Bay
Skyworld
Wed. Myett's - Cane Garden Bay

NOTES

NOTES

Fodor's

Looking for a different kind of vacation?

Fodor's makes it easy with a full line of specialty guidebooks to suit a variety of interests—from adventure to romance to language help.

Fodor's. For the world of ways you travel.

L@@king

⊚ FOR A
great place to go?

We know just the place. In fact, it attracts more than 125,000 visitors a day, making it one of the world's most popular travel destinations. It's previewtravel.com, the Web's comprehensive resource for travelers. It gives you access to over 500 airlines, 25,000 hotels, rental cars, cruises, vacation packages and support from travel experts 24 hours a day. Plus great information from Fodor's travel guides and travelers just like you. All of which makes previewtravel.com quite a find.

Preview Travel has everything you need to plan & book your next trip.

air, car & hotel reservations

vacation packages & cruises

destination planning & travel tips

24-hour customer service

© 1999 Preview Travel, Inc. Visitors estimated from Media Metrix 3/99 Key Measures Web Report. CST #2022036-40

previewtravel.com

preview travel

aol keyword: previewtravel
www.previewtravel.com